WHY
Bobby Jones
QUIT

A Literary Portrait

BOB THOMAS

Email the author: hoganbook@aol.com

Published by:
Bob Thomas Books, Inc.
PO Box 853
Black Mountain, NC 28711

www.hoganbook.com
www.changinglivesschool.com

Distributed by:
Ingram Book Group
www.ingrambook.com

Cover design by
Burning Frog prods

Library of Congress Cataloguing-in-Publication Data is available upon request.

Printed in the United States of America
10 9 8 7 6 5 4 3 2 1

A NOTE
FROM THE AUTHOR

I thought I knew a lot about Bobby Jones. After all, I've been in golf since August, 1947. But at the main library in Savannah, Georgia, on historic Bull Street, I looked up old Savannah Morning News files one day in 1998 – and was quite taken back by what I found.

When Bobby played in the Savannah Open in 1930, his Grand Slam year, he did it because lots of people placed personal display ads on the sports pages of the Savannah Morning News begging him to play. I'm not talking about one or two ads. There were dozens and dozens. Imagine my surprise when I saw those ads! I naturally wondered what else there was about Bobby Jones that I didn't know.

To me, a book serves two purposes: to entertain and educate. An author has to do both. If you leave out one or the other, you'll either have a very boring book or one which doesn't have a good base.

So, before I really got into my Jones book, I reread a number of my books about Bobby Jones, and I made a list of what I wanted answered about Dixie's Boy Wonder. To my surprise, I found that there were quite a few things not covered in any of the books about him.

For instance, I wondered what happened to Perry Adair, the boy Bobby grew up with. I wondered what happened to Stewart Maiden, Bobby's renowned Scottish teacher. I wondered if I could find the root cause of Bobby's great rhythmic swing. (Authors are very curious people!)

Like most people, I wondered why Bobby picked up his ball at St. Andrews in 1921. I had heard a couple of versions of the story behind Calamity Jane, Bobby's faithful putter. I decided that I wanted to know which one was real. I also wanted to find out how the Jones family could afford to send Bobby away for trips across the Atlantic every few years when Bobby made no real income from playing golf and when the grandfather Bobby was named after didn't easily share his wealth.

Most of all, I became intrigued with the reasons that Bobby gave for quitting. They seemed too simplistic for someone so successful and in love with his game.

I asked people why they loved Bobby Jones. They didn't have an answer. That made me really curious, and I felt as if Bobby was challenging me to come and do his story.

The answers that I found in my search for Bobby's story all but astounded me. Bobby was raised in a little village that gave him all he needed to become what he became in golf and in life. And that trend held. Bobby's story is all about love and cooperation…and what life could become for us if somehow we could all change.

Bob Thomas
Kure Beach, NC

Feel free to write to me:
Hoganbook@aol.com

To Pam Tanney
Who has the same heart
and the same high integrity
as the subject of this book.
Thanks for the help, Pam.

ACKNOWLEDGEMENTS

Different authors work in different ways. My efforts come off the work of those who have gone before me, whether they're reporters and columnists like Oscar Bane Keeler, Grantland Rice and William Richardson, or whether they're authors and researchers like Steve Lowe, Sidney Matthew and the especially talented Charles Price, whom I proudly met while I lived in Pinehurst. Without these people, my work would easily be twice as hard and not nearly so interesting.

I'd like to salute the old Atlanta Georgian and Atlanta Journal newspapers, and the New York Times and various newspapers like the Savannah Morning News and the Philadelphia Record. I cannot leave out the American Golfer Magazine and the old Golf Illustrated, which I found at the Library of Congress in Washington, DC. The Library of Congress is a fascinating place that everyone interested in the written word should visit.

Like Bobby Jones, I sometimes wonder if friends aren't what life is all about. If so, since I have become an author, I must be heading in the right direction because I have had many special people who seem to want me to continue my path as a published author. They were especially important to me when I ran into brutal problems with New York publishers.

I can't say enough good things about Don and Jeannie Horak of Pinehurst, North Carolina, and Pam Tanney of Newport Beach, California. Without them and my wife, Mary Anne, who discovered my writing talent, I would probably be anything but an author.

The special golf loving lady, Ilana Gavin of New York and Washington has been a wonderful friend to me for years.

Then there are the special folks in my life that I wish to thank like John and Leland Keyser of Maryland, Bob Hammerschmidt of Chicago, Harry Waddington of Beaufort, South Carolina, Jon Roth of Dallas, Walt Braxton and Mary Rose Busby of

Pinehurst, and of course, Robin Freer of Charleston, South Carolina. I'd also like to thank the wooden- shafted golf expert, Tom Irving of Indiana, the gifted creator of St. Mulligan, Chaz Henry of Cary, North Carolina, David Kramer of Chino Hills, California, the son of tennis great Jack Kramer, and golf's special teacher, Jim McCright of Charles Town, West Virginia.

Going further, I must stress my appreciation for my talented graphic artists. Thank you Tressa Foster for your original ideas, and thank you Kerry M. Scharf of the University of North Carolina at Wilmington for my cover portrait of Bobby Jones. Kerry is a talented and gifted art student with a proud father who loves the game.

Some people that I have to thank for being by my side in one way or another are Ron Soldo of Hilton Head, South Carolina, Bill Sharp of Gallatin, Tennessee, Charles Mitchell, Jr., of Lexington, Kentucky, and Dick Stearns of Savannah, Georgia. Dudley Warner of Nashville, Tennessee, could do his own book about Bobby Jones and what he meant to the South.

Thanks also to Sybil Hilton, of Bakersfield, California, a very gracious lady of golf, Sid Cooper of Gladstone, Oregon, Art Barr of Minneapolis, Minnesota, Ed Welles of Washington, D.C, a true prince of a man, Gary Biehl, of North Bend, Ohio, Glenn Haueisen of Blacklick, Ohio, a man among men when it comes to standing behind his thoughts, Michael Noyes of Huntington Beach, California, Robert Funke of St. Louis, Missouri, Tom Nakamoto of Wailuku, Hawaii, Jay Blint of Holly Lake Ranch, Texas, Donnie "Coach E" Etheridge of Fairfax Golf Club, Edmund, Okalhoma, Glenn Tonoli of Hacienda Heights, California, John Bowen of Atlanta, Georgia, Don McIlwain of Bradentown, Florida, Charles Kim of Palo Alto, California, Stephen Robinson of Columbia, Tennessee, Jack DeRuyter of Oberlin, Ohio, Mike Stevens of Tampa, Florida, Howard and Peggy Graening of Western Springs, Illinois, Bill Scheben of Union, Kentucky, Ted Cheron of Mission Viejo,

California, Wayne Ockovic of O'Fallon, Illinois, Johnny Miller of Cooperstown, New York, Michael Moser of Perth Amboy, New Jersey, Willis Black of Corbin, Kentucky, Bo Wilhite of Walhala, South Carolina, Jim Gibbons of Wilsonville, Oregon, Wayne McGinnis of Arkdelphia, Arkansas, Philip Hansen of Sedalia, Colorado, Brother Bill McCarthey of San Antonio, Texas, Bruce Fox and Frank Simutis of Watseka, Illinois, Kenny Smith of Winter Park, Florida, Keith Frederick of Morrison, Illinois, Mike McGuire of Powell, Ohio, Ronald Ajax of Key West, Florida, Ryan Brickley of Charlotte, North Carolina, Shawn Campbell of East Berlin, Connecticut. Without all of you, I wouldn't have stood a chance. I hope you know that.

Lastly, I wish to acknowledge a great Irish author by the name of Ivan Morris. He's a gift to our game and he has a huge heart.

CHAPTER 1

He was a man who faced his destiny with appreciation, which was not an easy thing to do considering the things destiny asked him to be. He was a golfer who always gave his fellow competitor his due. He was a human being who was willing to show his humanness to all who cared to look. He was a man who did things for the betterment of society and for the game of golf. He was a father and a husband and a son who loved and appreciated his family and community. He was the hero of the South, when the South needed a hero, and in fulfilling his destiny, he became a man who gave the rest of us something to look up to, forever.

In November of 1929 the summer heat of Georgia was dissipating, slowly. That month, the South's new hero, Bobby Jones, the golfing wonder, decided to take a hand in shaping his own life. It was taking a turn he knew he'd never be able to accept.

Bobby stood as the court was called to order. This would be the ninth time he had served as his law firm's litigator since joining his father's law firm the previous year. He felt so comfortable thinking and talking in front of people after all his years of golf that the firm of Jones, Evins, Moore and Powers jumped at the chance to use him as the firm's representative before the court. The move, when it came up for a vote in the firm, gave Bobby's father, the Colonel, as he was known in law circles, another chance to be, yet again, so very proud of his son.

Bobby stood watching as Judge Bears, in his judicial robes, came in from the anterior room, stepped up, and moved behind the bench. Bobby didn't expect it to be a long day. The defense was supposed to make a simple motion, and Bobby had no protest with the motion.

The hard day in this particular case had been the day before. Word-against-word cases were the worst. In a day when a man's word was expected to stand for something, contracts were often confirmed by a handshake.

The reason Bobby was in court was that his client, the developers of a land project, had one view of the handshake while the construction company had a differing view. Bobby liked cases such as these, even though they were difficult, because they brought out a person's character.

"Mr. Amos, there is something we need to address?" Judge Bears asked the construction company's attorney from his bench while he shuffled papers.

"Yes, your honor," the attorney, Richard B. Amos, replied. "We ask that we be permitted to take the time to bring in a very serious part of our defense tomorrow morning. We just found this witness' whereabouts, and we believe this witness will allow us to bring this process to a fair settlement." Amos moved slightly back and waited for the judge's ruling.

The Judge leaned his head to one side. "At this late a date, I hesitate to permit this extra time as you, yourself, call it." The Judge spread his elbows on the large judicial desk before him and looking out at Mr. Amos, he sighed. "You've had months to prepare."

"But, Your Honor, we just found this witness, whom we believe is utterly significant to the outcome of our presentation." Amos looked across at Bobby. "We couldn't find him until just recently although we were trying desperately due to his importance to the case." Amos tried a different tact. "It's not as if Mr. Jones didn't know about the witness."

The Judge reacted in disbelief, his eyes coming to life as they rested on Bobby Jones. "And what do you have to say about this situation, Mr. Jones?"

Bobby stood. He glanced over at his opponent, Richard Amos. "We have no objection to seeking the just outcome of this case, Your Honor. If it will only take another day, we would prefer to allow the stay so that both may present fairly the entire case. Further, as Mr. Amos stated, we did know about this witness. It just took Mr. Amos longer than anticipated to locate him." Bobby sat back down in one long, graceful movement.

The Judge shook his head. "Very nice of you, Mr. Jones. I might suggest that over the years you consider becoming more, shall we say, case-hardened."

Bobby rose again. "With due respect, Your Honor, I'm hoping that the long years I have put into becoming a decent person and able trial lawyer will suffice," Bobby retorted. "But I will take Your Honor's advice under strong consideration."

The Judge smiled and addressed Bobby's counterpart. "Well, Mr. Amos, it appears that you have a decent opponent. Let's reconvene here tomorrow morning at nine o'clock with your long-sought witness."

Amos stood. "Thank you, Your Honor," he said, and then he looked over at Bobby. "Thank you, too, Mr. Jones. And I'm sorry that we couldn't have negotiated a settlement prior to coming before the bench."

Bobby simply nodded. He bent over to pick up his briefcase, and after a few seconds, he heard a shuffling sound from behind him.

"This would be a great day to play a little golf."

Bobby turned to see the Judge standing there in his robes. "Not many days aren't," Bobby replied. "A good course is a great place to free your mind of complex matters. Especially at this time of year, with the color changes and the air thinning."

The Judge nodded. "Do you have any free time to take in a round after we finish with the matter before us?"

Bobby had been expecting a request like this. It seemed like they were becoming more and more frequent as his cases progressed. But since Bobby liked to play golf, it was very easy for him to accommodate the requests.

"They just finished sanding the greens at East Lake, but Druid Hills and Brookhaven are in excellent shape," Bobby said.

The Judge nodded, obviously very pleased. "How about if we plan to play at Druid Hills the day after we finish?"

Bobby smiled. "I don't see why not. I look forward to it." It was the third time a judge on one of his cases pursued a game with Bobby.

That night, Bobby went to Atlanta's big, old downtown theatre. These days, the theatre wasn't used much, and Bobby used the big stage at the theatre for a little shuttlecock game devised by Douglas Fairbanks that gave him enough exercise to keep his weight down over the winter months when he usually gained about fifteen pounds.

The game was a cross between tennis and badminton and often resulted in long exchanges, keeping the players running for long periods of time and therefore expending a great deal of energy.

Bobby's powerful legs, the seat of his power in the game of golf, were thick and strong and not suited for this particular game.

"I wouldn't dare play you on any course, Bobby, but I'll beat your ass anytime out here," Fairbanks snidely threw out.

Bobby laughed. "The only thing that allows you to beat me is your experience. Soon, I'll damn well give you all you can handle and more."

The next day, Bobby was back in court. He brought another attorney with him, James J. Hunter, called J.J., whose worth to Bobby and Bobby's firm was his great ability of sensing whether or not someone was being honest. Bobby wanted another opinion about the testimony of the witness he was about to hear in the case before Judge Bears, especially after his clients suddenly decided not to make this appearance in court.

"All rise" came the call as Bobby and J.J. rose. Bobby had watched Amos speak heatedly to a new person at his table and felt sure that he would be meeting the man shortly on the stand.

"Well, Mr. Amos. Are we all ready to go today?" The Judge spoke over his bench to the defense.

"We are, Your Honor, and we greatly appreciate the extra time to get our witness here." Amos seemed happy to lead him to the stand.

"State your name for the record, please."

"Ray Howard," the man said, getting settled in his seat and just possibly showing some nervousness.

"Mr. Howard, are you familiar with the construction firm known as Mellon and Walters?" Amos started.

Howard nodded.

"You have to use your voice to answer the questions, Mr. Howard," the Judge pointed out. "Speak up."

"Yes, yes. I am familiar with the firm. The construction firm, that is, of Mellon and Walters." Howard overreacted nervously. The Judge nodded along with Howard's answer like he knew what was coming.

"And are you aware of the construction project that is being completed on West Peachtree Street? The large apartment dwelling that was built there?"

"Yes, I am aware of the apartment building that was built on West Peachtree Street."

"And were you there when the meeting was held between the construction firm and the owners of the property concerning where they wanted the extra building to be built? The little out-building?"

Bobby sat forward, listening and watching very closely.

Ray Howard nodded. "Yes, I was there." He spoke easily now.

Amos walked around as if composing himself for the final questions. "And last night, although it was dark, you got back into town and walked the site of the construction on West Peachtree. Is that correct?"

Bobby thought, "He's leading him a little bit, but I'm gonna let it go this time."

"I got back into town after I heard that you wanted me here, and I went to the site and found it to be exactly like I thought it should be. The new streetlight the city put up on the corner made it very easy to see. The extra building was placed in the northeast corner, ten feet east and ten feet north of the main building. That's what I remember was decided at the meeting that was held between the owners and the builders. The site looked correct to me."

Amos thought for a few seconds. "If I were to tell you that there is now a disagreement on what some think was said at that meeting between the owners and the construction company, would that surprise you?"

"Objection, Your Honor. Irrelevant. Foundation." Bobby had quickly gotten to his feet, made his points, and just as quickly sat down.

"Sustained," the Judge practically sang out.

"No further questions." Amos now sat back and watched as Bobby approached the witness.

"Mr. Howard." Bobby nodded as a way of saying hello as he approached. "How is it that we haven't had the pleasure of your company until the very last moments of this case?"

"I was out around Chicago visiting some old friends of mine. I didn't even know that the case had proceeded to trial until a week ago. Then I tried to get back here as fast as I could."

"And you wanted badly to get back and speak for your friends?" Friendship was almost always at the forefront of Bobby's thinking.

"Objection, Your Honor. Leading." Amos said, and quickly sat.

"And how was it that you wanted to play a part in this trial?" Bobby tried again.

"Oh, I didn't. I didn't. I don't like being up on the stand having to go against anyone else's word." Howard shook his head. "It makes you feel so...so..." He looked off, obviously trying to find a word to fit his feelings.

"Exposed?" Bobby smiled.

Howard shook his head positively. "Just like you were for so many years."

That caught Bobby up. It was at times like these that Bobby was caught off-guard, when someone he didn't know identified him with his golf. Such intimate talk from a stranger would have startled anyone, and it especially startled Bobby.

Bobby thought. "So, in fact, you don't like going against the words of the property owners?"

Ray Howard saw the trap. "I don't like to disagree with almost anyone, Mr. Jones. Especially when I have to say that I think that they're wrong."

Bobby now felt that the man had some honor in him, and he questioned again why his clients didn't want to be here to confront this man. As Bobby knew, a lot of people tried to get away with things. They just didn't know how cheap it made them look or what it foretold for their souls.

"So, you went out last night to look the site over. What struck you about the site as compared to the discussion that you heard months ago about the future development of the site?" Bobby asked, trying the question another way.

"That the buildings on the site had been built in accordance with the meeting and instructions that I heard that day. The little out-building was to be built out and away from the main building. Ten feet east and ten feet north. It wasn't hard to mark that off and see that the building was right where it was supposed to be."

Bobby walked around for a few seconds. He knew not to rush when important things were at stake. He looked at the witness who was busy waiting for Bobby's next question.

"Are you in any way related to anyone in this case?" Bobby asked, searching for something.

"Nope." The man shook his head.

"Are you friends or enemies with either the building owners or anyone in the construction company?"

"Nope." The man answered and again shook his head.

Bobby looked at the Judge casually and saw that he was paying close attention.

"Is there any possibility that you could have heard only part of what the parties were talking about that night?"

The witness looked off. "Mr. Jones, I remember the conversation as clearly now as I heard it then. And after seeing the site, I don't know how anybody can think that the construction crew got their instructions wrong. I know someone is wrong here, but, obviously, the building was built where it was supposed to be built based on the conversation that I heard between the two parties."

Bobby looked at the witness and decided. "Witness dismissed." He had the feeling that the man was telling the truth, but he wanted J.J.'s input.

"What'd you think?" Bobby leaned over toward the younger attorney.

J.J. leaned toward Bobby so their conversation wouldn't be heard. "I think he's being honest. More so than the feeling I got about our clients." Bobby nodded his agreement and listened as the Judge spoke.

"I'll have my verdict tomorrow morning in this chamber at nine o'clock."

Bobby rose as the Judge left the chambers.

"Don't think the answer coming down for this one is going to make your clients very happy," J. J. said as they walked back down Cone Street away from the courthouse.

Bobby looked ahead, as was his custom. "I agree with you, but you have to take the bitter with the sweet at times. Never,

ever heard of an attorney who was so blessed that he won them all."

"What do you think the chances are?"

Bobby continued to look off. "Not very good. But then, maybe that's for a very good reason."

The following morning found Bobby and his rival attorney, Richard Amos, alone in the courtroom awaiting the judge's arrival.

"Good luck to you, Mr. Jones," Amos smiled.

"You, too." Bobby grinned as he always had in facing his opponents on the first tee.

The two attorneys quickly rose as the Judge entered.

"Be seated, gentlemen." The Judge had put on his robe, but it had obviously been a last minute thought, as it wasn't completely buttoned.

"Well, here in the case of Top South Developers versus Mellon and Waters Construction...." The Judge looked at the two attorneys seemingly glued to his words.

Bobby's four-leaf key fob was in his pocket and he found it and rubbed it for good luck as he had for years, although he felt this case was a lost affair.

The Judge took a deep breath. "I'm going to find for the Plaintiff's Top South," Judge Bears spoke out, and Bobby was stunned.

"But," Amos started and just as suddenly stopped as Judge Bears looked over his glasses at the direction of the sound.

"In matters where it's almost word-against-word, that's where we judges find ourselves doing our hardest work."

Bobby glanced at Amos and felt sorry for him. He knew the man had worked very hard for his seemingly honest clients, and from Bobby's spot, he probably should have won the decision.

"As I understand it, the full value of the building in question is $15,498. I leave it up to Mr. Amos' clients to either give the money for the building back to Top South or redo the building exactly as per the original wishes of Top South. I do not expect to hear anything further about this case." Judge Bears looked across his glasses again and tilted his head. "Am I fully understood?"

"Yes, Your Honor." Amos looked off, wondering how he could explain this outcome after being so positive about a victory.

"Yes, of course," Bobby simply stated.

As they left the court, Bobby continued to wonder about the outcome of the case. Just as he did for years when playing his golf matches, he felt for his losing opponent. Amos had some tall explaining to do to his clients, and Bobby knew it.

At Druid Hills, the next morning, Judge Bears took the first shot. Bobby watched as the Judge's drive just about made it to the start of the 1st fairway, and then he hit his drive with all the rest and strength that his last two months away from the game had given him.

"Beautiful drive, Mr. Jones." Judge Bears smiled knowing that he was going to enjoy watching Bobby play the game for which he was so famous. Behind Bobby and the Judge were about 50 people standing and watching them tee off. The Judge chuckled to himself. He was the one playing a full round with the great golfer.

"Thank you, Judge." Bobby gave his club to his caddy as they walked down off the tee. "It's always nice to get a decent start to a round."

As they walked, Bobby's mind drifted. He felt free to just enjoy the game. In tournament golf, he had to either win an Open or an amateur event or defend one of his national crowns.

Then, just as he learned so many years ago, Bobby's mind started sorting out things. He recalled his father making so many of his own decisions while thinking in the shower and singing with his great baritone voice.

"Awfully quiet over there," the Judge said after hitting his second shot.

Bobby smiled. "Just enjoying Mother Nature's breezes." More than that, though, Bobby's mind wanted to work on a decision he was in the process of making. It was a decision that he had only let out to his friend, O.B. Keeler, and it had come to the forefront of his mind because of the recent court decision from Judge Bears.

Bobby absentmindedly looked out over the links of Druid Hills. He smiled as he saw visions of himself as a young boy on the course while Donald Ross worked on East Lake back in 1913. Bobby had come to play Druid Hills through the auspices of George Adair, the very successful Atlanta real estate entrepreneur who had single-handedly built Druid Hills and had so much to do with the start of East Lake and Atlanta golf.

Bobby's mind came back to golf when he arrived at the spot where his caddy stood. A chill ran up his arms as he saw the shot. It wasn't a hard shot, but it was reminiscent of a shot that he had played with Adair during one of their last rounds together, a shot that at that time Adair had loudly praised but that Bobby knew could have been better.

Concentrating on his options, Bobby looked closely at the shot. He took out his choice of clubs and walked very smoothly and casually up to take his stance. In what seemed like an instant, he made his very rhythmic swing.

The ball started out just to the right of the target, and as it headed down, Bobby saw the differences between this shot and his shot back in 1921. This shot did what the shot from 1921 didn't do. This shot moved back to the left and went straight toward his target. This shot was hit the way it should be—with all his heart and mind wanting to pull it off. And the feeling that this good shot brought was one of total relief.

But this shot was free. This shot didn't have a lot of people yelling at him about how great the shot was or fighting for his divot or jostling to walk along with him down the fairway and wanting to strike up a conversation with him or betting a lot of money on him. This was a joy, a quiet, contemplative joy.

A shot to be savored personally and privately. A shot that was a singular joy for him, the Judge, and their caddies. A shot that was struck with the simple purpose of being an uplifting achievement to just a few.

But as Bobby thought about it, he thought about Adair and what the man had meant to his golf history. The memories caught in his throat, and he cleared it.

"Very nice shot," the Judge said across the fairway.

Bobby nodded his thanks but thought to himself, "You're right, Judge. There was someone very special in my life at one time that I wish had seen that shot."

The day passed casually as Bobby shot a very easy three under par. He could have played better if he had tried just a little bit more. But Bobby knew that if he tried harder, he would be taking some reserves out of his system—reserves that he was going to need this next year, the year of 1930.

After the round, Bobby and the Judge sat at a table on the veranda of the clubhouse.

"Well, you should be very proud of yourself. A victory one day and a great round the next." The Judge smiled over at Bobby.

Bobby looked off and then slowly faced the Judge. "I have a question for you, and I hope that you'll take it in the spirit in which it's intended."

"I'll certainly try, Mr. Jones." The Judge smiled at Bobby and put his drink down.

"You and I have a job to do at times because of our positions in life. Making our legal system work correctly is a very important matter for our citizenry." Bobby put his drink down and moved his left leg up and over his right leg very slowly and purposely. "To what degree," he began, "to what degree, if you will, was your decision in my recent case before you predicated on my being Bobby Jones the golfer, not Bob Jones the lawyer?"

Judge Bears was visibly taken back. "Not at all," he replied hastily. He paused, thinking for a few seconds. "And I'll forgive you for even asking me that question. I've been on the bench now for close to ten years. Long ago, I learned that any decision I make has to be totally in line with my objective findings. You're too young an attorney to know that, so I'll forgive you for asking." The Judge shook his head as he eked out a smile.

Bobby looked straight at him. "But the other side seemed to me to have a much better case. They even had an outside witness that seemed to be a very honest man in his own right, one who testified to the merits of his conviction."

The Judge nodded. "But if you are ever in my position, you'll see the story from a very unique perspective." The tone of his voice left no doubt that the subject was over. The Judge was satisfied. He was simply not willing to see what Bobby saw.

Bobby got to his office early the next day and began cleaning up some odds and ends. Shortly after eight o'clock, he heard his father come in. Bobby went through the special doorway that ran between their two offices, over to his dad's office, where they hugged to start the day as they usually did.

"I have something very serious to bounce off you," Bobby said, sitting on the corner of his father's desk.

The Colonel nodded and sat back in his chair and took out a cigar. "I've had some sense of something happening for a while now."

Bobby looked quizzically at his dad and smiled.

"Know what yesterday's date was?" the Colonel asked.

Bobby shook his head.

"It was this time, back eight years ago, when we last played with George Adair." The Colonel looked at him and watched as he thought. "Before he died," he reminded.

Bobby got up and looked out his dad's window at downtown Atlanta. "I've been thinking some of Adair lately." Bobby turned around. "He was really something."

The Colonel nodded. "That he was. For you and me and for East Lake and Druid Hills and golf in Atlanta. If it wasn't for him, we might not even be playing the game." The Colonel smiled. "Bet you haven't met anyone more ethical or moral than he was." The Colonel's memory of Adair brought a smile to both their faces.

Bobby grinned. "You know, every time I win something, I think of him and how glad he would have been for me."

"Paying your debts back?" the Colonel smiled.

"Just maybe what I'm working on now has something to do with Adair."

That was a message for the Colonel, and he sat up, lit his cigar, and paid close attention to his son, sensing that something big was coming.

"I think I might better step down as the firm's litigator."

The Colonel was silent for a few heavy seconds. "But I heard that you just had another great win."

Bobby stood up and took the chair across from his dad. "I'm not sure if you could really refer to what happened as a great win for the legal system though. I think the win should be credited to me the golfer, not me the attorney, and therein lies the problem."

The Colonel shook his head. "Not surprised at that. J.J. and Bill and I talked about the possibility of that happening. Guess it's hard for Atlanta to put behind it what you have done for the South. You may never be able to escape your aura as the South's hero." The Colonel looked off. "A lot of litigators would love to have this problem."

Bobby nodded in agreement. "I'll bet."

They were both quiet.

"What do you think I should do?" Bobby finally inquired.

The Colonel glanced out the window, then slowly back at Bobby. "This is a decision that you best make, son. This is a worthy decision that is going to be carried on your shoulders for a long, long time. But I'll tell you this; whatever you decide is fine by me and your mother, and I know that the others here will know that you gave it all the proper thought that was necessary."

Bobby looked at his dad. "I think I have already given this much thought. In the best interest of our legal system, I believe I should step down as the firm's litigator, so that the judges can go back to making decisions based on the merits of argument and law rather than allowing themselves to be swayed by some misplaced allegiance to someone well known for simply hitting a white ball around." Bobby looked back at his dad who was now sitting straight up in his chair. "I'll be glad to help J.J. take over, if you all wish me to."

The Colonel stood up as his son made a motion to leave. "Oh, Keeler dropped in yesterday. He said that one of his British reporter friends found out something that he knew you'd be interested in." The Colonel cocked his head. "Turns out that next year's British Amateur is going to be held at St. Andrews after all."

As Bobby took in the information, he faced his dad. "You know what that means?"

The Colonel gently nodded.

"Three out of the four events that I like to play are going to be held at courses that I first played at for a national title." Bobby looked questioning at his dad. "Do you think that's an accident?"

The Colonel responded. "I think that it's what they call very providential."

Bobby wandered out of the office and down the street. He felt good about his decision to step down as the firm's litigator. He knew that he had done the correct thing for the good of the practice of law, and his past experience told him that he would have made George Adair very happy.

Any thoughts about George Adair connected Bobby to golf. He had grown up in the game and now the game was almost running his life. If the United States Golf Association (USGA) or the Royal and Ancient, the organizations that ruled the game of golf, weren't contacting him about something, fans were constantly asking him for something for either themselves or their courses. Or he was the center of some very heavy betting or the object of scrutinizing questioning. He was glad he now had an office and a secretary who could help with all his fan mail and requests.

Then the truth of his feelings about his decision to step down as the firm's litigator came to him. It was a decision that was motivated by the fact that the position did not pan out the way that he had hoped, and he knew that his golf life hadn't gone in a direction he would have chosen had he had the right to choose.

That thought caused a chilling ripple to go up his spine, a ripple of feelings that told him he needed to do something. There was a part of his life that wasn't in alignment, and it was up to him, Robert Tyre Jones, Jr., to correct that before his life went totally out of kilter.

Three out of the four tournaments he had planned for the next year were going to be played at courses that he had played during his original years at big tournament play. That said something to Bobby. If he was simply able to carry his progress forward, and step up and step up again, to do better than he had done in 1921 and 1926, he might be able to win at least three of the big tournaments, which would give him the biggest year ever in the game.

Bobby grinned. Dare he even think of winning all four? He automatically shook his head. A silly thought about doing the impossible. To win all four in only his third try at playing all four in the same year would really be something.

CHAPTER
2

At the turn of the previous millennium, a lot of people were hoping for something to happen. When it finally did, few were quick to see it for what it was. Special happenings usually start out so small, it's easy for people to discount them.

It was another summer day cloaked in the heat and humidity of East Lake as the little tow-haired boy peered out of his living room window to watch the other children in his neighborhood run back and forth between the cottages. They were playing together as he so badly wanted to do.

"Little Bob!" the maid, Camellia, called from the dining room in her usually expectant tone. Quickly, the little boy pulled his elbows off the windowsill and climbed onto the big high-backed sofa and started to bounce back and forth with his pent up nervous energy.

"Now, I know that you weren't there a minute ago," Camellia said, coming into the room and pointing her finger at the boy, unknowingly shaking the duster in her other hand. "You can only spend some time at the window." She intentionally looked over at where the drapes were left parted. "You can't spend your whole day there." She pointed to the window.

The little boy sat quietly on the big sofa as he knew the maid wanted him to do. He had learned there were times that he could get away with some things and other times he just had to take his medicine.

Camellia went over to the new Victrola record player, wound it up, and played the German Opera records for which the little boy's mother had developed a daily preference. As she glanced over at the little boy, she noticed that he was quietly bouncing back and forth on the sofa in tune with the heavy Germanic tones of the opera music. She smiled to herself, knowing from past experience that as long as the record played she could count on the boy to be involved with the heavy beat and not allow himself to be pulled away to visit with his friends as a spectator.

It wasn't unusual at the turn of the twentieth century for a family that had lost a child to become overly protective of their other children. Medicine had made great strides, but losing a child or two or more was commonplace among many families, as was the lingering sadness that accompanied the traumatic losses. And this family was no different.

The first Jones son, William Bailey Jones, had died six years before, and shortly after the birth of their second boy, known as Little Bob, on St. Patrick's Day in 1902, they had taken the precaution, despite their son's six doctors' contradictory wishes, to rent a summer vacation home six miles outside of the city of Atlanta in a small rural town called East Lake. Here the air was considered more healthful than it was in the growing city of Atlanta, which only seventy-six years previously had its name changed from Terminus, Georgia. The family hoped that the healthful country air of East Lake would benefit their second son, the one they named after his very strict, religious paternal grandfather, Robert Tyre Jones, the big mill owner who owned most of the town of Canton in the foothills of northern Georgia.

Little Bob's father, having gotten his sickly son to the age of five, now only worried about common childhood diseases like polio and tuberculosis, which he understood to be a lot less common in the country than they were in the city.

Sadly, his second son had been almost as ill as their first child had been. It was only recently that Little Bob could be put on a regular diet. Until close to his fifth birthday, he had been on a strict diet of egg whites, tapioca, and pabulum at the direction of his doctors, fortified only by treats from his father who would occasionally sneak the boy some oatmeal or snap cookies. Now the youngster was eating regular food and growing very quickly, as if his skinny body wanted to catch up with his oversized head.

And Little Bob, with his newfound energy, wanted so badly to play with the rest of the children that he saw running around the neighborhood from his highly valued window perch.

"Li'l Bob, get your dirty little feet back down off the sofa!" the maid, Camellia, reminded strongly. The little boy wiggled his feet down off the end of the sofa, then bounced back against the old high-back sofa again in tune with the music coming out of the hand-wound Victrola record player.

Because of the child's improved health, and the fact that it was summer, there had been times that the little boy had been allowed out, but only to go over to the big green golf course across the little dirt lane with his parents. There, he followed his mother and father around as they played a new game called golf. It was his first introduction to a family outing and, partly because he was allowed outside, he loved it.

"Now, you keep up, Little Bob," the boy's mother, Clara Jones, warned again and again as the three of them spent afternoons, very warm Georgia afternoons, walking and playing East Lake golf course, one of only three new golf courses in the Atlanta area.

And of course when the new golf professional arrived, everyone lined up to meet him. "This is my son, Bobby," Bobby's father, Robert Purmedus Jones, said to introduce his son to Stewart Maiden, a recent immigrant who had come from Carnoustie, Scotland. Maiden had followed his younger brother, Jimmy, to East Lake. Jimmy had been the pro at East Lake, but he left his position to take another professional's job with a new golf course up north in Nassau, New York.

Maiden looked down at the youngster who was busy studying him from his position below. "Nace tae meet yer, Maister Robin." Maiden reached down to find the boy's hand, and failing to get that settled for patting him on the head.

The little boy looked up, and shading his deep blue gray eyes from the afternoon sun, smiled shyly, tilting his tow head.

"He's been following his mother and me around the past couple of weeks and seems to be enjoying the out of doors. We're hoping that it's good for his health. He looks like he's growing stronger, doesn't he?" Bobby's father smiled a profoundly grateful smile as he joined his hands happily under his suspenders.

Maiden nodded and handled a golf club from his workbench, watching the boy's eyes closely follow his activity. Maiden could see that the boy was very alert and interested in learning.

"What's a good age for the young'uns to start playing golf?" Bobby's father moved his eyes from Maiden back down to his son.

"Och onytime, onytime at taw," Maiden said, watching the boy's eyes travel with his every move. "Thae younger, thae better," he mumbled intently, watching the boy's reactions.

But destiny beat them both to the punch. "Here's for you, little one." Fulton Colville, a local boarding house resident who played at East Lake, had been watching the boy trail his parents for weeks. He arrived at the scene and handed Bobby an old cleek, a golf club used before 1930 that was the equivalent of a two-iron and very difficult to hit.

Bobby took the club and, fumbling, immediately put it down to hit an imaginary ball. But the length of the club prevented the boy from swinging it. Maiden reached over, took the club from the boy's hands, made a few quick measurements and adjustments to the club, and in almost no time had the appropriately sized cleek back into the child's waiting hands.

"Thare, Robin." Maiden gazed on the young child. He coaxed the boy outside and over toward an open area where he dropped a ball onto the ground. He watched the boy move naturally into a position to strike at the ball.

Maiden grinned at the child's willingness to get started quickly and with such ease.

"Nae. This," Maiden said, letting the little boy move into position again but this time stopping him while he addressed the ball. "Lak this," Maiden insisted, moving the boy's fingers about on the shaft of the club, and then having set them in place, he squeezed them so as to make an impression on the boy's mind.

"Nou, hat it!" Maiden commanded, backing away from the boy and patting him on the head.

Maiden watched, along with Bobby's father and Colville, as Li'l Bob took his first swing and sent the ball scurrying across the ground.

"Aff yer gae." Maiden pushed the boy in the direction of his ball and watched him scamper after it, dragging his club gaily behind him.

"Why, thank you," Bobby's father said. He smiled at Colville and nodded his thanks to Maiden.

"I sure hope he'll get some good use out of it. That darn club has been nothing but pain to me," Colville said, shaking his head and drifting off after picking up the rest of his clubs.

"I hope my son won't be a bother," Bobby's father said as he and Maiden drifted back into Maiden's little wooden-sided golf shop that sat away from the main building.

"Naet at taw. Naet at taw," Maiden said, picking up the hickory shaft that he had been working on. Then he looked over at Bobby's father, who was affectionately called Big Bob by his friends to distinguish him from his own father and later his famous son. "An this tis as guid a time as ony for him tae be l'arnin. Nou e'll growe up wi thee gemme as thay dae back in thee auld kintra."

Big Bob parted with a rare smile from Maiden that made him feel oddly relieved.

From that point on, Bobby became a fixture at the links of East Lake. At almost any time of day, except weekends, members would move aside and allow the little boy to pass through, playing his way to the next hole. Weekends were saved for men who had only weekends to invest in their new sport.

"Who is he?" one new member said to another as they stood watching the boy hitting small yardage shots while moving directly up the fairway.

"That's Big Bob's boy. The sickly one. But as you can see, the clean air and health of East Lake have cured him."

And it was a fact. The combination of better food and exercise and being out of doors were impacting on the boy's body. For a five-year-old, he was having a real growth spurt.

Because Bobby couldn't play on the course on weekends, he and his neighborhood friend, Frank Meador, created a two-hole course that they played, down across the wooded lane in front of their shared house. It was on this makeshift course that Bobby made his first hole-in-one, a shot that dribbled down the road and into the large rain ditch that the boys considered the second hole.

The Joneses shared a cottage with the Meador family that summer and Little Bobby couldn't have been happier. The Meador's son, Frank, was a very easygoing boy who, although two years older than Bobby, was a built-in follower. Whenever Bobby couldn't play on the course with his parents, he had Frank to play with on their little road course.

"C'mon, c'mon," Bobby would yell to Frank and off they would go. Bobby had also come by an old mashie-niblick and a spoon from his father that Stewart Maiden had gladly resized for the boy. Matching these clubs with his original cleek from Colvin, Bobby now had a workable set, for the cleek was a two-iron, the mashie-niblick was a seven-iron, and the spoon was a three-wood.

"Me first," Bobby claimed, putting his ball down on the road. Frank had no trouble waiting, as was his habit in life.

The little tyke's shot went along the road, but this time drifted off into a briar patch that was filled with black raspberries. "Pesky ball, damn pesky ball," Bobby shouted, as he had heard his father say. He spun around and swung his club. "That damn pesky ball doesn't want to behave."

Frank didn't know what to say. He had heard adults speak that way, but never another child.

Bobby got his ball out of the briar patch and in the process wound up with nettles all over his shorts and socks.

"Now you're going to get it," Frank offered, seeing Bobby's clothes.

Bobby scanned his clothes to see what Frank meant. "I'll go to Camellia," Bobby thought out loud, and he took off to get rescued by the maid who often helped him get out of his little-boy predicaments before his parents could see the problems he had gotten into.

The next day found a cleaned-up Bobby and Frank waiting for the ice wagon to make deliveries to their cottage. In hot weather, the boys always scooped the ice chips off the back of the horse drawn wagon to cool off while the ice man made his long call on the Jones house. The iceman's call on the Jones family always took a while because the iceman was Camellia's boyfriend.

They whiled away the time playing their new game. "I'm gonna make that pesky ball behave," Bobby said, taking another swat at the little white ball which bounced this time off the cottage before heading into the briar patch again. "Pesky ball. Damn pesky ball." Bobby danced around swinging his club, which just missed Frank. This time, Frank beat Bobby to the punch and rescued Bobby's ball for him, and just in time for Bobby to see his father turn up the dirt lane, returning home.

"Dad," Bobby bleated, and he ran to greet his father.

"Having a good time?" Big Bob asked his son when they reached each other and hugged his son to his stomach. He was so glad to see his son outside playing with another child, growing healthy and strong.

He was so glad, in fact, that he got the boy a Collie dog a few days later. They named him Judge, and it became the boy's responsibility to make sure the dog didn't wander off.

Day after day, young Bobby found himself chasing after the Collie that followed after almost everyone who walked past their property on the little lane alongside the East Lake Golf Course.

Big Bob had a decision to make. Seeing how strong and healthy his son had grown over time, which Big Bob credited to spending the summer at East Lake, he was struck with the idea that, just maybe, they should consider moving to East Lake permanently. Bobby's health was never out of Big Bob's mind.

"You know, Clara, I kind of miss our little family outings at that golf course out there in East Lake," Big Bob said to his wife one night after they were back in Atlanta. "Even if we were able to play only once every week or two, it would be better than sitting in this house in the damn city."

Clara looked at her husband and shook her head. "But it takes you so much longer to get home from your office when we live out there."

Big Bob looked at her. "Seeing you and our son enjoy the fresh air and the little community like you do is worth the extra trip to me. Maybe if we move out there permanently, I might be able to get off work sooner at times to cover the extra travel time." Then Big Bob smiled. "And just maybe before too long, we'll be able to afford one of those new cars and I can get right home at my own pace rather than waiting for the trolleys and then switching over to a hack."

Gazing at young Bobby, Big Bob continued airing his thoughts with his wife. "And look how our boy has grown." His mind ran back over his son's happiness at being outdoors, which had flowered into a big weight and size gain for the short time the boy had been in East Lake. It had cost Big Bob a lot of his well-earned funds to take that summer cottage, but he knew that he would do it again—and quickly.

Big Bob made his case and Clara agreed, and neither of them knew or had any true idea of what their actions would mean to their family, golf, or the South.

CHAPTER
3

Big Bob moved his family into a new, year-round home in East Lake. He began to take long walks to settle in, and he played golf and baseball with his son and fished with him off the pier at the busy recreational lake in their suburb, as well. Like most doting fathers, Big Bob was glad to see his son learn sports. He himself had painful memories of being deprived of sports. His father was a strict religionist. In his father's view, you worked six days a week and rested on the Sabbath. You didn't play golf or baseball. There was no mention of sports in scripture.

But baseball was the national pastime in America at the turn of the century, and scores of people were in love with it. Teams representing factories, towns, and villages got together to compete on neighborhood parks and playgrounds. Newspapers ran full pages of all the local teams and their activities, and the games and their box scores filled over fifty percent of the sporting pages in many of America's town newspapers.

Big Bob had bitterly regretted not having these kinds of experiences with his father. As luck would have it, Big Bob was good at baseball—so good, in fact, that when he attended Georgia College, he signed a contract to play professionally for the Brooklyn Trolley Dodgers. But his father put so much negative pressure on him about playing, he had eventually backed away from it. He spurned a baseball career to make his father happy, and he went on to graduate from Georgia College with a law degree. He was now a practicing attorney in the growing metropolis of Atlanta, which had a population of close to one hundred fifty thousand people.

But the hole that was left in his heart by his puritanical upbringing wasn't lost on him, and he promised himself that, if he ever had a son, he and his son would play together, his son would have his approval, and they would enjoy being related to each other as father and son—in life and in sport.

So, Big Bob worked relentlessly to earn his son's trust and, in the process, he became his son's best friend.

"Look, Dad, look," Bobby said, bringing his newly-caught fish to his father one day at East Lake.

"Damn good, my boy. We'll cook it for dinner," Big Bob said, patting his son on the head and then hugging the boy's head to his stomach. "Hell, now go back and see if you can damn well catch another big one." Bobby dutifully obliged.

Big Bob made good on his promises to himself. His son never went without the parental approval that he had so painfully gone without. He hugged his son before hugging was in vogue, he supported his son's feelings well before anyone knew how important that was, and he spoiled him a bit—buying Bobby a pony because there were few other children for Bobby to play with in the country. Bobby named the pony Clara after his mother, in a childish display of affection.

School time came around for Bobby. He attended the new Woodbury Elementary School with the few playmates in his neighborhood, and his love and appreciation for the outdoors soon became a problem.

"Now you go off to school. After school, you get to play on the course," Bobby's dad reasoned with him most mornings. "Besides, all your friends will be at school. You won't have anyone around to play golf with."

But that sort of talk didn't stop Bobby. He knew about a few outdoor things, like fishing off the East Lake dock, that didn't need friends. So on the way to school one morning, he created the perfect alibi. En route to school, he walked through every mud puddle he could find until his shoes were totally dirty and his feet soaked to the core.

"Go home and get those shoes and socks changed before you catch your death of cold or worse," his teacher said, knowing of the Jones family plight in raising a healthy child.

"Yes, Ma'am." Bobby almost saluted as he skipped all the way home thinking only of the fish that he would catch and the praise he would get from his father for his catch. Once he got to the house, he laid hands on his fishing pole and off to the dock at East Lake he went.

"Woo, woo, woo," Bobby cried as he worked to pull in what looked to him like the biggest fish he had ever seen. His efforts to land the fish were met by the fish's efforts to stay in the water.

He moved closer to the edge of the dock to bring the big fish in, then closer still, until there wasn't any more dock left. Into six feet of water the young boy went, without any semblance of an idea of how to swim.

Bobby floundered in the water, until the man attending the boats swiftly came over and pulled the boy to safety.

That night was a terrifying one for the Joneses as they realized how close they had come to losing their second son.

"Robert, you damn well come here this instant," Big Bob commanded, having heard what happened from the boat manager.

Bobby was not used to his father addressing him that way, and he approached his father with trepidation.

"Young man, you scared the living hell out of your mother and me today. We were damned lucky you didn't lose your life out there, alone on that dock. Now I am going to have to do something that I do not ever want to damn well have to do again." With that, Mr. Jones paddled Bobby over his knee and then sent him to bed early with no fatherly hug.

The following morning Big Bob was still mindful of what

had transpired the previous day as he fixed his son's breakfast. "The next time you play hooky from that damn school, you will get another firm paddling." But Big Bob was hoping mightily that the day would never come.

It wasn't just the paddling that affected Bobby. It was the fact that he had made his father, who was his best friend, upset. That bothered Bobby more, and it made him more aware of their friendship.

Fishing and baseball were nice sports, but Bobby and his father played golf more, for golf provided Big Bob with more reasons to encourage his son.

"Damn nice shot, my boy," Big Bob would say, with the littlest provocation, and Bobby correctly sensed that his father was always pulling for him even when they played against each other. Big Bob was not about to bestow an easy victory on his son though. His days in baseball had shown him that no one ever really got a reward out of an easy victory.

But unbeknownst to Big Bob, young Bobby was getting a boost from a source other than his father. Bobby's development in the game was also progressing because of the lessons, some quite mystical, that he was getting from the new Scottish golf professional, Stewart Maiden.

Bobby's home was near the 13th green. It was called the mule house because it had previously housed a few mules that were used on the grounds when the area had been a park. But the mules were now long gone, and the Jones family occupied the second floor that had a commanding view of the course.

Whenever Bobby wanted to know who was playing golf on the course, all he had to do was look out one of his second floor windows. The newly-arrived Scottish professional, Maiden, became one of Bobby's targets. Bobby loved to watch Maiden play.

"I'll be back, Mom," Bobby would say, and off he'd go as soon as he saw Maiden in the distance. Bobby would follow Maiden for a few holes and watch everything the Scottish professional was doing. After a few holes, he'd break off the routine and head over to his house near the 13th green to hit the same kind of shots he had seen the professional golfer hit. It was Bobby's way of improving, by watching the best player around, and it became his and Maiden's own little silent ritual.

Secretly, Stewart Maiden had been paying close attention to Bobby's game. Whenever he saw Bobby having problems with a particular part of his game, he would set himself up to play some of those shots. That way, he could teach Bobby about a particular shot without giving him a formal lesson. Maiden often watched Bobby head off to work on the shots, and his face wore an insightful grin long after the boy was out of sight.

Evenings at home were spent listening to the phonograph or talking or playing games. There were card games, and occasionally board games like chess and checkers, and even participation games like charades and the popular memory tests, and of course the old favorite among the children, Hide-and-Seek. Games tested and stretched people's minds or their reflexes. There was always someone who knew the heavens and all the stars or someone who knew all the trees and their leaves.

But Bobby had a different game to offer. He had learned to mimic a lot of the players at East Lake while trying to swing as they did. So, at night, he entertained his father and others with his rendition of various member's swings.

"Guess who this is, Dad," Bobby said to his father and some of their neighbors who gathered one night on the porch awaiting the heat of the day to expire as the sun dropped below the trees of East Lake.

Bobby grunted as he grabbed his golf club and swung, and

then stepped quickly forward in the fashion of the club member he was mimicking. He swung the club again, grunting, hoping that someone would be able to tell who it was that he was portraying.

Big Bob broke out into a belly laugh, recognizing the swing of his fellow neighbor. "Go get Frank," Big Bob insisted to a neighbor on the porch.

"But what's Frank going to say, having a youngster making fun of him?" the woman returned in a hushed tone with her arms crossed over her chest.

"Oh, peeshaw, woman. He's just mimicking him. It's a damned compliment for Christ's sake." Big Bob took another swig of his whiskey and went in to get his wife. "Clara. Come out and see what the hell our son can do."

Bobby continued swinging as some of the neighborhood children gathered to watch.

"Do that swing that you did before," Big Bob ordered arriving back on the porch. He wanted everyone else to see what he saw and to be as proud of his son as he was.

Finally, the man being mimicked arrived. When he saw Bobby perform his swing, he almost keeled over. "That's me?" he asked.

Big Bob laughed. "If anything, he damn well looks more like you than you do, Frank." Big Bob's laugh became a deep belly roll.

"How about Stewart? Can you do the old pro?" Big Bob inquired with a bit of inside knowledge.

Bobby very easily showed a version of the golf professional's swing which was, for all purposes, an exact likeness.

"Very, very good, my boy. Very good," Big Bob said, and after another fatherly embrace, Bobby was released to play with the other children.

Bobby enjoyed his newfound fame. It seemed to cover him like a warm quilt. It endeared him to his parents and the other adults around, but also the acclaim made his new friends look up to him and admire what he was capable of.

But as much as mimicking grown players at the club brought him attention, it was Bobby's actual game that was becoming his father's pride. After every round, Bobby searched out his father, and together, they'd go over his final score and discuss in detail what he did on each hole.

They also scoured the newspapers together for news of golf.

"Guess what was in the newspapers today?" Big Bob would frequently say to his son as they spent nights enjoying one of Atlanta's six daily newspapers. Electric lights had come to their neighborhood, and it gave families more options in the evenings.

"Now, let me think," Bobby would throw back at his dad, knowing full well what his father was referring to. "The paper had a story about golf in it?"

"Correct." Big Bob smiled and enjoyed the repartee with his son. "Now guess what kind of golf story the paper had?"

Bobby rubbed his index finger over his lips. "Hmmm. Let's see." Then he'd look out of the corner of his eye to watch his father who was busy watching him. "How about a story about the National Open?"

Big Bob shook his head. "That's not going to be played for six more months."

Bobby tried again. "How about a story about foreign golfers?"

"Close enough," chucked Big Bob. "This is a story about one of the home-bred professionals which, as we know, is different than the foreign-born professionals who came over here from Scotland."

Big Bob read the story about Johnny McDermott who was busy blazing a path through the American golf scene. Big Bob favored the stories about the American golfers because they showed that an American could meet or beat the players from the old countries.

One of the interesting things about the stories he read was

the fact that golf reporting was often done by sports writers who had never played the game themselves and who might be covering their first golf tournament or golf story. Having never played the game, many of these reporters had a tough time seeing any merit or ability in hitting a little stationary white ball from place to place, and because of that, Big Bob found himself constantly helping the reporter whose story he was reading.

"How about this?" Big Bob said chuckling out loud. "This reporter writes that the game must be harder than he thought because all the players seemed to miss their first two or three swings at the ball." Big Bob laughed again.

Bobby had a puzzled look on his face, so Big Bob explained.

"The reporter didn't know that the players were taking practice swings," Big Bob laughed. "Can you imagine having that reporter along to count up your scores?" Big Bob shook his head. "You'd wind up with scores in the hundreds."

Big Bob rustled the paper in his lap. "When you were about three or so, there was a local newspaper guy who really understood all the sports. His name was Grantland Rice. Now he knew what he was talking about when it came to sports, and especially golf, because he played golf himself," Big Bob told his son.

Bobby looked up at his dad trying to understand, and a few things began to emerge as Bobby and his father read the sports pages together.

"Looks like there's a battle looming over who is going to run our game," Big Bob said to his son. "A new group called the Western Golf Association has come out with its own set of rules and is signing up courses and members just like the United States Golf Association is doing." Big Bob grinned knowingly. "Whenever something new comes along, you'll find people who want to get in on it one way or another."

CHAPTER
4

No one ever knows how good they can be in golf until they give it their all. When Bobby found that out, he began to draw favorable circumstances to himself.

Before Bobby was seven years old, he got a golf champion to play with. She wasn't a champion yet, but she was destined to be. Her name was Alexa Stirling, who eventually won three Women's National Amateur events. She was five years older than Bobby when she moved to East Lake.

Bobby had been playing with George Adair's son, Perry. George Adair was the guiding light behind the development of East Lake. In preparing for his real estate career in golf, George Adair had taken many trips back to the old country of Scotland. There, he saw how the Scottish people got their children involved in the game early. He was delighted when his own son, Perry, became so infatuated with the game that he learned it quickly—including the rules, an area most players find boring. But knowing the rules gave Perry insight into the game that other players did not have, and it gave him power because of it.

Alexa's father had come to Atlanta to serve as the British Consul. He and his wife were not used to the rural South, and they worried that Alexa would not find anything to occupy her time. So, Alexa's father signed Alexa up for golf instruction with Stewart Maiden. He had no idea how far she would go. Alexa was a very good student, and in a very short time, she became Maiden's best pupil.

Bobby's foursome was rounded out with his first playmate in

East Lake, Frank Meador. Bobby was the youngest of the group. Alexa was five years older, as was Frank, and Perry bested him by three years. The Stirlings, the Adairs, the Meadors, and the Joneses all played golf at East Lake, just as families did in Scotland.

East Lake, a small town hidden in the depths of the languid, unnoticed South, was becoming the perfect breeding ground for great golfers.

"Now, here are the rules for the tournament," Mrs. Meador said as she addressed the young foursome on another hot, humid Georgia day. "You play out to the 3rd hole and come back on the 16th, 17th, and 18th. The boy or girl who has the lowest score for the six holes wins this trophy." Mrs. Meador held up a little three-inch vase and the kids looked at it."Who goes first?" Perry Adair asked, certain he would be first since he was the oldest.

Mrs. Meador didn't know the rules of golf, but she was a champ at improvising. "Oh, let's play ladies first," she said.

Bobby and his father had spent time reading about the great champions and the history of the game. Suddenly, he found himself in a tournament just like he imagined his father had been talking about, and his excitement peaked.

"Who's keeping score?" Alexa asked Mrs. Meador.

Mrs. Meador had no trouble deciding that point. She had recently had talks with her son about accepting responsibility. "Why, Frank will be happy to keep scores." Hearing his mother, Frank's head sunk. He wasn't great with numbers or keeping things straight.

"Okay, off you go," Mrs. Meador encouraged. "Lemonade to everyone after the winner is picked."

Bobby stared at the trophy. He saw that the little three-inch vase was within his grasp, and he almost reached out to it right then and there.

"I go first," Alexa said proudly. She had a great chance to win. She had beaten all the boys before and felt she could do it again.

The four youngsters teed off, and Mrs. Meador watched them walk down the first fairway. She headed toward her kitchen knowing that the youngsters would be busy for the next hour or two.

Out on the course, the children worked their way from hole to hole. Their idea of the rules were not yet grounded, so they just did the best they could. Frank tried to keep the course scorecard, but he wasn't used to keeping score for himself let alone three others. Nonetheless, the children enjoyed being in a tournament, and despite the heat, they had a great time.

When they arrived back at the Meador home, Frank handed the scorecard to his mother. "You didn't add it up," Mrs. Meador groused.

Frank shook his head and took the card from his mother. He sat down to add up the scores. Everyone kept their own scores in their heads, of course. Alexa had done the best of the group, and she believed the tallied scores would confirm that.

"Here." Frank again handed the card to his mother who looked at the bottom tallies. Frank had added each three-hole total and had then added the two totals together for the six-hole scores. Mrs. Meador looked at the scores and double-checked Frank's figures. She announced the winner.

"The winner is Bobby," she grinned.

Bobby looked at the others to see what they were going to say. But everyone just stood there, and finally, Mrs. Meador placed the trophy in Bobby's hands.

"Wow," Bobby thought. He had visions of showing the trophy to his father as soon as he got home.

"Let's see," Alexa commanded.

"Now, can we have some lemonade?" Frank asked, glad his scorekeeping job was over.

The children drank their lemonade and talked about a lot of things, but every now and then, Bobby took the trophy out of his pocket and looked at it. It was having quite an effect on him.

That night, Bobby sat on the front porch waiting for his father to come home. He saw him walking up their lane, with his dog Judge behind him, and he ran to meet him.

"Look, Dad!" Bobby held the trophy out for his father to see.

"Well, damn, is that the trophy for the tournament Mrs. Meador was having for you children? Did you win that?" Big Bob asked, taking the trophy and looking at it while they walked.

"Yep. We had a tournament just like you talked about."

Big Bob smiled. "Well, you sure did." Then he pulled his son to him. They stood there for a time, father and son, happy to be in each other's company. "You sure did," Big Bob repeated. "Let's go into the house and you can tell me all about it." Big Bob had known about the tournament, but didn't think Bobby would outperform the others.

When they got inside the house, Big Bob reached into his valise and pulled something out. He grinned at Bobby while he handed him a book. "Is it about Mr. Travis?" Bobby asked.

"It certainly is," Big Bob answered. "It's Travis's golf book. I may have to read most of the book to you, to, eh, sort of help you completely grasp what Travis is talking about."

Bobby had been using a putter just like Walter Travis used. What a special day this was! Bobby had received two special gifts in one day.

That night, Bobby took his trophy up to bed with him, and spent time looking at it close-up by the light of his single lamp. When he finally climbed into bed, Bobby put the trophy on one side of him and he put the Walter Travis book on the other.

Bobby's next entry into tournament golf came in his ninth year, when he played for the Junior Championship at East Lake. Because so few Juniors entered, all who signed up were automatically forwarded into the tournament.

Proud to be involved in a tournament sponsored by a legitimate golf association, Bobby went through eighteen-hole match after eighteen-hole match with his head held high. One thing that helped was the fact that no one was smaller than he was. That was something he was used to at East Lake.

"Well, how'd my boy do?" Big Bob asked Bobby, but he could in fact already tell from the smile on his son's face.

"I won, Dad, I won!" Bobby blurted out.

Big Bob stopped and looked with wonder at his son. "And by how much did you win?"

"4 and 3," Bobby said. "Mr. Adair said he was proud of me for winning against someone much bigger than I was," Bobby added gleefully. "And older."

"Well, I'm proud of you too." Big Bob gave Bobby one of his fatherly hugs.

"Dad, Perry almost broke 80 today. I wasn't with him; I just heard about it."

"Well, when you're his age, you'll be breaking 80, I'll bet."

"I hope so. I'm close to breaking 90, but I want to be with Perry when he breaks 80, so I can see how it's done."

Big Bob nodded.

"Are we gonna play with Perry and his dad on Sunday morning?"

"George and I already talked about that. Yes, I expect we'll play with them again this Sunday morning."

"Oh, good." Bobby almost skipped along with his dad as they arrived at their cottage.

"Hey, Dad?" Bobby started. He had something special to say to his father. "What do other people do on Sundays if they don't play golf?"

That innocent childhood statement caught Big Bob off-guard. After thinking for a second, he started laughing. Bobby couldn't understand, but his father was enjoying a moment of validation. He realized that he had put his upbringing behind him and his family.

The next day, Bobby had his picture taken with the runner-up. He took the picture up to his bedroom and wrote "Champion" on it under his image and he wrote "Runner-up" under the other boy's image. The pride he had in himself was obvious by the bold way he wrote the titles.

Moving to East Lake had been good for the entire Jones family, including Bobby's father. Big Bob himself was making progress as a golfer. He had always been a good athlete, so he had strength on his side, and he developed a full swing and learned how to score well. But no matter how much he applied himself, Big Bob found that his nine-year-old son was in the process of passing him. Big Bob began to realize that he had something special on his hands. And unbeknownst to him, he had chosen the perfect golf course for his special charge.

East Lake was no easy golf course. The 1st and 3rd holes were par-threes while all the rest were par-fours, about half of which measured over 400 yards. It was no easy test for a nine-year-old, but Bobby, after getting his first par on the short par-three first, kept at it—and he was close to breaking 90.

The style of golf that was played when Bobby was nine also helped. Match play was the preferred method of golf at the time. Most golfers are familiar with medal play. In medal play, the lowest score for 18 holes wins. Match play is a competition by holes. You win a hole by having fewer strokes on the hole than your opponent. The winner of the first hole is said to be 1-up, no matter how many strokes he wins by. A hole played in the same number of strokes by both competitors is said to be halved; it has no bearing on the outcome of the competition. When one player has won more holes than are left to be played, he wins the match.

But match play didn't give Bobby much of a chance to feel like a winner. Because of the age and skill difference between him and his regular playing partners, there was very little hope that Bobby could win. That made him try harder, and his effort paid off suddenly in 1911 when he was still nine years old.

Bobby began to have the occasional round where, no matter how many holes he had been given by Perry, they weren't necessary. So, Bobby started making his move, and Big Bob noticed.

One day that year, Big Bob had the pleasure of seeing his son achieve his first personal golfing goal.

"I did it, Dad! I broke 90!"

Big Bob hugged his son, told his golfing group what his son had accomplished, and left the group to walk to the clubhouse to celebrate the 89 that was on his son's scorecard.

"Let's go," Big Bob said, and they were the words Bobby wanted to hear. Off father and son went to a private world of scorecard talk, lemonades, and companionship.

CHAPTER
5

For those who believe that pain in life must be endured for success to be obtained, Oscar Bane Keeler would be a standing monument to that concept. Keeler's life before he met Bobby Jones had mostly pain in it, but that was about to change.

O.B. Keeler stared out the window of his hot Georgia office, his chin resting nonchalantly in his cupped hand. The twenty-four-year-old man watched as a lonely straggler walked past his office window. But Keeler didn't have the spirit left in him to bother wondering what the stranger was doing or whether he was happy or not, as he once may have done. He knew that he was close to being depressed again, and that depression was fast becoming his lifestyle.

Born in Wheaton, Illinois, in 1882, Keeler's family moved to Atlanta when he was four. He still missed the Illinois winter snow that he barely remembered, but had learned to deal with the heat of Atlanta that seemed to reside in every corner of the building where he worked. In his numerous mental ruminations, Keeler often wondered what Atlanta had ever done to survive the heat before electric fans were created. There was an electric fan on every desk in the big office where he worked as a cashier at a fire insurance company.

His job was so boring, Keeler had thought many times about throwing a rock into the Chattahoochee River and not letting go. But being a cashier he felt was better than his previous job as a stock clerk at the railroad. For that, he was truly grateful—but not much.

It was Keeler's wife and two children that were responsible

for him still being alive. Keeler had started on a family a mite early, after falling for a Southern lady. He often thought that his early marriage might have been another escape from his boredom.

Keeler's saving grace on the job were the people who came in to pay their bills (they always had a story to tell) and of course, the newspapers that he read daily from front to back. Three papers in the morning and three in the afternoon—almost the total of Atlanta's output of local and national news at five cents a copy.

The Atlanta Georgian struck Keeler's fancy more than the other papers. There was something special about the Atlanta Georgian to Keeler, and he made it even more special by writing the occasional verse, sending it to the sports editors, and seeing his lively words appear a few times in the paper's sports columns.

The sad part of Keeler's daily trip through his newspapers was the way he compared his life to those of the happy people in the articles. Keeler always found ways to dwell on the good news, but it was the good news of others that made his own life pale in comparison.

When he was younger, Keeler had fancied himself a sportsman, but that dream ran into the reality of his poor hand-eye coordination, and the ultimate addition of glasses to his face made his self-image even worse. So, baseball, tennis, and boxing were out. Should he try that new game, golf? It seemed to be sweeping the country, causing parkland to be converted into golf courses everywhere. He asked himself the question nonchalantly and just as nonchalantly, he decided to give it a try. He hoped it would be easy.

It was only a matter of a couple of tries before Keeler realized that his forte didn't lie in golf either. The moment Keeler held the club and addressed the unmoving ball, the flag seemed to retreat into the distance as if to laugh at his lack of self-confidence.

Keeler had never broken 100 until this past summer, and that happened, he thought, by pure, blind, dumb luck. But he stayed with the game for fun and diversion. He had to have something. He had no social life, and playing golf was a means for him to mingle with fellow Atlantans and get out in the fresh air and green grass and dream of better possibilities.

As Keeler knew, golf was growing in America. There were now three golf courses in Atlanta, including another new course out in Atlanta's suburbs, East Lake. Rumors were that two more were soon to be built. Some people even said that golf might someday surpass baseball and become our national pastime, but that was unthinkable to Keeler. He saw how many people played baseball every day in the newspaper write-ups, and he figured that half of those people would have to switch to golf for golf to win out over baseball.

The daily box scores on the local baseball teams usually took a whole page or more in the Atlanta Georgian, but the Georgian now had two columnists covering golf. Almost every day, there was a story of one local golf tournament or challenge match being played between professionals or talented amateurs.

One day, as Keeler reached his spirit's breaking point again, he forced himself to visit Mr. Dudley Glass, the Atlanta Georgian's City Editor, who had been approving his verses for publication.

Keeler waited patiently in Glass's office. He had worn his best suit and had even had his shoes polished at the corner shine parlor.

"Well, well, if it isn't our local poet," Glass said, coming back into his office from a tour of his charges at all the desks in the sports bureau.

Keeler stood up. He could hardly believe that he had gotten the nerve to apply for a position, and a minute later, he doubted himself. "Eh, Mr. Glass, I'm thinking that I might apply to work in the newspaper business."

Glass's feet went up onto his desk and his hands immediately fell into a locked position behind his head. His office chair groaned beneath his weight shift. He was a portly man.

This was a story that Glass was used to. "You and everyone else, Oscar. With papers being as popular as they are, nearly everyone wants to either work here on staff or be a telex operator."

Keeler shook his head at the mention of the telex. "I want to report on the goings on in Atlanta. The people, the events, the results." Keeler could see himself covering all the wonderful people and happenings he couldn't take part in.

A grin grew out of the side of Glass's mouth. He knew he was in a strong position where hiring was concerned and knew how to take advantage of it. "Tell you what, Oscar. I need some new spirit in this office. Someone to go out and get the job done instead of just sitting around waiting for the story to come in over those damn wires. But you are an unproven reporter and if you're willing to take a chance and show me what you're made of, well, I might even hire you."

Keeler just wanted a chance, so what Glass was saying was music to his ears. "I'll do it," Keeler shot back without even knowing what the conditions were.

Glass chuckled. "You'd better wait till I'm done before you accept." He put his feet back down on the floor. He knew he had Keeler hooked. "You work the first two weeks to prove yourself—even bring in your own typewriter. If after two weeks both you and I are happy with you, well...."

Keeler had already stood up. His mind was working out where he could obtain a typewriter and how quickly he could get out of his old job at the insurance company. The pain of his current position had made Keeler more action-oriented than usual.

"Okay, that's all I want. A chance. Just a chance," Keeler said.

Glass stood up as Keeler was already heading out the door. "And one other thing," Glass shouted after him. "Only write what you can make interesting, understand?"

Keeler stopped. "You'll be hearing from me soon, real soon," he threw back over his shoulder as he flew out the door.

Glass smiled at Keeler's back, shook his head, and grinned, enjoying the power his position gave him. He had no idea that, in this case, the chance he offered was so monumentally perfect.

Keeler started work for the Atlanta Georgian on January 4, 1904. Although it would take a while before Keeler's real destiny with the newspaper made itself known, the start had been made. For someone like Keeler, who was very loyal, the start was usually the important part.

Keeler's first assignment had him covering a Southern Evangelist named Dr. Len G. Broughton. Dr. Broughton spoke on therapeutics, the psychic healing of physical illnesses. It was one of the dying speeches of spirituality, and it would have looked that way in the newspaper write-up if any other reporter besides O.B. Keeler had covered it. Keeler's writing—so personable—made the event a front page story, above the fold, the most prestigious position in a newspaper.

With one swift blow, Keeler was in the newspaper business and causing heads to turn. He had discovered his gift, and those who read his columns discovered it too. Words didn't flow from Keeler yet, but they tumbled out in a joyously intimate fashion. That made his columns the talk of Atlanta.

So Keeler had his start. His newfound grasp of words surprised him as much as it made others joyful. He had success for the first time in his life, in the newspaper business, the leading form of media coverage as the nineteenth century turned into the twentieth century.

But the relationship between Keeler and the Atlanta Georgian was not a bed of roses, although it should have been. Keeler was not the only man willing to work for two weeks for no pay. Free workers were plentiful and promotions were hard to come by. Those ahead of him at the paper had no plans to leave or to move over to make room for this newspaper phenomenon. So Keeler left Atlanta for Kansas City, where luck and fame found him.

He got a job at the Kansas City Star where he was assigned a story about Dr. Bennett Clark Hyde and Hyde's murder of a man named Swoop, together with his attempt to kill Swoop's family with diphtheria. This story stormed the city's moral decency in such a way that it made the front page. For the first time in its history, The Kansas City Star gave a byline, and Keeler became a household name.

But Keeler's best was yet to come. It was the historic year of 1912, when the Titanic went down on April 16th. Keeler rose to the occasion.

The Titanic took 1,300 down!

That is what the broad and heavy black headlines said and it was as if the morning papers came to the waiting doors, bearing with them a knot of crepe.

The Titanic took 1,300 down!

There was a sound in the line as of a bell of death tolling somewhere out on the broad Atlantic, a thousand fathoms above the sodden twisted wreck of what had been earth's proudest ship.

The Titanic took 1,300 down!

Breakfasts were left untouched after the unfolding paper left bare the hideous intelligence. There was a hush in the streetcars, a suggestive quiet in the subdued greetings at the offices, a dearth of laughter; so that the light unconsciously merry voice of an unthinking child jarred and somehow hurt in the burdened atmosphere of gloom.

The Titanic took 1,300 down!

Under the settled melancholy, that terrible line hammered away at the imagination with a ceaseless irritation. How did they meet it, this fearful thing?

What did the men do, called on to face a ghastly death in the cold hours before dawn? Were they calm and steady, or were they a shrieking merciless mob, fighting for places in the lifeboat? Did they help the women and children to places of safety with cheerful comforting words that it was only a precaution—that nothing much was wrong—as men should who face the end as men? Or was the shame of La Borgoyne on their last moments—the beating off of women from the crowded boats—the maniacal rage of fear?

Brief as the last dispatches were, they showed there were heroes on the doomed ship.

"The survivors were mainly women and children," the dispatches said.

And there, in that single line, is as fine an epitaph as could be written for the men passengers and crew who went down with the ship. That line tells of a captain with his first and last thought for the passengers in his care; of a crew that made ready the lifeboats with never a hint of delay, and sent them clear of the floundering vessel with business like precision unshaken by the doom their experienced eyes saw only too well. That line tells of the manhood of Great Britain and America almost buried, it seems at times, in the sordid struggle of an unromantic and unheroic age, yet flashing out as brightly at the grim need, as ever it shown when knighthood was in flower.

The survivors were mostly women and children.

It is the brightest line of that grim story, the stirring martial chord in the terrible dirge beginning.

The Titanic took 1,300 down!

Keeler's story was a fitting epitaph for one of the biggest stories of 1912, and it ran in most of the national newspapers in

America. The story, as it was written and portrayed by Keeler, was used for years in journalism classes all over the country as a good example of how a reporter should communicate with his audience.

With his newfound success as a lead reporter, Keeler's popularity jumped overnight to magical proportions. Keeler had his own byline at a time when bylines were rare. Keeler felt powerful, but he also felt homesick for his adopted Southern hometown of Atlanta, Georgia, birthplace of his wife and his favorite newspaper, the Atlanta Georgian. He would always remember Kansas City fondly, but the South was his home and his mission down the road lie somewhere between there and his future.

As Keeler looked at his experiences at the Kansas City Star, which included working and socializing alongside reporters like Ernest Hemingway, he smiled knowing what he had accomplished. However, his memory was tinged with a feeling of not being fully appreciated for the long hours and effort he had put in. They were mixed emotions of the purest type.

So, Keeler went back to Atlanta like a battle-worn warrior returning home. He had done so well in Kansas City that he had forgotten about the famous office politics of the Atlanta Georgian—the free two weeks. But no matter; Keeler was his own man now.

Keeler had just settled back into his job when destiny came calling.

It was on a late ride home one night not far from Marietta that Keeler made a grizzly discovery, and his nose for news netted the people in Atlanta something special in the way of a story. He discovered the body of a man who had been duly tried and found guilty, but was now hanging from a tree. The governor had commuted his sentence, but the vigilantes who hung the man had a different opinion of the man's guilt. The hung man was Leo Frank, and Keeler's part in the story started when he found the grisly body.

The following day, after Keeler told the world his story in

his ablest way, another strikingly sad part of the story unfolded. A package was delivered to Keeler containing the hung man's wedding ring, which someone wanted Keeler to return to the man's widow. In delivering the ring, Keeler experienced a part of a reporter's job that he had no wish to ever experience again.

But sales of the Atlanta Georgian soared, and Keeler poured himself and his words into Atlanta's local scene with an enthusiasm that was totally missing from his life just a few years before. He knew what a good story was and what it could do.

Baseball was the biggest news of that day, and most reporters covered it at one time or another. The Atlanta Georgian had ten reporters on the baseball beat with half assigned to major baseball news and half assigned to all the local factory, church, and association leagues. There was even a special reporter who covered Ty Cobb. Cobb was from Georgia, and he was considered a local boy.

But Keeler did not want to cover local baseball news. Covering the local baseball scene meant getting around Atlanta and its now growing suburbs mainly by trolley or the more flexible two-horse hack, or for those in shape, a bicycle. Keeler hated the smell of riding behind a horse-drawn hack. He considered it as close to uncivilized as it was possible to get.

Boxing and horse racing were a possibility, but they were well covered. The only sport that had incomplete coverage was the new game of golf. Other reporters that occasionally covered golf didn't have any experience at the game. In fact, many of the Georgian reporters were heard to make fun of the game. To them the game was a white ball that just sat there waiting to be hit. No one seemed to see any reason for the game other than as a social affair, or light exercise sport, or an excuse to spend time outdoors in one of the converted parklands. To Keeler, though, golf was another way to get ahead.

He had heard through his cultivated grapevine that the great British players Harry Vardon and Ted Ray were coming to East Lake to play an exhibition match with Willie Mann, the professional at the new Druid Hills golf course, and Stewart Maiden, the professional at East Lake. The match was set for thirty-six holes on each course. The lowest score on a hole by a member of either team would win the hole.

That intrigued Keeler. It was the same instinct that had taken him so far already in the newspaper business, and since no other reporter seemed interested in the match, Keeler decided that he would be there.

CHAPTER
6

Many people think fireworks are set off when the main characters in a magnificent story meet for the first time. That may be true in some cases, but in this case, it didn't happen that way. The two main characters in this story were both too hesitant. Perhaps they knew how great their story would be, and were awed by it.

Keeler walked around the stately East Lake clubhouse and took a look around. He looked forward to seeing how real professionals played the new game of golf.

"Do you know what time the players will be teeing off?" Keeler asked a man coming out of a little wooden house, his sleeves rolled up to his elbow.

The man glanced at him quickly, sizing him up. "Aboot an hour."

Keeler decided that he'd better work on his reporting principles of who, what, when, where, and why. "Do you know any of the players that will be involved?"

The man nodded.

"Are any of them around yet?"

The man nodded again.

Keeler was getting a bit frustrated. "Would you mind pointing one of them out to me?"

Stewart Maiden thought about that for a second as he stopped work on the golf club he had in his hands. Then he thought some more. Finally, he pointed his finger out from himself, and collapsing his elbow back inward, he pointed his finger at his chest.

"You're one of the players?" Keeler was surprised.

Maiden nodded. "Wha is it that yer needin, Maister newspaper mon?"

Keeler's frustration mounted. All this man was capable of was questions. "How do you know I'm with a newspaper?"

Maiden shook his head. "Dae ye think ye're the first newspapermon A hae 'ere rin intae?" Then he explained, economically. "In Scotland, we eddicate thee senses first. Thee rest follows naturally."

That comment flew right over Keeler's head, but he quickly recovered and got down to business. He asked Maiden to fill him in on the details of the match.

"H'it's fower baw," Maiden responded, knowing that the man would be perplexed.

Keeler asked what that meant, and spent the next five minutes trying to understand what the Scottish professional was telling him, all the while pushing Maiden's patience to its limit. "Och, ust pey notice to whit is goin on as thee roond is played. Ye'll unnerstaund it frae that." Maiden spat out the words, finally out of patience.

Keeler took a breath and put his pad and pencil back in his pocket. "Are any of the other players around?"

Maiden walked Keeler to the door of his workshop, glad to be rid of him, and pointed out a man who was putting on the green. "Tha's Willie Mann frae Druid Hills. E'll be mae pairtner." Maiden added," E'ss frae Scotlund."

Maiden walked outside and pointed down the fairway. "Tha's Maister Harry Vardon, an the big mon ta his left tis Ted Ray. Thay are thee Inglis Champions." With that, Maiden disappeared into his shop, leaving Keeler to fend for himself.

Keeler walked over to the two British champions to watch them hit a few shots down a fairway where two caddies were running back and forth gathering their balls. He didn't know much about the game, but he could sense their professionalism.

When he followed them back to the clubhouse, he realized

he wasn't alone. There were 250 people, including 25 children, gathered around the clubhouse. People seemed to be everywhere, and some even drifted over towards the lake or sat under one of the large live oak trees.

A man with a megaphone came out and made an announcement about the match: eighteen holes starting in fifteen minutes, followed by time off for lunch for the contestants; then another 18 holes. The same procedure would be followed the next day at Druid Hills.

There was a smattering of murmur as people picked up interest in what was going on. First the British champions drove off, then the two hosts, the professionals of East Lake and Druid Hills.

The man with the megaphone worked pretty hard the first couple of holes trying to keep the spectators back from the field. People seemed to want to push forward toward the players, who continually needed to have a path cleared for their shots. Slowly, the spectators learned, and they stayed out of the path of play.

Keeler watched closely. He noticed everything that was going on. He was amazed that the players seemed to make the ball do whatever they wanted it to do, and he noted a number of spectators that seemed to follow one player over another. That told him a lot. Fans were obviously more knowledgeable about the game than newsmen.

Keeler's jacket came off as the sun rose. Children drifted over the golf course from hole to hole. They'd watch a player, then drift back into talking with each other. A few boys seemed very intent on following the great champion, Harry Vardon. Vardon walked along as if he were playing a game all by himself.

But it was clear from Vardon's scoring that he was the best of the players. Vardon scored around four strokes on every hole he played—a drive onto the fairway and an iron shot onto the green or around it. Vardon usually took two putts if he landed his second shot onto the green; one putt if he had to chip his third shot.

As Keeler watched Vardon play, he became mesmerized. The man was the picture of consistency. Keeler wondered how he could duplicate his efforts on each and every hole while playing with a coat on.

Bobby was at East Lake for the match, and he was in golf heaven. He and his friend Perry watched their local hero Stewart Maiden tee off with the great British duo of Vardon and Ray. From the start, Maiden's game was very close to that of the British professionals. Most people didn't know that Maiden had competed in the National Open, later called the U.S. Open, five years before and had finished tied for 42nd place. He had also done well in the North Carolina Open played in Charlotte the previous year.

"Did you see what Vardon did back there on seven?" Perry said to Bobby. Their excitement was building, hole by hole.

"How about Ray's second shot on twelve?" Bobby countered.

A lot of people were taken with Ted Ray's approach shot at twelve. He had out-driven the other players again, but his ball had wound up in the right rough with a very tall tree seemingly in line with his necessary play to the green. Ray looked around the tree to the right and to the left, then back again to the right side. Fade or draw seemed to be the question.

The drawn-out decision-making just built up the drama for the two boys. Neither of them could have made the shot Ray chose.

Ray decided to go straight up and over the forty-foot live oak tree even though everyone thought he was too close to the tree to get his shot up that quickly and still reach the green.

But Ray had obviously hit a shot like this before. He simply hit down with his mashie-niblick with his considerable strength and watched the ball shoot almost straight up and over the tree and onto the back of the green.

What took Bobby's breath away was the size of Ted Ray's divot. As the caddy replaced it in the ground, Bobby could tell that the divot was bigger than Ray's foot. It was the biggest divot Bobby would see for a long time to come.

Bobby and Perry were totally caught up in the match. To Bobby, it was as if the great champions were there to show him the best way to play the East Lake golf course.

Perry was fascinated by the easy movement of the four great players. Because he had played the course so many times, it was easy for him to relate to what the players were doing.

But the real story was Harry Vardon. At the close of the morning round, Bobby sensed something about this player that no one else did. Vardon seemed to be in his own world. Although he was playing with three other golfers and in front of what was now close to 350 people, Vardon seemed isolated. As Bobby watched, the other players seemed to carry on conversations and intermingle while Vardon kept totally quiet.

In addition to this difference, Vardon's consistency caught Bobby's eye. "He's always around four on each and every hole," Bobby said nudging Perry in the ribs.

"And he's never out of play on a hole," Perry added. "He's the one whose game I'd like to have. No wonder he's won the Open over there so many times."

It was a very special day. Bobby and Perry were able to compare their games to the games of the four professionals that played at East Lake that day. As the boys went over the match hole by hole, they recalled every shot the four players had hit, and their comparisons to their own games became a driving force in its own right.

That night, comparisons of the players kept right on going at Perry's house as Bobby, Perry, Alexa, and Frank Meador told their parents how great the players were. No one's opinion was left out.

There was a full moon that night, so Bobby and Perry

went over to a practice green near the clubhouse and putted until the moon had shifted away and no more light remained. Sleep that night was a blessing for the boys. They were both exhausted.

But even in sleep, something was happening to the young Bobby Jones because of his special day. In laying his eyes on Harry Vardon, many of Vardon's traits—like Vardon's ability to score so evenly and to be in his own world—were already modifying Bobby's game. Bobby's ability to mimic was coming in handy.

At times, it must have seemed to Bobby that situations seemed destined to work in his favor. When you're raised in the spirit of cooperation, you get to the point where you believe that helping is the way life should be.

"Do ya think your dad will let you come with me and my dad to Montgomery for the tournament if my dad asks him?" Perry Adair asked Bobby in the spring of Bobby's twelfth year. Bobby had grown rapidly the past four years and was now looking rather chunky for his size.

Perry and Bobby were finishing a round on the old East Lake setup before Donald Ross arrived to redesign the course, which would make it longer, yet play to an easier par of 72. The old layout had attracted its share of grumbles from the membership about the difficulty of play, so East Lake started negotiations with Donald Ross to redesign the course. East Lake wanted a more appealing course that also afforded a well-rounded scoring test.

"I hope so," Bobby answered Perry. "I want to. I want to see a course where they play a lot of tournaments," he added, "but my dad's pretty busy these days."

George Adair's business enabled him to take his son, Perry, to some of the hot spots of golf in the South to play in tournaments. With only three finished courses in Atlanta, experienced golfers wanted different layouts on which to test their game, so they often traveled across state lines to play a different course or tournament.

And Perry's success in tournament golf was spreading. By the age of fourteen, Perry had gotten the nickname "Dixie's Boy Wonder" for his golfing prowess in tournaments in Alabama, Tennessee, and Georgia.

"Aw, your dad is so easy he'd let you come even if I ask him about it," Perry said, knowing how much Bobby's father doted on him.

But Big Bob was never really easy. He said yes to his only son frequently, but only if it was for something he thought he should say yes to. Big Bob's strict upbringing still ruled his psyche, even when he didn't want it to. He hovered over his son's health and safety—yes, he did—but he borrowed some of his father's strict child-raising philosophies as well.

Some people might have thought Bobby was spoiled with all the attention he received from his father, but he was not. Part of the reason had to do with Bobby's personality. Bobby rarely asked for something for himself. Then again, he didn't usually have to. With friends like Stewart Maiden who would repair his clubs after he broke them or even make him a new club to suit his growth, and George Adair who was always talking to Big Bob about taking Bobby to some tournament, Bobby's wants were taken care of naturally, through cooperation.

Bobby broached the subject of the tournament with his father that very night. "If Mr. Adair wants to take me to the golf invitational over in Montgomery, will you let him, Dad?" Bobby squirmed, wondering what his father would say.

Big Bob folded his paper and put his drink aside. "Now what did you score today?"

Bobby leaned on the fat arm of his father's chair. "85."

Big Bob took a sip of his drink. "85, huh?" Big Bob moved around in his chair. "And when is the tournament in

Montgomery?"

Bobby thought. "I think it's the middle of next month."

Big Bob smiled. "How about, you can go if you break 80?" Big Bob watched his son's face for a reaction.

Bobby jumped up and smiled. "Then I can go?"

Big Bob's face showed his incredulity. "You mean you can break 80?"

Bobby smiled. "If it's that important, I can. You'll see, Dad."

It didn't happen as quickly as Bobby wanted it to, but he got a helping hand from Stewart Maiden who handmade another set of clubs for the youngster. This set featured iron heads from a well-known shop in Scotland, and Bobby fell in love with the new clubs.

"You'll hae tae stop thrawin thaim gif ye want me tae be makin ye mair," Maiden said to Bobby as he watched the youngster take his first few shots. Bobby had started becoming known for a hot temper when his golf shot didn't do what he wanted it to do.

Bobby smiled, but shook his head. "Well, I'll bet these clubs give me no reason to throw them." And he hit another shot, reveling in the solid feeling of the well-made clubs.

"Na maiter. Dae na brak thir," Maiden said, and he headed back to his shop.

Bobby's second set of clubs were special. Maiden had made them like they make clubs in Carnoustie, Scotland. He had also reshafted Bobby's Walter Travis-style "Schenectady" putter, which had been declared illegal by the Royal and Ancient rules body in St. Andrews.

Bobby broke 80. He worked hard to get it, and Big Bob saw that. He also saw that Bobby was scoring better than anyone else at the club except for the club professional and Perry Adair.

"You know, I've been thinking that maybe you and I ought to go with the Adairs to Montgomery," Big Bob smiled. "Let me see what I can work out."

He wasn't able to do it. His business was growing, partly because of new business coming in from a new soft drink maker by the name of Coca Cola. He had a partner in his law practice now, but he really couldn't take time off.

"I've been thinking about Bobby and me going with you and Perry to Montgomery," Big Bob said to George Adair one night at the club. "But it seems that I have a lot of business that I best take care of."

"So, instead, you're going to let Bobby come with us?" George continued.

"You know, I never even thought of that." Big Bob looked off. "I'd have to check with Clara about it." Big Bob continued his thoughts. "Not very sure she'll want us to have him so far away before he's fully grown."

Surprisingly, though, Clara agreed. "Clara said it's okay for Bobby to go, so I guess you'll have three chances to bring a winner back to East Lake, if the offer is still open," Big Bob said to Adair within the week.

Adair smiled. "Both Perry and I will make sure that he knows the ropes and is safe," he said. "Don't worry. Montgomery is pretty civilized these days." Adair smiled and rubbed his hands together.

And so it was that the Jones family watched their only son leave home after eleven years of working to keep their son safe from harm. Big Bob gave his son money for the trip, but as would be the case time and again over the coming years, Bobby had money left over when he arrived back home. George Adair was never short of money or help for Bobby Jones.

Expectations were not high for his big organized tournament, but Bobby didn't know that. Bobby's heart and mind were on representing Atlanta and East Lake.

The Montgomery Invitational was a big tournament for

its day. First, you had to be invited. George Adair, with all his contacts, took care of that. Next, you had to qualify over two rounds. Bobby did that. But his score qualified him for the second flight, which didn't sit well with him. He considered second flight a lowly proposition. Then, too, the play was match play, a harder game than medal play. Here, Bobby tripped, but he quickly recovered.

He lost in the first round, which threw him into a consolation flight. Then he caught on. He won match after match and lost in the consolation final flight while Perry Adair was winning the championship flight. It was a very successful trip for the families from East Lake.

Bobby and the Adair family were greeted at the train station by a very happy Big Bob. Bobby had his prize ready to show his dad as soon as he alighted from the train.

"You won that?" Big Bob grinned at the returning golfers, so glad to see his son safely home.

Bobby nodded. "I didn't qualify for the championship flight though."

Big Bob smiled. "I never heard of prizes being awarded to damn losers. Looks like you did great to me." In Big Bob's mind, his win was a big success. To go to a strange course where everyone was older than he was and play well at the age of eleven; that told Big Bob, again, that his son was truly special.

Lower scores came a lot easier for Bobby after his return to Atlanta. This fact wasn't lost on Big Bob. Having seen an excellent course in Montgomery that had a few par-five holes was a real eye opener for Bobby, and it released another gift within him that took his game up another notch.

The year 1914 brought some tragedy to the world and more steady progress to the young Bobby Jones. The governments in Europe seemed, at times, to be at such odds with each other.

"What do you think of my son's game?" Big Bob asked Stewart Maiden one day while he was over at East Lake course.

Maiden looked at him in the far-off way that he seemed to use when he didn't think too much of a question. "Och, h'it's comin. H'it's comin."

Big Bob looked at him. "But you grew up with a lot of people who started early in the game back in Scotland," Big Bob scratched his head. "Well?" Big Bob continued, hoping for something, but not quite knowing what it was.

"He's l'arnin," Maiden smiled. "An we best lea' h'it at tha." Maiden turned back to his work, and Big Bob took the hint.

Big Bob had been thoroughly taken with what his eleven-year-old son had done in Montgomery. Now, no matter what the Scottish pro thought or didn't think, he decided he should start feeding Bobby more experiences in golf.

"Really?" Bobby exclaimed. Big Bob had just told Bobby that the Southern Amateur was going to be played at East Lake and that Bobby was chosen as the fourth man of the East Lake team to compete.

"Well, you did so well in the Montgomery Invitational that when the other players brought up your name, I thought we may as well see how well you can do in a tournament on your own damn course. You'll be a great addition to the team."

Bobby was still close to numb. "Part of the team?"

"Yep. There's two parts to the tournament this year. There's the individuals, which are played as match play after qualifying, and there's the team play that takes place during the qualifying rounds. George Adair, Perry, and Will Rowan asked that you be named the fourth player on their team. I decided that they had good reason based on what you did in Montgomery." Big Bob grinned. "You might take notice that they didn't ask me."

Bobby hadn't thought of being part of the team to represent East Lake in the Southern Amateur. It caught him off-guard and caused him to become flustered. He had dreamed of playing in the Southern Amateur, but representing East Lake and all his friends was beyond what he had considered.

Bobby had always played a tournament like this in his mind, but this time his heart was involved. He was playing for East Lake, with other good East Lake players that he liked and for which he had a lot of respect. As Bobby finished his qualifying round, he felt as though he had struggled. He would have said that he hadn't been able to get his game going at all. So, it was a big surprise when his score of 83 was posted and he was listed as sole third behind the two co-medalists who tied at 82. He had the lowest score on his team.

"You did great representing East Lake." Big Bob hugged his son to his chest.

But Bobby didn't feel that he had done well. There were so many putts that could have gone in. He figured there were five.

The next day, during individuals, Bobby won his first match and then he met one of the icons of Southern golf, Commodore Bryan Heard of Houston, Texas. The Commodore was well past his most productive years but had a golf game that was known to be tenacious when on.

The two went at it, age against youth, steadiness against exuberance, experience against desire. It was one of Bobby's greatest early rounds, but he lost on the 17th green, 2 and 1. It was his first experience against a great stickler of a player. The Commodore was in the fight for every hole, and Bobby felt the pressure the whole way.

Because he had qualified so well, his loss only caused him to be dropped into the second flight where he won his next three matches. This got him into the finals against Frank Clarke, a hot-shot golfer from Nashville. At the end of the morning round, Bobby was 3 down. At the end of 27 holes, Bobby found himself 4 down. It didn't look good.

Then, Bobby's mother and father suddenly showed up and an affected Bobby poured on the heat and won the next four holes.

Bobby was so proud of his accomplishment in front of his

parents that he gloated over his comeback. Frank came back and Bobby lost, again on the 17th green, 2 and 1.

Nonetheless, a twelve-year-old boy had played some of the best golf ever seen, and Big Bob was no fool about what lay in store for his son.

☙

"Are you coming with us to Birmingham to play in the Roebuck Springs Invitational?" Perry asked Bobby as they sweated under the hot Georgia sun.

"I damn well hope so," Bobby answered. "I want to play those damn par-five's and do better on them. Now that I've played some long holes in Montgomery, I'll know how to damn well play them better."

"Want me to have my father ask your father?" Perry smiled.

"I've been talking to my dad for a while about going to Birmingham. He missed not going to Montgomery. I think he'll want to go this trip. This time, all four of us will represent East Lake."

Bobby was correct. Big Bob wanted to go to Birmingham and play with his son and neighbors. He didn't want to be left out of a special golf trip that he had heard so much about. Plus, Big Bob's law firm had done a lot of work for the new Atlanta soft drink manufacturer, so much so, that Big Bob was thinking about getting one of those new cars that would enable him to get home faster to his family after work.

This time, in Birmingham, Bobby was at his best. Playing for East Lake in the Southern Amateur had given him the experience he needed to go all the way at Roebuck Springs. Bobby met Perry Adair in the second round and beat him 2 and 1. Then in the finals, Bobby met a much older player who wouldn't give in, even though Bobby had the lead the whole way. At the end of the match, they were tied.

The first playoff hole yielded no change, but the third one

did. Bobby won on the 21st hole. It was his first big win.

"Now do you see what I mean?" Big Bob said to Stewart Maiden when he got back to East Lake. "Winning the whole tournament at the age of twelve has to stand for something." Big Bob huffed.

Maiden shook his head. "Young Tommy Morris wan thee Open at thee age o only seventeen. Nou, whit daes 'at tell ye?"

"Then, what should we do?" Big Bob tried to make sense of it all. "To help him, I mean."

Maiden just stood there. "He's la'rnin. Lea' thee lad alane. Lat'em dae hit is awn wey."

Bobby did it his own way, wrapping up 1914 by winning the Davis Freeman Cup at East Lake, then the East Lake Club Championship, and putting his mark on 1915 by winning the Club Championship at the new two-year-old Druid HIlls Golf Club across town. He didn't know it then, but 1915 would be the last year his name was known only on a regional basis.

CHAPTER
7

Bobby and Perry dominated the Montgomery Annual Invitational in 1916. No one seemed to be able to stop either one of these East Lake players.

They actually met in the semifinals of the tournament, but Perry came out on top after overcoming Bobby's 3-up front-nine lead with a hot back-nine of his own. First Bobby shot his 33 on the front nine to take his 3-up lead. Then Perry showed why he was called the Dixie Boy Wonder. He came back to blister the back nine with his own 33. Perry won on the 18th green, 1-up. It was written up as the match of the century because of all the great golf the two boys played.

Big Bob's response to Bobby's play in Montgomery was to increase his schedule as he had done the year before.

Bobby went on to win in Birmingham, shooting a tournament-best 69. He won in Knoxville with a final match play round of 73. And he won the first East Lake Invitational. The name Bobby Jones was spreading. He was just fourteen.

Big Bob glowed, but Perry was still being called the Dixie Boy Wonder. Sometimes circumstances change on their own and sometimes changes need a tournament or two to come to fruition.

"A new state gawlfing organization haes ben stairted," Stewart Maiden mentioned to Bobby and Perry while wiping his hands on his ever-dirty apron. "Hits gaun tae haud thee first state amateur in Georgia this Augist."

"What course will it be played at?" Perry wondered.

"The Brookhaven coorse o thee Caipital Ceety Club," Maiden murmured. "Ye gaun enter an git yersel some mair lessons?" To Maiden, golf for his boys was all about lessons.

Bobby and Perry both looked at each other. "If I'm allowed," they said together, and all three of them laughed.

"Thare will be ah lot o players comin intae Atlanta for this," Maiden continued. "Thee first stae amateur shoud be uphauden by awbody tha lives in Georgia." New events always won Maiden's approval. He wanted his boys to get as much experience as they could.

A few weeks later, the notice about the tournament was posted in the men's locker room. It read: The First Georgia State Amateur.

"This should be fun." Perry smiled at Bobby. "My dad says there was a man from the United States Golf Association at Druid Hills yesterday," Perry continued. "He's trying to get some entries for their amateur tournament up in Philadelphia this fall."

Bobby listened.

"They want to get more people from the South to come play in the National Amateur Tournament."

"That's a long way to go for a golf tournament," Bobby thought out loud. Concern for his parents and their fears about him were never far from Bobby's thinking.

"But, it's a national event. Not just a local or state tournament," Perry explained. "My dad's thinking maybe we should go."

"I never even thought of playing in one of those." Indeed that was true. Bobby was so happy playing with his friends that his imagination didn't reach to national events.

But Big Bob had a different take on the matter. "Chick Evans, an amateur out of Chicago won the National Open, up in Minneapolis."

"An amateur won again?" Bobby wondered.

"That's three out of the last four Opens that an amateur has won. Must have something to do with the fact that they just play for the love of the game and not for the money." That was the common thought then. Professionals were often looked down upon and thought to be corrupt because they played for money. At the time, this maxim applied to all sports, not just to golf.

Bobby looked off.

Big Bob also saw another article. "Francis Ouimet is no longer an amateur."

"He isn't? So he turned professional?"

Big Bob shook his head. "I don't know what he is. The paper said the USGA took his amateur rights away and that he can't play in any USGA tournament as an amateur." A look of consternation came over Big Bob. "But they can't label him a professional because, I think, they don't have that power." Big Bob shook his head. "Sounds confusing to me."

Bobby had hoped that his father could explain it to him. After all, Big Bob was a lawyer, and a good one at that. If he didn't understand it, who could?

Bobby and Perry easily qualified for the first Georgia State Amateur Tournament. Maiden had told them that the field was full of promise, and Bobby and Perry played with a lot more than just promise.

Excitement at East Lake built partly because Bobby and Perry qualified in different brackets. If they were to meet at all in the Georgia Amateur, they would have to meet in the final —and that's what everyone on the local scene wanted.

Bobby's bracket contained some of the really good players like Simpson Dean. Dean was a couple of years older than Bobby and he was headed to Princeton. He played out of Rome, Georgia, where his golf was very well respected.

Bobby had to get over Dean in the semifinals if he wanted to meet Perry in the final. Both boys wanted that to happen, but their play had to bring that about.

Perry won his semifinals match, but he didn't face the kind of danger Bobby faced.

Bobby's semifinal round with Dean started out well. By the end of nine holes, Bobby was 3-up and showing poise and confidence.

But by the end of play on the 13th hole, Bobby was dormie. That is, he was 5-up with five to play. He could only lose if the match went into sudden death.

Then Dean found the game that he was known for. He won the 14th, 15th, and 16th holes in runaway fashion. Suddenly, the gallery was thinking that the final would be Perry against Dean. Bobby looked like he was on the ropes.

"What do you think?" Big Bob said to Maiden who was watching the play with inordinate interest.

Maiden never lost his focus. "Hush. La's la the gowf speak for itsel. For Robin tae e'er become something in gowf, this is thee exact seetiation he needs."

They played the 17th, and Dean was looking at a five-foot putt to win another hole. Bobby stood aside looking as though he had nothing left in him.

But Dean missed. He left the ball right on the very front door of the hole. The young man was exasperated. He had wanted so badly to be playing in the next day's final.

"On the front lip. I can't believe what I just did." Dean had his head down and was shaking it.

That night, the clubroom at East Lake was full of happy people. They had both finalists in the first state amateur. Tomorrow would be a great day for East Lake.

Bobby and Perry grinned at each other on the first tee at Brookhaven. They had faced each other countless times before and both were prepared for the match of their lives. But with the pressure and honor behind the importance of this match, it was almost as if they had hardly played before. Only this match mattered now.

Almost half of the people following the match were friends of the boys back at East Lake. That fact created a very quiet final round. The gallery didn't know whether or not to clap. If they clapped when Bobby won, they'd be rooting against Perry. So they remained silent.

It was Perry who was slowly pulling ahead. He was playing very solid, steady golf while Bobby, at times, lost his demeanor and ranted and cursed over one missed shot or another or threw a club.

Bobby never cursed his fellow player. He put all the blame on himself, his equipment, or the course. He even threw a club a few times and had to go chase it, making himself look rather foolish. Nonetheless, no one stopped pulling for him. He was three years younger than Perry and, for a lot of people, that meant he had a good reason to act like a child.

Bobby could out-drive Perry, but Perry had the better short game. So far, on this day, Perry's short game was more than a match for Bobby's driving. Perry took a 3-hole lead into lunch. Quite a few people thought that Perry had the match totally in hand and that the afternoon play would simply continue as it was going.

Maybe it was the new spectators that showed up in such numbers that encouraged the tournament chairman, Ralph Reed, to speak to the crowd on the first tee of the afternoon match. He simply told both boys to continue their fine play, but rumors circulated that Reed had asked Bobby to continue play on the bye, or back nine holes, after the match was over to make sure the large gallery saw as much golf as it could. Many thought it meant that Reed believed Perry would win, and Reed had a lot of influence. So, a buzz went through the crowd.

Bobby lost the first hole of the afternoon round to go 4-down. Some in the gallery thought the three-year difference between the boys was showing up in their play, but they didn't know Bobby.

Bobby got angry at himself for losing the first hole, and this time he played up to his own expectations and won the 3rd hole with a birdie. 3-down. He won the 7th hole with another birdie. 2-down. The match was tightening up.

Perry missed a three-foot putt on the 8th. The hole was tied. Still 2-down, and it stayed that way though the turn. Nine holes to go.

The strain began to show in Perry, and he played poorly on the 10th hole. 1-down.

Bobby was now on his game. He scored par after par, and Perry made another mistake and they wound up on the 18th tee, all square.

The pressure was on, and it was felt by everyone who was there.

Bobby continued playing well on the finishing hole while Perry struggled a bit. But it was enough of a struggle to give Bobby the match, 1-up. Bobby was the first Georgia State Amateur Champion. He was fourteen years old.

A tired Perry walked over to congratulate Bobby on his win; his face carried a thin, worn smile. After all their time together and all their rivalries, Perry had a simple message to relay to Bobby, and it was an important one.

They shook hands as they had done so many times before, but this time Perry looked at Bobby full of appreciation. "Bobby, you're simply the best."

Bobby was caught by surprise, and he didn't have anything to say back. So, he walked off the green with Perry into the gallery and right into hugs from their families and friends. Big Bob glowed.

A tall bespectacled man walked up to Bobby, forcing Bobby to take a break from all the congratulatory messages he was receiving. "Bobby, I'm Oscar Bane Keeler with the Atlanta Georgian." Keeler watched the boy's face try to make sense of his words. "I'm a reporter."

Bobby nodded. The hard work of 36 holes under pressure in the hot August, Georgia sun was hitting home.

Keeler asked the boy his age and how long he had been playing the game and he asked about the rivalry between Bobby and Perry.

"You know, I followed Harry Vardon over these links and his score wasn't much better than yours was today. I figure you shot a 76, even with the rough six you took on the first hole this afternoon." Keeler looked at the youngster. "Did you know that?"

Bobby didn't have any idea what Keeler was talking about. He looked away as if the conversation didn't mean anything to him.

Keeler watched Stewart Maiden hug both Bobby and Perry and laud them for their efforts. Joy was in the air.

"You're the guy who played in the match with those two English professionals at East Lake a few years back," Oscar said, and then, as if remembering something, stopped.

Maiden nodded—his choice over speaking to outsiders.

"So, you're the teacher of golf for the two boys who just finished playing?"

Again Maiden nodded.

"I just read where Alexa Stirling, a member of East Lake, won the Women's National Amateur." Keeler watched the shorter man closely. "And she's your student too?"

Something about that caught Maiden's fancy and now he grinned slightly.

Keeler noticed the change in the golf professional's face. "Quite a record for you as their teacher, isn't it?"

Maiden's face returned to normal.

"Where did you get your golf information?"

"Back hame in Scotland."

"But where in Scotland?"

Maiden's head lowered and came slowly back up as if thinking. He looked at Keeler. "At Farfirshire gawf schuil in Carnoustie."

Keeler had grabbed the note pad from his back pocket. "Far For Sure golf school in Carnoustie?"

Maiden shook his head. "'Far-Fir-shire schuil. Na wan can promise ye 'Faur for shuir' unless ye dae awthing richt in thee sweeng." Maiden slightly shook his head. "A canna think on ony real Scot wha wad pit sic ah name on a schuil."

Keeler nodded vigorously. He had the man talking. "You must be proud of what you've done with your students."

Maiden slightly shook his head again. "A'm prood o whit ma students ave duin. Guide gowf tis ayeweys up tae thee player, nae thee teacher."

"So, has anyone called you, 'Kiltie the Kingmaker' yet?"

"Are ye here tae play or juist tatter?" Maiden was finished with the interview.

Unbeknownst to Maiden, a few people milling around had heard his conversation with Keeler. They took to calling him "Kiltie the Kingmaker" after that. Maiden always let out a puff of air when they did.

"George Adair wants to take you up to Philadelphia to play in the National Amateur Tournament," Big Bob announced to Bobby a few days later.

Bobby looked over at his mother. "I knew Mr. Adair and Perry were thinking of going."

"Well, Mr. Adair thinks you should be allowed to go, too." Big Bob risked a glance at his wife, Clara. He knew she wondered if she could allow her son to go so far away from home, to the North of all places.

Addressing his wife, Big Bob said, "George thinks the experience will do both the boys a world of good. They'll have a chance to put Southern golf on the map." He added, "I think Bobby will do just fine."

"I think I'd like to go." Bobby looked at his parents. "Stewart even helped me make an old pair of army boots into a pair of hobnail golf shoes. We put nails in the bottom of the shoe.

Stewart said they may never come out."

"Sounds to me like we have a decision to make," Big Bob smiled.

"Be very careful up there," Clara ordered. "We hear so much about Yankees that you just don't know what to believe."

"Can I get some long pants to play in?" Bobby asked. It was customary for boys to wear shorts until they passed the age of twelve.

Big Bob nodded.

This trip was beyond Bobby's imagination. He had read what he could in the newspapers about the national golf scene but, for the most part, this trip was a trip into the unknown. He had heard a lot about Yankees, too, about how they cheated you and were rude, yet he had met a lot of people from the North and none of them had seemed that bad to him.

The train left bright and early and Bobby left the station with the tears of his parents and the friendship of his friends pulling him in different directions. The train went through Richmond, with a changeover at Washington's Union Station. From there, Bobby and the Adairs boarded a train for Broad Street Station in Philadelphia, the second largest city in the nation.

Bobby was totally entranced. History seemed to be passing him through the windows of the train and, for the moment, he thought nothing about the upcoming tournament.

The travelers had never seen such a grand and glorious rail station as the Broad Street Station in Philadelphia. There were signs leading to trains heading out to places all over the country.

Their next stop was the Bellevue Stratford Hotel. George Adair was used to traveling in style and the Stratford was one of the finest hotels on the East coast with services and decor that others could only strive to copy.

The morning after their arrival, Adair had breakfast in his room while the boys went down to the main dining room and began to enjoy the big city. This was a dream neither of them had even considered a few weeks ago.

"Let's go," Adair called out to the boys as he arrived in the lobby of the gracious hotel. Their golf bags were already standing under the canopy of the hotel. They would be taking a taxi to the suburban train station to go out to the course to practice before having to play 36 holes over two courses to qualify for the tournament.

Adair was a smart one. He arranged things so that the boys would have four good practice days before their scores would count. When Adair gave thought to anything, it usually worked out very well.

"We're here to represent the South," Adair said to Perry and Bobby as their train headed toward Ardmore. "No matter what, you have much to be grateful for and much to represent. Let's make the folks back home proud of us."

Bobby and Perry looked at each other, wondering whether they were in over their heads. Perry's father had always been serious, but this time he seemed even more so.

The boys stood with Adair inside the clubhouse as they registered. The registrar couldn't believe he was registering a fourteen-year-old boy to attempt to qualify.

"You two go ahead and warm up and get a tee time for yourselves." Adair pushed the boys out the door. "I'll finish up here." Then Adair turned back to the official. "I didn't want to say it while the boys were here, but those two were the finalists in the Georgia State Amateur a couple of weeks ago. They both grew up in the game. You'll certainly see that in a couple of days."

Over the next few days, Bobby and Perry played golf as if they had just fallen in love with the game. Whenever a tee time was open and they were available, they were away and playing. East course or West course, it didn't matter. They delighted in playing their first Northern golf courses.

The grass on the courses was much thicker than it was back home and the greens were very fast, but they tried to adjust.

After all, it was just golf to two young boys who had found friendship through it.

To top off the experience, Adair did something he thought Big Bob wouldn't consent to, but he did it anyway. He got the boys caddies. For the first time in their lives, Bobby and Perry experienced someone else carrying their bags.

"This feels so strange," Bobby remarked to Perry as they headed off the tee behind their caddies.

"Last night, I was hoping that it wasn't going to be hot carrying my bag," Perry laughed. "Now, I don't care how hot it gets."

"Aren't you Bobby Jones, the son of Colonel Robert Jones?" a man asked the young Bobby after the boys had completed their round.

Bobby nodded, shading his eyes from the sun.

"Well, the last time I saw you, you were about three years old and struggling to keep anything in your stomach," the man continued.

"Bobby, I'm Grantland Rice and I hope you know my name." Rice smiled. "And maybe even read my columns now and again."

The light in Bobby's head went on. "Oh, you write 'Tee Times.'" Bobby grinned. He had been reading Mr. Rice's columns for almost three years in the Atlanta Georgian. "Yes, I read your columns, Mr. Rice."

"Yes, I write 'Tee Times.' And 'Sports Talk.'" Rice smiled proudly. "But you can call me Granny like everyone else does. Granny like Grandma." He smiled at his own nickname. Grantland Rice was considered the dean of American Sports Writers. His columns appeared in over 150 newspapers every day. Philadelphia itself had nine dailies, and Rice was in most of them.

Tournament time was very special to Grantland Rice. He played the game of golf well himself, and he knew golf's intricacies, which a lot of the other reporters didn't.

"How's your golf coming?" Rice asked. "I understand that you are a real fine player."

Bobby smiled shyly. "Oh, it's coming, if I can ever get my damn ball to do what I want it to." Bobby looked away. "These two courses are a real challenge. The greens are real smooth and very fast."

Granny nodded. "Think you gotta chance?"

Bobby shrugged. "I guess I never really expect to win. That way if I do win, I get a great surprise for me and my dad."

"Well, from what I hear, you've been giving him some great surprises." Rice put his hand out to shake goodbye and Perry came back, wanting to take Bobby away for some more golf. "So, tell your dad I said hello, will ya?" Granny finished. "Your dad was one hell of a third baseman."

Bobby grinned as Perry pulled on his sleeve.

Challenge or no challenge, Bobby and Perry fell in love with the four-year-old Merion golf course. Already revered by golfers, it was one of the only golf clubs in America with 36 holes. The boys found it highly playable and visually beautiful. If they could only learn to putt its fast greens, they might make some great scores.

Playing Merion was their first meeting with bent grass greens. In the South, courses mainly had Bermuda grass greens or sand greens due to the hot temperatures. Bent grass found Southern temperatures close to intolerable. Besides, bent was a recent discovery for greens.

More than a few people had heard about the young boys from the South and went out of their way to see them play. One of them was Walter Travis, the author of the book Bobby slept with when he won his first trophy. After being educated in Australia, Travis moved to the States at the age of twenty-four. He took up golf at the age of thirty-five and fell in love with the game. He set his goals very high and went on to win the National Amateur in 1900, 1901, and 1903. He went to Britain and was the first person outside Britain to win their Amateur by playing nearly flawless golf in 1904.

In winning the British Amateur, Travis had made a lot of putts in the 20- to 30-foot range—so many that it startled the British players and the press. The British, in trying to find an excuse for why an outsider won their amateur, looked at his putter and promptly banned it from play in any British golf event. Travis's center-shafted Schenectady, the putter he played with, stayed banned until 1952. In many ways, the ban was a tribute to the man. He was the only amateur champion who had had a golf club banned by the Royal and Ancient.

The first day of qualifying in the 1916 National Amateur found Bobby and Perry ready to go. Bobby was the first to post his score. He shot a 74 on the easier East course.

"He shot what?" were the words heard all over the course when people learned Bobby was only fourteen years old. "He's going to run away with the tournament," they said. The boys had heard it all before, and so, they took it in stride.

But while Bobby was eating lunch, the spectators rushed to see what time he would be playing next. It was bedlam. That afternoon, when Bobby showed up on the West Course for his tee time, over 1,500 people were there to watch him play.

Bobby couldn't believe his eyes. He had never played in front of more than 150 people before. Now, the gallery lined the first hole almost all of the way down and around to the green. It was intimidating.

As Bobby looked at the gallery, he realized that he knew no one in it. He felt terribly alone and exposed and on exhibit.

That afternoon, he didn't play well. His putts were more off line than they had been since he got to Merion, and his shots, not like his morning shots, were troubled. He played so badly, he almost missed the cut. His total was 163 for the two rounds, just 5 shots from missing the qualifying. His score swung 15 shots between his morning and afternoon rounds.

Perry shot 167 and was in a playoff for the final qualifying spot. Luckily, he won the spot, but he was not having a very good tournament either.

The boys met at the scorer's table. When they learned they both qualified, they grabbed each other's hands and spun around and around like on a maypole.

"We did it, we did it," they sang.

"Congratulations, you two." Adair brimmed with happiness. "You both done good."

Grantland Rice interviewed the boys, and he wasn't alone in doing that. Quite a few newspaper reporters wanted to interview Bobby.

"It wouldn't bother you to see your name in my column would it, Master Jones?" Rice asked Bobby as their paths crossed. Rice did not want to hurt young Bobby. He remembered what Bobby's parents had to do to bring the boy up.

Bobby shook his head shyly. A number of people were asking him questions that he felt he had no good answer for. He was still fourteen and only a golfer.

People were talking about Bobby, and they were talking about more than just his golf. He had brought with him the one pair of long pants his father had bought him, and he wore them every day. Now, six days later, along with his worn and dusty army shoes, he looked like a straggler. He didn't know the hotel would have cleaned his pants overnight if he had wanted them to.

Adair didn't notice Bobby's appearance. Things like that weren't important to him. But the reporters noticed, and they put in their stories how the boy from Georgia must be a farmer back home because of the way he was dressed.

Bobby's cursing was coming under scrutiny too. Bobby had

no problem cursing even during ordinary conversation, and it was bothering some people. In 1916, most people were very religious and believed cursing was immoral and sinful. Bobby had no idea his habit of cursing was grating on people's nerves, because no one told him.

All of that had to be put aside, however, when the National Amateur got underway.

"Bobby," Adair began, "you'll play Eben Byers and you, Perry, will play L.B. Paton."

Bobby and Perry stared at each other over the menu at the Bellevue Stratford Hotel. They didn't know if Perry's father's statement needed a response.

"Just remember what you were told back at East Lake by old Mr. Fitzsimmons," Adair brought up. "The bigger they are, the harder they fall." Bobby wondered why the statement was needed.

"Who is Eben Byers?" Bobby asked.

"Oh, he won the Amateur back in 1906, I think it was." Adair smiled.

Bobby looked across at Perry whose face was buried in his menu.

Adair bid the boys good luck and hurried off to see something he didn't want the boys to know about. It was something he had heard about the night before.

He walked into a smoky meeting room crowded with men a few blocks over, in another hotel. On the wall was a listing of all the players that had made it into the tournament. A man in front called out one name after another while those in the room bid on that player. It was a calcutta, a form of gambling, and the name Bobby Jones was being thrown around because of his opening round of 74. Adair wasn't sure he liked what he saw.

The following morning, Bobby met his opponent and they teed off only feet from the front door of Merion's clubhouse. A good-sized gallery was on hand.

As they walked off the tee, Bobby turned to his partner.

"Like a stick of gum?"

Byers mumbled "no" and also flicked his hand at Bobby as if rejecting his gesture. Bobby was shocked. No one had ever rebuffed him like that before. He didn't know what to make of it.

Byers, for his part, may have been working on the fact that he was playing the youngest contestant who was also the gallery favorite.

But play went on and Bobby found that he and Byers had some things in common. They both threw clubs and they both swore. As a matter of fact, they often threw clubs almost together, one after another. The gallery was alarmed. Even other golfing groups on the course noticed.

Bobby played some good golf and some bad golf. Maybe he should not have won, but he did; 3 and 1. It was an inauspicious start to his national career, but it was a start.

As he walked off the course, he couldn't have known that some fans in the gallery would have preferred he lose because of his swearing and club throwing. Days later he would find out.

Perry lost his second match and was out, and so, he was in the gallery to watch Bobby's next match which was against another golf veteran, Frank Dyer. Dyer was a state champion and he also held a few district honors. He was not a shoe-in win for Bobby. He was there to play.

Almost before Bobby knew it, Dyer had him 5-down. Out of the first six holes, Frank missed winning only one. It looked like the youngster would be going home early.

Then Frank made a few mistakes and gave a few holes back to Bobby. It was almost as if he felt sorry for Bobby. He shouldn't have.

Bobby came back on the back nine and, shooting a 32, tied the score. He and Dyer started the second 18 all square. This time Bobby made fewer mistakes. He won 4 and 2. In time, Bobby would grow to prefer 36-hole matches. Good golfers like Dyer could get hot at any time. With more holes to play, Bobby had a better chance to win.

Bobby's next opponent was the defending champion, Robert A. Gardner, from Chicago. Along with Gardner came a bigger gallery. This was a match people were talking about. Since Perry had lost, the hopes of the South were all on Bobby.

The two opponents looked dramatically different on the first tee. Gardner was nicely dressed but Bobby, well, Bobby still hadn't found out about his hotel's cleaning service and shoe shine shop. One was young; one was not so young; and Gardner towered over Bobby who was only five foot four.

Still, Bobby held an advantage. Gardner had an infected finger.

After five holes, the match was all square. Both players had gotten off to a great start. Bobby shot a 76 on the first 18 and was in a 1-up lead. This was the type of golf where Bobby felt at home. He was in his swing groove and everything was clicking for him.

It was time for lunch. Bobby topped his off with apple pie a' la mode.

$$\text{\textbf{Y}}$$

By the 6th hole of the afternoon round, the contest was back to all square. The match was the buzz of the course. Everyone wanted to see it. But Bobby was caught up in the game and didn't notice the large gallery following him.

On the 8th hole, Bobby's approach stopped ten feet from the cup while Gardner's approach went over the green into an awkward lie. Bobby thought he would get back to 1-up, but Gardner pitched his next shot four feet from the cup and sank the putt. Still tied.

On the 9th hole, Bobby's approach was fifteen feet from the cup while Gardner's approach was way off to the left. Again, however, Gardner came back and put his shot next to the cup.

Another tie.

Bobby just shook his head. "This can't go on," he thought.

On the next hole, Bobby's approach was close to the cup while Gardner's was closer to the next tee. This time Gardner's chip just reached the green.

Bobby thought, "Finally!"

But he celebrated too soon. Gardner dropped his long putt and Bobby had to make his to tie. Bobby was breaking. He was angry that for his great golf, he had gotten nothing. He had just played three holes of absolutely perfect golf and his opponent had barely scraped it by and yet had tied him on all three holes.

Bobby lost five of the next seven holes. Gardner won 5 and 3 on the 15th green in "his" style. He had driven out of bounds on the tee shot and yet had come back to sink a twenty-foot putt for the par. It was over.

News reporters said that Bobby walked gaily back in after the match thinking only of his coming dish of ice cream. They had noticed his penchant for sweets.

In fact, Bobby was trying desperately to figure out what had happened and why he had lost. He had never had an opponent like Robert A. Gardner before in an important match. Bobby felt all alone and, in addition, misunderstood. This was a type of golf that he hadn't met before.

He was also trying to figure out how his best golf didn't win out against Gardner. Bobby had thrown par after par at him but had lost.

Walter Travis spotted Bobby in the gallery watching the other matches play out. "I'd like to have a word with you, if that's okay," Walter said. Both George and Perry Adair were with Bobby, and George Adair was happy to meet Walter Travis again. He had a great deal of respect for what Travis meant to the game's history. Adair nodded his approval, and Bobby gave up his mental questioning.

Bobby and Adair followed Travis to a spot where there were

less people.

"I've been watching you play your matches. You have quite a fine tee to green game." Travis watched the boy's face. "As a matter of fact, from my perspective, your tee to green game cannot get much better. You are about the equal of anyone playing in this tournament. But some day you will learn to hit your shots a mite better."

Bobby looked at Travis and then back at Adair. He was a little surprised at the accolades Travis was throwing at him.

"But your putting is less than it should be. It doesn't go along with your fine irons and woods play." Travis now looked at Adair and their eyes met in a smile.

"I'd like to be of help to you in your setup, your grip, and your putting stroke." Travis stopped and caught his breath. "If I am correct, and I think I am, I can help your putting be the equal of the rest of your game."

Bobby was nodding, so Travis continued.

"I'd like to meet with you here tomorrow morning at eight o'clock and give you a lesson on the practice green."

"Okay," Bobby nodded. Adair was stunned. He couldn't believe Bobby was about to receive such a gift.

"At eight then."

Bobby nodded and watched Walter Travis walk away.

"Now, how about that," Adair smiled. "A putting lesson from the man that most people think is the best putter in the country."

"At eight," Bobby reminded.

"At eight," Adair said.

The following morning though, they all woke up late. They didn't get to the train station until almost eight-thirty and it took the train almost a half hour to get to the Ardmore stop. By the time Bobby got to Merion, they were late and Travis was gone. Travis was a very punctual man and had little to no respect for people who weren't. Bobby had missed a date with his destiny.

Adair kept the boys over for the finals. In between rounds,

they saw some of the great sights in the city of Philadelphia. He didn't want to take the boys home with a bad taste about their first trip North. Adair sensed that Bobby would have the need to come North again and again.

Bobby also used the extra time to talk with Grantland Rice who was in the boy's corner. He also met Chick Evans, who won that year's National Amateur and became the first golfer to win both the Amateur and the National Open in the same year.

And Bobby ran into Robert A. Gardner again. "You gave me one hell of a fight," Gardner said. "I could never have played the golf that you played at your age."

That made things better for Bobby.

"Did you ever see Francis Ouimet?" Bobby asked George Adair as they were settled in their coach seats.

Adair looked at him. "I didn't really expect to after the USGA changed his status. Something tells me that changing Ouimet's status was a big mistake for that organization to make. It doesn't seem right to me, but maybe there's something I don't know."

Perry asked about the calcutta. Where he learned of it is anyone's guess.

"Did anyone bid on Bobby or me?"

Adair quickly picked up his newspaper. "I didn't stay that long. Once I saw that it was just another form of gambling, I left." He didn't want to tell Perry that indeed Bobby had been sold and that Perry went as part of the field. There was no way, short of being forced into it, that Adair would have told either one of the boys that there was $20,000 riding on Bobby's play. That was the equivalent of $250,000 in twenty-first century terms.

Adair turned to his newspaper. He had grabbed copies of all the newspapers he could find for the ride back south, and all of them became a source of embarrassment for Bobby as he read what the reporters wrote about his dress, his beet-red face, his club throwing, and his swearing.

But more than once, Adair told both boys how proud he was of them, and pride was the thing most mentioned after they arrived home.

"You would have been very proud of him," Adair said to Big Bob as they walked about the grounds of the East Lake club. "In his match with the defending champion, there must have been close to 2,500 people following, and Bobby never flinched. I think he got used to having that many people around watching him play."

Adair swallowed hard over what he had to say next. "You're not going to like this, but there was a calcutta gambling pool for the tournament." Adair looked up at Big Bob who had a quizzical look on his face. "It's a simple set-up where after the qualifying round each player is offered up for sale to the highest bidder." Adair tried to soften the news with a smile. "I was shocked at some of the bids for some of the players. I think Chick Evans and Robert Gardner went for the most, about $4,000 each."

"$4,000!", Big Bob exclaimed. "That's a lot of money."

Adair shook his head. "I'll say. Most of the field wound up going as part of a package if they didn't get a bid of at least $500." Adair looked directly at Big Bob. "Bobby went as an individual, but Perry went as part of the field. I didn't tell the boys about the pool until we rode home on the train."

"Smart move."

CHAPTER
8

The First World War postponed golf in 1917. Men signed up to fight, and everyone else held parades and gatherings of all sorts to get their fellow countrymen to either buy War Bonds or help the troops in other ways. But the National Amateur Champion and National Open Champion from the previous year, Chick Evans, figured out a way to help the war effort that involved golf—and it didn't require shooting a gun.

Evans drove all the way to Guelph, Ontario, and played in a match for the Canadian Red Cross which drew thousands of spectators and made a lot of money for the Canadian War Relief Effort. Soon, Bobby and Perry would be called on to do the same for the States.

"Now that's how you can help," Big Bob remarked to Bobby one night as he saw the newspaper notice about what Evans was doing.

"Play golf?" Bobby was amazed. He couldn't see how playing golf could be of help to the soldiers that were doing the hard part, the fighting.

"Oh, it's not just simply golf. It's golf with a purpose. Ever since Grantland Rice put you in his columns, you've become famous in some circles. You and Perry could set up some matches and help in your own way." The last thing Big Bob wanted was his son to go off to war, and that's why he made the suggestion, but he had no idea how big his suggestion would turn out to be.

J.A. Scott took the lead. Scott was head of the Wright and Ditson Company, makers of golf equipment outside Boston. He got in touch with George Adair, who in turn got in touch with Big Bob. Bobby would be leaving home to play golf, but he wouldn't be going overseas. He'd only be going up North. Some Southerners thought that was even worse.

Bobby had company. Perry and Alexa Stirling were going with him. Alexa was now the Women's Amateur Champion, and she was taking Elaine Rosenthal, the recent winner of the North South Women's Invitational, along with her. Elaine's mother was invited to act as chaperone for the women; Bobby and Perry were planning to stay with Grantland Rice and his wife, Kit, in New York.

"Well, we meet again, young Bobby Jones," Rice said as he welcomed Bobby to his apartment in New York. "Mr. Adair, nice to see you again," Rice said to Bobby's constant fellow competitor. Bobby and Perry grinned as they all shook hands.

"Of course, one of the unspoken arrangements of your stay here in New York is that my golf game will have to show some improvement or I, for one, won't consider your trip up here to have been as successful as it might have been."

Rice smiled in his well-known way. "Of course, also being a reporter like I am, although some think of me as a glorified form of reporter in being a columnist, I cannot promise you that whatever you say and do, or that your successes and failures, won't appear in bold naked print."

Bobby nodded and looked at Perry. "Best we talk nothing but golf. Maybe that way we can throw Mr. Rice off." They all laughed.

Rice was from the South, that helped Bobby and Perry become comfortable in his presence. He also had well-known sport celebrities over to his apartment to talk sports; that helped, too. Nights were spent talking golf or other sports with Rice and his drop-in friends; days were spent at golf courses all over New York, northern New Jersey, Connecticut, and Massachusetts, with side trips as far north as New Hampshire.

Bobby and Perry's names appeared even more regularly in

Rice's columns. Matches were played with Bobby and Alexa against Elaine and Perry—either alternate shot or best ball.

Bobby took his matches very seriously, and his cursing and his club throwing made the spotlight more than a few times in local papers.

"Damn, damn, damn," Bobby screamed out after one shot that didn't do what he wanted. He threw his mashie into the rough and Alexa expressed her thoughts by shaking her head. Bobby noticed her unhappiness and felt very badly about what he had just done. It was the beginning of Bobby's awareness of his behavior. Alexa was someone Bobby looked up to.

The fact that the youngsters had Rice in their corner helped a lot. Rice often put the information on the Red Cross matches in his columns and people flocked to see the group play. It was the perfect promotional setup and Bobby's fame grew because of it.

One of the group's best days was spent at the Nassau Country Club in Nassau County, New York. There, Bobby, Perry, and Alexa renewed their acquaintance with Jimmy Maiden, the golf professional brother of Stewart Maiden. Bobby delighted in meeting Jimmy Maiden. His voice and demeanor followed the pattern that Bobby had heard so many times before with his teacher, Stewart Maiden.

"Thee laest time a saw ye, ye were trying ta overcome a sairious ailment," Jimmy Maiden smiled at the now-stocky young man.

Bobby nodded. "I hardly remember," Bobby answered—and he was so healthy now, he truly didn't remember being so sickly.

With all other golf activities brought to a halt because of the war, it was mainly the Dixie Kids who provided the fodder and gossip for golf columns all across the country. Large galleries came out to see them play, and so, after the success of their first trip, Bobby and Perry were invited to Chicago to play against Chick Evans and Robert A. Gardner, two of the best amateur golfers in the country. That trip was another huge success, and it was extended to meet a few other golfers in Kansas City and St. Louis.

The boys were getting to be the best-known golfers in the country.

The world just couldn't get enough of the Dixie Kids, so War Relief matches were created with amateurs set against professionals. The matches were played at a few of the better-known courses like Baltusrol, Siwanoy, and the home course of Walter Travis—Garden City.

The makeup of the teams was Amateurs, American Professionals, Scottish Professionals, and British Professionals. Play was foursomes or alternate strokes, and finally, individual match play.

In the first match, at the end of the first day's play, the scores stood: English Pros, 44; American Pros, 39; Scottish Pros, 14; and the Amateurs, 13.

The next two days of the first match were only marginally better for the amateurs. Some of the professionals played better.

"Well, Bobby Jones, how goes the struggle?" Grantland Rice said that night when they arrived at his apartment.

Bobby looked at Perry. "We had our tails beaten off us. We came in damn last."

"But he didn't do too badly," Perry nodded at Bobby. "He's the only amateur unbeaten in singles play against the pros and single's play is where you can blame all your problems only on yourself."

"Kudos to you, Mr. Jones," Rice beamed. "I'll see to it that everyone back home in Georgia knows how well you played."

One of the those back home reading Rice's column was O.B. Keeler. He had read about the Red Cross matches and now the War Relief matches and was anxious to get some good copy for himself on his hometown hero.

Keeler had been fighting to travel along with Bobby ever since Bobby did so well in the last National Amateur, but he was having a tough time getting funds for travel from Dudley Glass, his editor. Glass and Keeler had gone around and around about the need to cover local heroes at away matches, but Keeler felt no closer to convincing him than he had been two years before. Glass had a very tight budget.

"We don't have room to pay for what might be," Glass shook his head very firmly. "We need to cover the big guys. That's what our readers are interested in. Not some would-be golf prodigies."

"Then I'll damn well pay for it myself," Keeler almost screamed at his boss after one meeting. "Now, will the paper afford me the time to spend my own money to go get the story?" Keeler shook his head and turned to walk away. He knew the Bobby Jones story was getting bigger and he did not want to miss out on another major tournament. He felt the next one might be the youngster's breakthrough.

"You go, but you had best come back with the sports story of the century," Glass said to him as Keeler continued walking down the hall.

Keeler turned back to Glass. "Wasn't it you who thought Ty Cobb would never make it to double A?" Keeler brought up an old story that proved Glass's inability to forecast success.

"Keeler, you come back with the best story of the year or don't come back at all." Glass got the last word in for now.

Keeler wasn't well-received with his news at home either.

"You mean your job's on the line, you're spending our money for your work, and you have to travel out of town?" Keeler's wife asked. She was incredulous. "You do remember that you have four mouths to feed to go along with your big ambitions, don't you?"

Keeler sighed. Sometimes it felt to him as though the world was against every big story that came along. But he reminded himself that even before this occurrence his marriage had been in trouble, and he took off after his story.

Keeler took the night coach to Washington, D.C., and made the early morning connection to New York. He arrived at Rice's apartment, disheveled and a little too late to catch up with the boys before they left for the day. But he did catch Rice who was in his den preparing copy for his daily columns.

It was obvious to Rice that his fellow scribe was working on something.

"Now you understand why I left the South," Rice said to Keeler after he heard Keeler's story about his ordeal with his newspaper. "I love the South. It's my home, but I just wanted to accomplish more. I heard about the news syndicates that were being put together up here and it sounded so right."

Keeler nodded. "A great story is not far away and the Atlanta Georgian doesn't want anyone to bother with it. Just makes no sense to let something so good get away from us. My competitors at the Atlanta Journal or the Constitution won't stay home too much longer. They'll see what I see too."

"Well, I can't leave here because what I am doing is going so well, but someone has to cover the kids. Why not you, if they don't have you on something else that's special?"

"Because Glass doesn't think the kid is going to pull it off. In twenty-three years of play, no fourteen-year-old ever did what he did in the Amateur." Keeler sighed and looked at Rice. "And now, he's older and stronger and more experienced."

Rice shook his head.

"Could I be wrong?" Keeler asked Rice. "Do you see what I see in this developing story?"

Rice lit his well-worn pipe. "What do you see? Maybe I can confirm your thoughts."

Keeler took another sip of the black coffee that Rice had poured for him. He was very serious when he spoke. "There's a lot of luck in this story. A kid is born and just about lives. His parents move him to a golf course and he flowers. The family has little money but they have a real estate friend who has it made financially and takes the boy to tournament after tournament. The son of the real estate guy is three years older than our hero but they provide each other with heads-up competition. A little-known but excellent Scottish golf professional takes over at their course and the kid mimics his swing and starts to win and win big and he's damn well only fourteen years old."

Keeler took a breath and continued the story for Rice. "Then the world steps in to help. The world goes to war, but it's too soon for the boy because he's not old enough to be called up. The golf associations cancel out their tournaments, yet people work to get the boy top-level competition to compete against." Rice raised his eyebrows. "And to top this all off, the top sports writer in the country picks up the boy's cudgel and proceeds to make him a household name."

Keeler sat back with a sigh. "I've never been around a developing story before, but if I had, I have a funny feeling that it would be just like this. This boy can do no wrong. His stars must be in alignment or something." Keeler shook his head.

Rice sat back. "You should have seen Bobby at three years of age. He was frail and wobbly. I would never have bet on him surviving, let alone growing up to be something special for any sport." Rice took a drag on his pipe. "I was working at the Atlanta Journal, but his father and I used to play baseball against each other. He was at Georgia and I was coaching Vanderbilt." Rice paused. "His dad, the Colonel, was one hell of a ballplayer. If it's true about our genes being passed down, Bobby is going to be one really determined golfer."

Silence settled in the room as they both took in what had been said.

"Golf is so new here that I don't comprehend it all. Do you?"

"Nobody does," Rice continued. "It's a real old game that seems just to tease those who latch on to it. It evidently started in Scotland back when knights were still jousting. Even Harry Vardon and Ted Ray said that they don't really grasp it."

Keeler looked off. "So, who's the expert here? Who can tell us whether we're onto something or just being teased?"

Rice chuckled. "No different than anything else. You just have to take your chances with it. As we've heard so often, time will tell."

Keeler finally caught up with the boys and wrote one heck of a story about what they were doing to help the war effort. Keeler reported that the boys's efforts garnered over $150,000 for the War Relief program, an amount that Bobby and Perry were themselves in awe of but could not really grasp.

In 1918, the war was finally over. The armistice was signed on November 11th, outside Paris. In another year, Bobby would have been eligible for the draft.

The next year, 1919, started out slowly for Bobby. The golf world had done its share for the war effort and now felt free to launch its own life again, but the engines were slow to start.

Bobby entered the Georgia Institute of Technology. He wanted to become an engineer. Of course, he also had golf and because of Rice and Keeler, he had become one of the best-known golfers in the country.

Keeler switched his byline to O.B. Keeler and now had a column called 'Oh O's by O.B.,' but his situation with the Georgian was still not settled. Glass and Keeler had merely called a truce to their squabble. It was similar to how the war ended, and Keeler knew that shortly he would once again have to challenge Glass's authority. Keeler knew this story wasn't going away.

With his father's permission, Bobby went to New Orleans and qualified to play in the Southern Amateur Championship again. He did well until he met another golf stylist named Nelson Whitney who beat him 6-5 over 36 holes.

But his real lessons were saved for the next tournament

he entered, the Canadian Open in Hamilton, Ontario. There, Bobby played very well, coming in second, tied with the winner of the first Professional Golfers Championship from 1916, Jim Barnes. Bobby and Barnes were 16 strokes behind a record setting effort by Douglas Edgar—a record that would last for more than a half a century.

Bobby followed a very hot Edgar for more than half of that round. Bobby watched a very talented golfer play his ball's fades and draws to get the lowest score of its day, a 66. Bobby's mind was nearly boggled.

His next outing was at East Lake where he finished just a shot behind Jim Barnes in the Southern Open Championship. It was a real letdown for Bobby. He didn't win on his own home course.

But the locals were able to watch their favorite player in a tournament after years of hearing about what he had been doing elsewhere around the country, and they were delighted by what they saw.

And O.B. Keeler was able to show his boss what it was like to have full tournament coverage for the sports pages.

"So, Bobby, do you think Barnes being a professional and your being an amateur had anything to do with his 1-stroke victory?"

Bobby tried to fathom both his loss and the question. "I think what won it for him was the four strokes I lost over the three holes from the 4th to the 6th in the third round. Barnes went birdie, eagle, birdie while all I could do were pars." Then Bobby threw out a statement that didn't sound like him. "I don't think the balls and clubs he played with knew whether Barnes was a professional or an amateur."

Bobby wasn't trying to be sarcastic. He was just passing on the teachings of Maiden, his teacher who had spent years looking at the game of golf and its players.

"What's next on your golf calendar?" Keeler asked for his readers, but also for himself. He needed to know what to fight Glass for.

Bobby's eyes glazed over a bit as he thought. "The National Amateur that's going to be played at Oakmont in Pittsburgh, I hope."

Keeler also wondered if he was going to be able to go to that tournament. Glass never showed his feelings ahead of time.

After the Southern Open, Stewart Maiden played a round with Bobby and Perry. At the time, neither boy knew it but this would be a round that they would remember forever.

Maiden seemed to be working mentally on something else as they played.

"Lat's tatter," Maiden said in his brisk, no-nonsense way after they had put their clubs back up.

Bobby raised his eyebrows and looked at Perry, asking if Perry knew what Maiden wanted to talk about. Perry just flinched his shoulders, as if to say, "Nope, don't know a thing."

"Ye twa hae become grand gowfers despite yer ages," Maiden started. "It hae been ma pleisur tae knaw ye." Maiden glanced at the boys to watch their reactions. "Bein here a East Lake watchin ye growe in baith life an thee gemme mey weel . . . ." Maiden seemed to have trouble clearing his throat. "Weel, it's been a pleisur for me."

He continued. "Ye knaw, in life, ye hae mony changes." Maiden looked down for a second. "Thee elieven years A hae been here . . . ."

A dread came over Perry and Bobby. This was a serious talk.

Maiden cleared his throat again. "Watching ye twa play in this past tournament shawed me tha ye baith are ready for whitiver ye want tae git frae gowf." Maiden shook his head slightly, then made his point.

"A've decided tae tak ah poseetion at thee St. Louis kintra club." Maiden let out a breath. "But A winna be verra faur awa.

In thee winters, A'll be free tae gae tae whauriver A want tae."

Bobby and Perry looked blankly at each other. Neither of them had even considered losing Maiden. It had never even been in the far reaches of their thoughts. But it was now fore-most in their minds, and they were both at a loss for words.

After a minute or two, Maiden got up—slowly—and walked off. After he had walked about ten steps, his head dropped down. It was obvious that he needed to be alone.

"You've got to let me do this," Keeler started in on Glass. He just had to convince his boss to let him go to the National Amateur coming up at Oakmont Country Club in Pittsburgh. "The other papers are following golf more and more. We need to show our readers that we're on top of what's going on in golf. And with one of the local boys about to break loose."

Glass cut Keeler off. "Tell me you're kidding." Glass shook his head. "The local boys haven't even won something of worth yet." Glass sat back down in his seat. "If you were responsible for turning a profit with this paper, you would see this thing from a better perspective."

"Haven't won anything of worth! Do you know what Bobby Jones did at the age of fourteen? He won about six regional tournaments. Six! And he was only fourteen. Now, he's stepping up and it won't be long before he wins a national event. Hell, even Rice manages to put an article about him in his columns every day or so."

"I'll bet you think his future is forecast in the stars," Glass chuckled as he put his feet up on his well-worn desk.

Keeler looked strongly at him. "I have a right to my opinion. This kid is going to be to his sport what another Georgian, Ty Cobb, is to baseball. We need to get in on the start of his career, not step in halfway down the road."

Glass thought. "I don't know if I can get the powers to be to give me the money or the authorization for that."

Keeler shook his head. "With all the newspapers in this town, we either take the opportunity or some other paper will. That's a given." Keeler walked off. He believed he was right. There were no doubts in his mind, none at all.

Bobby wanted to play in the upcoming National Amateur at Oakmont like a lot of golfers did. Oakmont was one of the top courses of the day.

Built by retired, wealthy steel executive Henry Clay Fownes in 1903 just outside Pittsburgh, Oakmont was known for both very fast greens and its large and plentiful bunkers. The bunkers were groomed with a special implement to leave them with deep ridges in the sand, making them very hard to play out of. No other golf course ever took it upon itself to do what Oakmont did to its bunkers; they were that fearsome.

CHAPTER
9

In the game of golf, sometimes problems never cease. It's golf's greatest curse as well as it's greatest joy.

"I'm having problems with my damn driver, and I can't figure out what's wrong," Bobby said to his dad one night. "I wish Stewart were here since my damn swing is just like his."

Big Bob wasn't sure whether the problem was with Bobby's swing—or whether it was with his heart. He knew that Bobby missed Maiden, who had been more than just a teacher to him for the past eleven or twelve years and who was now out in St. Louis.

"Does anyone else have any decent idea about what the hell you're doing wrong?" Big Bob had put his newspaper down. He knew how important the upcoming National Amateur was to Bobby. Unless Bobby was able to do something special in his second National Amateur, this would be the first year since he was fourteen that he had no wins in the game.

"I wish. Everyone is coming up with ideas and suggestions, but nothing works. I've tried everything. I just have no consistency with my damn driver." Bobby was visibly upset. "It just goes all over the place. If Stewart were here, I'd get him to make me another driver."

Big Bob gave Bobby his full attention. "That might not be the answer. Is Perry going to the Amateur?"

Bobby lightly shook his head. "I don't think so. I think he's had enough of big-time golf for a while. The crowds finally got to him. You should see how many people go to this tournament." What didn't strike Bobby was that with Perry pulling back, Perry's dad would probably be pulling back too. He'd be there alone.

"What else did he say?"

"He says that to him, he'd rather stay home and play here. He doesn't like a lot of people walking beside him and asking him questions."

Big Bob nodded. "Well, what do you want to do about your golf problem?"

"I want to fix it." Bobby stood back up. "Somehow." Bobby sighed deeply.

"How about if I send you out to see Stewart?" Big Bob's business was going much better and he could afford it.

"To St. Louis?" Bobby was caught off-guard.

Big Bob nodded.

"That's a big trip to get a damn driver problem fixed."

"Well, hell. You know another way?"

Bobby shook his head.

"Do you think Stewart can fix it?" Big Bob asked.

Bobby smiled. "If anyone can, he damn well can."

"Let's find out the train schedules and connections."

Bobby arrived in St. Louis a few days later.

"Weel nou Maister Robin,we hiv ah problem wi oor drivin dae we?" Maiden smiled as they met. With Maiden, any problem a student had was a problem he, himself, had.

Bobby nodded. He was still trying to shake off the click, clack, click of the train.

Rounds later, Bobby still could not overcome his driver problems. Maiden had come up with some insights into the problem, but for some reason, the problem remained.

"How about coming to the National Amateur with me?" Bobby asked Maiden on their fourth day together.

Maiden tilted his head forward and rubbed the back of his neck with his hand. He had some work scheduled but he also wanted to see Bobby play Oakmont. He looked away, then faced Bobby. "Okay, lat's gae."

They arrived at Oakmont together, spent their first day at Oakmont working on Bobby's problem, and then Bobby played the course to get the feel of it.

Maiden was amazed by all the reporters that wanted to talk to Bobby and by how many people came up to the boy as if they already knew him. To Maiden, all that took away from the game.

Bobby played in a practice round with Chick Evans, his partner in a few war matches and the defending champion of the National Amateur in 1916. He also met Francis Ouimet again.

But Bobby's drives were still not what he wanted them to be —and Maiden was getting very frustrated.

"Here's whit A want yer tae dae." Stewart had formulated his plan to fix the problem. "Hat thee baw as haurd as yer can."

"Even if it's not going right?" Bobby lamented.

"Listen, laddie." Maiden looked firmly at Bobby, putting his hand on Bobby's shoulder. "Hit haes ta gae somewheer. E'en gif yer git aff thee fairway at laist yer'll be closea tae thee hole."

Bobby played his qualifying match the next day. The USGA had a new format for this event. On Saturday, all entrants played 18 holes to qualify to be one of the lowest 64 players. Then they played 36 holes on Monday to reduce the field to the lowest 32 players that would go into the match play format. It was a sort of double qualification.

Keeler showed up to cover Bobby's matches, and in a surprise move, Big Bob showed up too. It was comforting for Bobby to hear his father singing Old Man River in the bathroom while he shaved. Big Bob had a broad, strong baritone voice and loved to share it with the world.

Perry and his father showed up too. It was like a gathering of the East Lake clan.

"How's it playing?" Perry asked, giving his head a nod toward the course.

"Long and hard, and I mean hard," Bobby answered. "They have more bunkers on this course than on any course I've played. And it's damn long to boot."

"How's the driver?" Perry added.

Bobby shrugged. "Stewart told me not to worry about it, so I guess I'll just hit away and hope for the best."

"It's not fixed?"

Bobby shook his head slowly. "Not completely."

Davidson Herron of Oakmont Country Club led qualifying on Monday along with two other players with a score of 158 for the two rounds. Bobby was one stroke behind at 159. It was a lot better than he had hoped for.

The big problem for golfers that day, besides the great course itself, was a hailstorm that dropped large hailstones everywhere. Word had spread that Ouimet had scored an 8 on the 18th hole because the hail on the green kept him from getting an accurate roll on his putts.

"Aw richt, laddie?" Maiden asked Bobby as they met at the scorer's table.

Bobby chuckled. "Whatever you recommend usually damn works, somehow."

Maiden nodded. "But, yer thee wan that did h'it. A juist git credit fa thee nudgin an pushin yer." Maiden smiled.

But Bobby didn't really feel good about his driving, and he certainly didn't feel good about his putting—he never had. He felt like something was missing. Ever since Walter Travis had wanted to give Bobby a putting lesson, Bobby's belief that his putting was lacking something grew stronger.

Like Maiden had taught him, he putted to have the ball die at the hole. A ball that was just about moving when it got near the cup was much more likely to go in—and according to Maiden, it had four sides in which to do it. Bobby and Perry made fun of the concept of "four sides," but they always practiced it.

Bobby was becoming very good at having his ball die at the hole and never leaving himself long follow-up putts. But still, something nagged at him about his putting.

Bobby won his first match, 3 and 2. He played a big match with Robert Gardner next, whom he had lost to in 1916, and won 5 and 4. Then he won another match 3 and 2 and then 5 and 4 over Henry Fownes, also of Oakmont. Fownes was the son of the man who built the course, and he had won the National Amateur in 1910.

With that done, Bobby was into the final round of the National Amateur. It was only his second effort.

Perry qualified, but barely. Then he lost in the second match. It would be the last time he qualified in the Amateur. His reign as the Dixie Boy Wonder was ending.

The weather for the final was close to perfect. Bobby was playing David Herron for the championship, and large crowds showed up to see the new Dixie Boy Wonder do it.

Herron was on his game, but Bobby's driver was working now, and the match was hard-fought. They were all tied after the morning 18; the afternoon round would have to provide the answer.

After lunch, Herron's local knowledge started paying off when he sunk three really long putts. With seven holes left to play, Herron had Bobby 3-down.

Bobby worked to pump himself up, and on the 12th hole, a long 600-yard par-five, he out-drove Herron while Herron bunkered his drive. No great champion ever gives up. Standing aside, Bobby watched as Herron managed to recover from his bunkered situation—but just barely.

It was time for Bobby's second shot. He reached for his brassie and managed to hone his eyes in on the green. He felt fluid and confident as he took a practice swing.

He addressed his ball and started his swing. But on the start of Bobby's downswing, a marshall speaking into a megaphone a few feet away cautioned the gallery to stop its movement. Bobby flinched, and the shot was ruined.

Bobby had a chance to cut back into Herron's lead; instead, he lost the hole. He was 4-down. He lost the match two holes later, 5 and 4. His year was over with no wins.

The ride home was a long one. Stewart Maiden went back to St. Louis, and Bobby had to say good-bye to him once again. But when your destiny is built around friendship, one friend arrives just as another one leaves.

"Not the kind of year you had expected?" Keeler said to Bobby as they took their seats for the train ride to Washington to connect with the East Coast line.

"I had hopes for at least one win. Who can stomach all seconds?" Bobby looked out the window as the train started moving. Big Bob went for his hidden stash of illegal hard drinks. Prohibition was in. "Even the papers keep saying I should win every time I play in one of these national tournaments."

"A lot of seventeen-year-olds would be very happy with the record you had this year," Keeler assured.

Bobby just shifted in his seat. Bobby's legs stung at times and his veins swelled up. It was one of the many things he shared with O.B. Keeler. Keeler's own left leg pained him when he walked a good deal.

"But you must feel pleased about moving up in the Amateur?" Keeler reasoned. "That was progress. And you beat Gardner this time."

Bobby nodded slightly and watched as his dad poured a drink. "I had it too easy in all my lead-up matches." Bobby shook his head. "But then, Herron had it easy, too." He paused. "He just had the game for the course."

"Local knowledge?" Keeler threw out, and Bobby nodded.

"Familiarity has to help. It makes you feel more comfortable on the course, which makes you relax. You can get more out of your swing."

Then Keeler asked the question of the day. "Did that megaphone on the 12th really end your effort?"

Bobby grimaced but shook his head. "I can't give the megaphone credit for Herron's win. He got what he deserved, that's for sure. He played like he was ready. He dropped some putts in the afternoon that were beauties to watch go in." Bobby shook his head again, more vigorously this time. "But someone should do something about those damn noisy horns. They can make you flinch five fairways away."

Keeler looked at Bobby closely as the boy stood up. "Are my eyes accurate? You look a little thinner to me." Bobby was ten pounds thinner.

Bobby put his hands inside his pants and tugged them up. "I did lose a few pounds." He tugged his pants some more and Keeler saw the room that was now obvious in the garment.

"But I saw you eating a good-sized lunch a few times."

Bobby grinned. "The food there was great."

Bobby went to stretch his legs.

"He's really something for a seventeen-year-old," Keeler remarked to Big Bob. He and Big Bob were fast becoming good friends.

Big Bob nodded. "That he is." He looked conspiratorially at Keeler. "I'm very proud of him."

Keeler smiled. "I'm proud of him, and I'm not his father."

"I only wish my father could appreciate what he's doing."

Keeler wondered. "Trouble in the family?"

Big Bob sighed. "My father, Bobby's namesake, is a religious tyrant." Big Bob shook his head. "The man believes that the perfect person spends twenty-four hours a day working or praying, which doesn't leave much room for anyone or anything else."

Keeler didn't know what to say except, "I'm sorry."

When Bobby returned to their car, Keeler had an idea.

"You know, Bobby, in every round I saw you play where you had just eaten one of your big lunches, it seemed to me that you had to play four or five holes before you could get your game to where it was before your lunch break."

Bobby thought. Then he nodded. "But those lunches were so good."

"Seems to me as though you're going to have to decide between pie a' la mode and winning a hole or two." Keeler grinned.

"We can always make up for your lost lunch at home," Big Bob smiled. "Camellia will be only too damn glad to cook some more for you."

Bobby thought the process through. "Worth trying."

As the ride went on, Big Bob and Keeler shared what was left of their illegal liquor. Keeler, being Keeler, brought up subjects he thought Big Bob would comment on.

"Did you ever think in your wildest imagination that your son would some day be playing for a national title at the age of seventeen?"

Big Bob shook his head. "Never. Damn never." Big Bob grinned. "He held his own. He stood the gaff."

"That he did. Seventeen and already a runner-up in a national event. And with all those people walking beside him and chatting in his ear or asking him for things."

"Asking him for things?" Big Bob questioned.

"I heard one lady ask him for a handkerchief and someone else asked for one of his used balls."

Big Bob laughed. "Wonder what the hell that's all about?"

"People think that he's going to be something and they want a souvenir, a piece of him, so to speak." Keeler chuckled. "One person even picked up one of his divots."

"Just like one of those damn movie stars."

"Just like them." Keeler smiled.

Then Big Bob recalled something of note. "Recently, at East Lake, we've had some people walk right onto the course and walk along with Bobby while he's playing." Big Bob laughed. "They think it's just parkland, I guess."

"They walk right on?"

Big Bob nodded. "He sometimes winds up with six or eight people following him around the course." Big Bob grinned. "It doesn't bother Bobby to have those fans along, but it sure bothers some of the people that he plays with."

Keeler shook his head. "Some people just need to be alone while hacking around."

"I sure do." Big Bob guffawed and Keeler joined in the laugh.

The train ride kept hurtling back to Atlanta.

"Bobby was sold for close to $3,000 in the calcutta," Keeler mentioned. "Total pot was close to $30,000."

"Not surprised about that. I'm only glad he didn't hear about it."

"Some people have great expectations of him. Leading qualifying in the first round of the last Amateur got Bobby noticed. And just missing the medal for low qualifier in this one kept it going." Keeler grinned. "Our friend Rice helps too. Bobby's on the lips of every golfer in the country now." Keeler thought. "You know, there was a great young golf champion back in the 1870's. A very young champion."

"Tommy something." Big Bob sat up straight in his Pullman sofa.

"Morris. Young Tommy Morris. Son of the green keeper at St. Andrews." Keeler now leaned back, learning to enjoy the ride.

"But something bad happened to him. Right?"

"He died. But not before he won his fourth Open. His wife died in childbirth, and they say Morris died of a broken heart."

Big Bob looked out the window remembering his own family's childbirth problems. "I hope they do something to stop the calcuttas. Someone could use that thing some day to slant the results of a tournament. Do they have a calcutta at the National Open?"

Keeler nodded. "I heard they do. About the same size, I guess." But Keeler had yet to attend a National Open, and he didn't really know. The calcuttas at the Open were bigger because of the professionals playing in it, and rumor had it that some of the biggest gamblers were the professionals themselves.

Keeler's professional problems were still building with the Atlanta Georgian and came to a head in the fall of 1919.

"Don't expect to be trailing that youngster around any next year," Glass said across the desk. "With all the money we have to spend covering the Black Sox scandal, we'll have nary a dime for you to become the next Lewis and Clark."

"That youngster is now close to eighteen and is going to be doing something special for the South, and Atlanta in particular. If you don't want your paper to have the lead in this story, so be it." Keeler expired air. "This is a story that may well overshadow all the other stories over the next ten years as the boy grows into a man and golf grows into importance."

"He's that good, eh?" Glass muttered weakly.

"He's who they talk about at the National Amateur. I wish you could have come with me to see it all and how well he handles himself even though he hates being fawned over." Keeler let out another long breath. "This 'boy' is not out for stardom. He just wants to win a national tournament, and he has the drive to do it."

Keeler saw Glass sit up. "If he misses, just slightly misses a shot, he swears an oath and throws clubs and gets totally upset with himself." Keeler paused. "He asks more of himself than anyone else out there."

"Well, he better win something before he goes to hell in a handbasket. Smart people know that perfectionists do not always survive what they ask of themselves."

Keeler walked around the block to his favorite watering hole, The Leather Bottle Cafe, where unbeknownst to Glass he had often met with the editor of the Atlanta Journal, Major John Cohen.

"Is your offer still open?" Keeler said to Cohen as he caught him heading out the door.

"How about right after the start of the year." Cohen stopped quickly in his tracks.

Keeler nodded. "That'll do."

Cohen grinned. "Just bring your heart and soul."

"Till death we do part," Keeler threw back at Cohen.

"It better be, after all the ruckus I'll have to create to get you the expense account you want."

Keeler joined the Atlanta Journal, and his stock rose—and it rose a bit more when Grantland Rice was named editor of the American Golfer magazine and extended Keeler an invitation to join his staff. Keeler was happy to oblige.

Keeler's first article for the American Golfer was about the Dixie Boy Wonder and what he had achieved so far in his young golfing life. In some ways, the article cemented the relationship between the two rising stars: Jones in golf and Keeler in golf reporting.

Bobby turned eighteen on March 17th, 1920. He was now a sophomore at Georgia Tech, studying engineering. With the smell of spring in the warm Georgia air, his thoughts naturally turned to golf, but he hadn't swung a club since the previous season when he decided he couldn't let his no-win record stand and he entered and won two small events. He won the Morris Country Club Invitational and then he and Chick Evans beat Harry Vardon and Ted Ray 10 and 9 in another exhibition match.

"Gonna try out for the Open in Toledo?" Bobby asked Perry as they played their first round of the new season. Bobby had received a personal invitation from the Inverness Club, the host of the Open that year.

Perry shook his head. "I don't like all those crowds of people looking over you while you play in the National. To me, that's not the golf I know. They get under my skin when they ask questions and take my mind off play."

Bobby understood that very well.

"It's hard sometimes, even with the ropes on the back of the greens and the tees, getting to the next tee," Perry remembered. "And I'm afraid of hitting someone." Perry shook his head. "These balls are hard. God only knows what they would do to someone who got hit in the head with one of them.

Bobby felt that danger at times, too, but Perry took his fear to the next level and Bobby now knew why Perry didn't do well in his matches. Worrying about hitting a person would naturally make you back off of a shot.

Before Bobby went to Toledo, he warmed up by going to Chattanooga, Tennessee, to play in the Southern Amateur Championship. Perry had suddenly decided to come to the Southern, too, saying that the crowds there probably wouldn't be too much for him.

Bobby won the Southern handily even though, for the first time, his hands showed the effects of hard fast practice sessions by bleeding. Because of that, and partly because it was being played not too far away in Memphis, he decided to enter the Western Amateur too.

After qualifying rounds of 69 and 70, which set new records for the Western, Bobby started winning his way through the matches until he met Chick Evans in the semifinals. It was the first time Bobby met Evans in a serious tournament in match play. Evans was a perennial favorite in the Western.

Evans, for years, had played for and helped promote Midwestern golf through the Western Golf Association. Raised around the Edgewater Golf Club on Chicago's north side, and starting out in the game as a caddy, Evans went on to win eight Western Amateurs, two National Amateur tournaments, and one National Open, plus many more smaller tournaments. His contributions to the game through his demeanor and his scholarship programs had made him a standout among the game's boosters.

But it was Bobby whom the crowd, obviously a partisan Southern crowd, rooted for. The South needed a hero after its defeat in the Civil War, which was not far from any Southerner's memory.

Bobby and Evans were the top amateurs of their day. Bobby was the hero of the USGA while Evans was the hero of the WGA, the Western Golf Association.

The morning round was a washout. Play was tight. But in the afternoon round, Evans slowly built up a 3-hole lead. With seven holes to play, the outcome of the match looked certain until Bobby suddenly won back three holes in lightning fashion, squaring up the match with four holes to go.

Halves on 15 and 16 left the tense outcome to the last two holes. On 17, the 35th hole in the match, both players showed the effects of the strain. Evans had a putt of twelve feet for birdie and Bobby had a six-foot putt to save par. Evans, never known for his putting, was not favored.

But Evans made his putt and Bobby his. One hole to go and Evans was 1-up. They both parred the 18th hole; Evans had won. It had been a stirring first meeting for the two. Evans went on to win the Western Amateur while Bobby headed back to Atlanta to prepare for the upcoming Southern Open to be played at East Lake.

"It was a thrill to watch you and Chick Evans battle it out like that," Keeler said to Bobby on the way home.

Bobby nodded as he looked solemnly out the window.

"You okay?" Keeler asked after he hadn't gotten an answer.

"I hate to lose when it's due to hitting inferior shots. I know I could have done better." Bobby breathed hard. "But he played well. I don't mean to take anything away from Evans and his victory." Bobby shook his head. "Hell, if I had played better, he may just as well have played better, too."

"We'll never know now, will we?" Keeler threw out.

Bobby looked sternly at Keeler. "The hell we won't. Let's see what happens the next time we meet."

Keeler nodded. That was the kind of fire in the belly that made him a believer about the boy.

Bobby worked on his legs, which had been bothering him.

"Thanks for coming," Bobby smiled gently. "It was great having company."

"I saw that you ate less between rounds."

Bobby grinned at him. "I played better too."

Big Bob met them at the Brookwood Station in Atlanta and heard the whole story from Keeler.

"Well, Evans will never damn well beat him again," Big Bob huffed and grabbed a bag to take to the car.

Bobby's golf quietly swung back into its natural rhythm. He played in the company of friends during their regular Sunday games together, and Camellia cooked up a storm for him. This was the way golf should be played.

When the time came for Bobby to get ready for his first-ever National Open, he felt good about his game. He had scored a new low record of 68 on East Lake and threatened record scores on both Druid Hills and Brookhaven.

Keeler would accompany him to the National Open. It was going to be held at the Inverness Club and Keeler had heard a little about the course. He thought it must be a good one because it was a recent Donald Ross designed course—as East Lake was.

Bobby immediately felt at home. There was Bobby's familiarity with a Donald Ross-designed golf course, and the Inverness Club had gone out of its way to make the contestants feel at home. It provided both transportation and housing, and it was the first host course to do so. The players couldn't say enough good things about the club when the tournament was over.

Bobby played practice rounds with both Harry Vardon and Ted Ray the second day he was at Inverness, and he ran into Keeler when the round was finished.

"Hi, Bobby," Keeler said. It wasn't lost on Keeler that Bobby was playing with the two players most expected to challenge for the title, and he wanted in on the action.

"Hi, O.B."

"How'd the round go?" Keeler fell into his reporter mode.

"It went fine. This is a great new course."

Keeler nodded to Vardon and Ray as they walked on by. "How did they do?" He tossed his head in their direction.

Bobby looked after the British players. "Like two great English professionals."

"They say Vardon is too old to really challenge here."

Bobby shook his head. "He plays very smoothly and consistently. I wouldn't cross him off the list of possible winners."

The next day, Bobby met Gene Sarazen, who was also playing in his first Open, and the great Scottish amateur, Tommy Armour. He played with and became good friends with a professional named Leo Diegel who had one of the strangest putting stances Bobby had ever seen.

"Still going okay?" Keeler asked Bobby as he caught up with him later.

"Pretty good. I like the course and it's fun meeting some of the golfers I've heard about."

"I didn't know that Vardon had won the British Open six times," Keeler mentioned. "Or that they call him the 'Greyhound' over in the British Isles."

Bobby smiled.

"Did you know that?"

Bobby shrugged. "Vardon hardly ever talks on the course."

Keeler smiled. "As a matter of fact, I got that from Ted Ray. Vardon hardly talks much off the course either."

Qualifying was a great lead-in to the Open. First, the players would qualify by playing 18 holes two days in a row on Tuesday and Wednesday. Then, the Open would be played over 36 holes for two days in a row ending on Friday. It was a test of stamina as well as one of skill.

Bobby's first round with Vardon went nicely. The first nine holes, Bobby actually led Vardon by three strokes. He kept that lead until the 18th hole where Vardon birdied and Bobby got a double bogie. Their even scores put them both in the running.

In the second round, Bobby was again in the lead until the 7th hole where both he and Vardon took the dangerous route on a short par-four over some tall trees. They both pulled their shots off and were left with just forty-yard pitches. Vardon went first and pitched beautifully while Bobby skulled his ball and watched it scurry across the green into trouble on the other side.

Bobby stood there steaming as Vardon slowly started walking past him. "Mr. Vardon," Bobby started. "Did you ever see a worse shot than that?"

Vardon coldly replied, "No." Vardon's answer agreed with Bobby's own analysis.

They both qualified. They were the youngest and the oldest competitors in the group.

Bobby didn't know it, but his bad first round brought into play two problems that were to haunt him year after year. First, he met up with a feeling he would come to know quite well. He had done most of his competitive playing in match play situations where he could see his opponent. But in medal play, his opponent was not necessarily in front of or beside him. That slow realization gave Bobby a feeling of stress that built—and the stress caused him to feel tight, which made all of his muscles react in unfamiliar ways.

His putting was a problem too. It was the one part of Bobby's game that had never been looked on favorably by other competitors or the reporters that knew the game well, like Grantland Rice.

"Welcome to the Big Show, kid," Bobby heard from behind him as he entered the locker room after qualifying. He turned to see a very well-dressed player grinning at him.

"Why, thank you," Bobby grinned back.

"Walter Hagen." Hagen stuck his hand out and Bobby easily reacted.

"This is your first Open and the first is always special, like the start of a long, wonderful love affair."

"I wish my first round would have been something better than what I had."

"Sure, kid." Hagen smiled. "We all do that." Hagen pulled his foot down off the bench. "Say, how'd you ever get Rice to put you in so many of his columns?"

Bobby smiled. "Just being friendly, I guess."

Hagen nodded. "I'll have to give that one a try. Rice did you one great thing in getting your name out there like he did." Hagen looked past Bobby to another player. "The club really did some great things in setting itself up for this tournament, didn't they?"

Bobby merely nodded and smiled.

"Well, see ya around, kid." Hagen had no idea how true that statement was.

Bobby's third round of 70 moved him into a tie for fifth, just four strokes behind the new leader, Vardon, the great "Greyhound." Bobby's descending scores of 78, 74, and 70 had also put him ahead of Chick Evans by one stroke. At that time, Evans was the top amateur in the country. He felt a lot of things were possible for him in the last round.

"Sure you want to finish all that?" Keeler said to Bobby as they shared a table for lunch. Keeler had noticed how much food Bobby had ordered.

Bobby shook his head. "I'm so hungry, and this is so good."

Keeler let out a breath of air. "But your stomach is not far from your muscles. You cannot ask your body to do so many things at one time and expect them all to be done well."

"Last time," Bobby had started to put his fork down. "If I don't do real well today, I'll change things."

Keeler shook his head.

"Last time," Bobby repeated. "Unless I get my 68."

"I've heard a lot of players suffer either a bad third round or a bad fourth," Keeler offered not really knowing if he was help-ing or hurting.

"I hope that my bad round was my first. Now I have a chance to do something special."

In his heart, Bobby felt he could do something special in his fourth round. But both the pressure of the tournament and a few bad strokes caught up with him. He tried to make up for those few bad strokes, and that caused its own pressure. The result was a 77, which put him into a tie for eighth, just five strokes away from an outright win.

The fourth round was fought through a torrent of wind and rainsqualls as a front moved through. Scores rocketed. Vardon seemed to show his age by losing six strokes to par over his last five holes. He lost out to Ray by one lonely stroke. Many people said that Ray won because of his girth since the squalls couldn't affect him.

Bobby was dismal as he posted his worst score.

"Hello, Bobby Jones," Bobby heard from another golfer whose stature was slightly smaller then his own.

"Gene Sarazen." The man offered his hand and Bobby extended his.

"Nice to meet you, Mr. Sarazen."

"My first Open. I can't wait to get back to another. Too bad that we have to wait a whole year."

Bobby nodded.

"Now, if we were Walter Hagen over there, we'd be getting ready to go over to the Isles and play in the old Open, the original."

Bobby glanced over to where Sarazen's eyes were looking and saw Hagen in another nifty outfit. "He sure wears some nice clothes," Bobby noticed.

Sarazen nodded. "That he does." Sarazen smiled. "He's something else, something else."

The long ride home was one of introspection for Bobby. "If I had shot just a 72, I would have won it," Bobby said to Keeler as they rode back together.

Keeler nodded.

"It was a strange feeling to be so tight in my backswing and that nervous over my putts," Bobby continued.

Keeler wanted to add something but wasn't sure what he could offer.

"I shot 70 in the third. One more time around with a 70 and I would have that big cup to take back home to my dad."

Finally, Keeler found something. "If you had just shot a 72, you would have won it. Did you ever think that the tournament pressure was affecting others the same way that it was affecting you?"

Bobby shook his head. "I wanted to get a 70 or better. I felt that others would score better on their final round."

Keeler shook his head. "Like I said the other day, the last two rounds are pure pressure. At least that's what I've heard. I don't think that anyone scored what they wanted to, especially with that weather."

Bobby nodded and thought.

"Oh, the others are watching you all right. Did you hear what Vardon said about you?"

Bobby shook his head, but his thoughts were of his missed approach that he had played on seven when he was paired with Vardon.

"Well," Keeler started out slowly. "He said that someday you'd be one of the greatest players the game ever produced."

That threw Bobby into a slight shock. For years, people had told him of his great game, but this statement came from Vardon, the best player in golf.

"He really said that?"

Keeler nodded. "If you have trouble believing it, read my columns over the next few days."

CHAPTER
10

I want to win one national tournament," Bobby exhaled. "Just one damn tournament," he said on the train to compete in the National Amateur in 1920. It was the first year Bobby played in both the National Open and the National Amateur. He was speaking to his dad, Big Bob, and his friend, O.B. Keeler, whom he had taken along. They knew Bobby wanted to make up for what he considered his first round failure at the National Open.

The world seemed to agree that Bobby should win a national tournament. He was the favorite of everyone who spoke or wrote about it. "A champion in the making," one columnist said. "A sure thing," said another. But it took the New York Times to really make everything official. In a ranking of amateur golfers commissioned by the Times, Bobby was placed second.

He huffed as he looked out the window at the moving scenery and stretched his legs. The veins in his left leg were giving him trouble again.

This National Amateur had drawn a small British invasion. It was being held on the East coast, at the Engineers Country Club on Long Island—easy to get to from Great Britain. Cyril Tolley, the Amateur Champion of Britain, Roger Wethered, a well-known player, and Lord Charles Hope had come over. It was as if the British were still trying to make up for Walter Travis's unpopular victory in the 1904 British Amateur. They disliked the fact that one of their coveted trophies had gone across the Atlantic for even one year.

Bobby had grown more mature in many ways. He understood tournament golf in a deeper, more comprehensible way, but as his understanding grew, so did his worries about winning. As such, this tournament occupied a bigger place in his mind.

To make matters worse, as if what he did in his first two National Amateur tournaments weren't enough to get him media coverage, especially considering his young age, Bobby tied Freddie Wright for the co-medalist of this National Amateur with a score of 154. The medalist is the golfer who shoots the lowest score in qualifying. In this case, two golfers shot the lowest score.

There were two camps of thought about the importance of being the medalist. Some people felt that the medalist should be favored in the regular tournament and others thought that once qualifying was over the real tournament began. To this second camp, qualifying meant nothing.

But it was a known fact that winning the medalist honors was special. Some medalists went on to win and they were remembered for being both the medalist and the tournament winner.

Gossip went around that Bobby had this tournament in the bag. The calcutta which was held in the smoky ballroom at the downtown hotel illustrated that. Bobby was sold for the highest price.

But Bobby didn't know about the gossip or the calcutta. As soon as qualifying was over, he switched on his match play mode and met and beat two players he had met in previous matches by the same scores of 5-up and 4-to-play. One player was the previous National Amateur Champion, Robert Gardner, who had knocked Bobby out of the tournament at Merion.

Bobby met his co-medalist, Freddie Wright, and won that match 5 and 4. He was on a roll. And this match had a little more riding on it than usual. Bobby and Wright had decided that whoever won this match would get to keep the medal for low qualifying score. Bobby was now a medalist for the National

Amateur; he had his first USGA medal.

"Look, Dad." Bobby held the medal out for his father to inspect, just as he had for years back in East Lake.

"Very nice." Big Bob held the medal by its little loop and turned it around in his fingers. Then they hugged as usual.

Keeler reached out to see the medal. It was just a tiny, round, shiny medal. "Amazing what some things are worth," Keeler said while looking closely at the object. "Congratulations, Bobby." He smiled at the young man. "You know, of course, some people move heaven and earth for years to get one of these and are never successful."

Bobby smiled humbly. He had a bigger medal—the Havemeyer trophy, given to the winner of the National Amateur—on his mind, but he wouldn't dare say it.

Bobby ran into a match with the man who had the distinction of being both a hero and a friend to Bobby, Francis Ouimet. Ouimet was the hero of the 1913 National Open over Vardon and Ray and the winner of the 1914 National Amateur. That combination took Bobby out of his concept of match play. Bobby had always had trouble beating people for whom he had kindly feelings. He had not yet separated friendship from simple competitive play.

Common thought about match play was that you beat your fellow opponent by hitting better shots than he did. If he hit a great drive, you hit a better one. If your fellow opponent hit a great approach, you had to hit your approach inside his. The object was to always be between your opponent and the hole. That was impossible to do if you looked at your opponent as your friend.

Ouimet didn't have a problem separating friendship from competition. He looked at Bobby as he should have, as an opponent. By the end of the morning round, Bobby was 3-down. In the morning round, Bobby even missed a two-foot putt on the 18th green.

The afternoon round included an instance on the 7th green

where Bobby was both chased by and the chaser of a bumble bee which held up play until Bobby, out of breath, ran the bee off the green. He then had to catch his breath and settle down before completing his putt. He missed. Then he missed again. People laughed at the episode, but it cost Bobby another hole.

His concentration lost, Bobby lost 6 and 5 to Ouimet. He was out of the tournament.

"Damn it," Big Bob said in a huff to no one in particular as he walked down off the slope to the green.

"Sorry," Keeler said to Big Bob as he tried to help.

"I didn't come all this damn way to watch my son lose." Big Bob let out a blast of air and looked off. "You know, I've had the gut feeling that my being here brought Bobby absolutely no good luck. I wonder if I'm a jinx to his efforts."

"I don't see . . . ." Keeler started, but was cut off.

"I'm around, and he loses. With golf being the way it is, maybe if I had stayed home, he would have had the finesse that he needed to bring off the shots."

Keeler remembered the strained relationship that Big Bob had with his own father and decided that he'd better stay out of Big Bob's thinking.

"That's it. I'm not coming to one of these again until Bobby brings home one of these tournament wins that he wants so badly." Big Bob huffed again. "I don't want to be my son's jinx."

"You're not even . . . ." Keeler attempted again.

"Damn, nope." Big Bob cut Keeler off and headed in the direction of his son to congratulate him for his fine overall effort.

The tournament was not a total loss for Bobby. He was able, for the first time, to comprehend what was going on with a number of other players as they played tournament golf.

In particular, Bobby watched as Chick Evans won his first match very handily, 8 and 7. Then he watched the next day and saw Evans's second match. It had Evans on the ropes, fighting to stay in the tournament. It looked hopeless for him. Bobby reasoned that Evans had yet to come onto his game.

Reginald Lewis had Evans 1-down and simply needed to halve this last hole to get his win. It was an exiting adventure for the spectators.

Neither player was able to hit his best tee shot on this last hole, and after mediocre second shots, Evans was short of the green while Lewis was over the back. Evans's ball lay in a batch of clover, one of the worst lies from which to hit a controlled shot.

But Evans put his approach fifteen feet from the hole.

Lewis put his approach just inside Evans's, and the match turned when Evans got his long putt down on the last turn of the ball while Lewis took two putts and lost the hole. The match went into extra holes.

For five extra holes, Evans showed some weaknesses and could have found himself beaten a few times, yet he won on the 41st hole.

A thought came to Bobby. It was as if Evans's play in the tournament had been predestined. Just one spooky shot had separated Evans from ultimate victory and ignominious defeat a number of times.

The putt Evans sank on the 18th hole seemed to be the starting point from which he rallied through the rest of the tournament, and as Bobby remembered it, a feeling came over him about the inevitability of a tournament. Bobby remembered hearing some of the pros say "it was his tournament to win."

Now, Bobby felt like he was witnessing the golfer's proverb. It was as if the hand of providence had willed Evans to win. Bobby saw it and even felt it. This was a part of a tournament that Bobby had never even imagined existed.

The day after the tournament, Bobby went to another nearby golf course and gave an exhibition. His dad went home. He didn't want to jinx Bobby's exhibition, too.

Keeler went with Bobby and, for the first time, Bobby and Keeler shared a room. It was the start of their many shared trips together. Keeler didn't sing in the shower like Big Bob did, but he recited poetry.

Traveling home on the train with Keeler, Bobby showed Keeler the extravagant gift he got for doing the exhibition. It was only the most recent gift Bobby had received. Since he was an amateur, Bobby wasn't allowed to charge for his exhibitions like the professionals did, but he was allowed to receive gifts. Often, the gifts Bobby got were worth much more than the money he would have received.

Keeler surveyed the gift and smiled as he handed it back to Bobby. "Now I know what Hagen meant when he said that there are days he would have preferred to remain an amateur."

If the nineteen-year-old Bobby Jones knew what was going to happen in 1921, he might have wanted to skip that year and go on to 1922 or especially 1923. Just five years previously, Bobby had no wishes or hopes of ever playing in a national tournament. He had qualified for the 1916 National Amateur at Merion in Ardmore, Pennsylvania, after his win in the Georgia State Amateur, and the rest naturally followed.

Now, though, Bobby had high hopes to win at least one national event. He had seen some of the awards ceremonies and he wanted to hand his dad one of those big trophies. This year, 1921, those hopes spread to the British Isles.

A lot of people were proud of the contribution that golf had made to the war effort for the Great War. Quite a few of them gave the victory, or the result of the armistice, to the English-speaking countries, and they felt that the best chance for world peace rested with the United Kingdom and the United States. Consequently, they wanted to build up contact between the golfers of these two countries.

This thinking was not unique to any one side of the Atlantic Ocean. The impetus for this thinking, indeed, may have gone as far back as Harry Vardon's first trip to the States in 1900. The growth of the game of golf after Vardon's tour around the East Coast had been phenomenal.

But it took George Herbert Walker, the President of the USGA, to commit these hopes to action. Walker put up a beautiful trophy, which others quickly named after him, for an amateur match to be held every other year between the two countries. Now the British authorities would have to agree to the premise of regular team play during the upcoming journey to England and Scotland.

The plan was to send eight of the best American amateur golfers to Britain for a match with their counterparts from the British Isles. Many of the British looked at the coming invasion as an American push to claim the British Amateur trophy, as Walter Travis had done in 1904.

"Are you going over there?" Perry said to Bobby as he reported on the news of the match.

"I just don't know how I would ever pay for a trip like that," Bobby said simply. It was an unusually nice spring day at East Lake, and the young men chose to play golf. But now, the game was over and they gathered their thoughts about bigger things.

"It said in the paper that the USGA may be paying for the trip," Perry pointed out.

That didn't happen, though, and Bobby learned that he'd have to come up with almost $1,500 if he wanted to go.

Bobby had heard from many players how the golf courses over in the British Isles were different than the American courses, that they were great learning experiences.

"That's a lot of money," Bobby told his dad when they received the invitation.

"It is, but the experience probably more than justifies the expense." Big Bob's mind was already drifting into ways to get some of the funds.

"Then you think I should go?"

Big Bob had yet to work out the details, so he simply nodded.

Once the word spread around the little village of East Lake that Bobby had been picked to represent the United States on a golf team in the British Isles, people dropped by the Jones house to wish the young man well. But only one person could really advance Bobby's trip with solid information about what the game was all about back in the old country—and that was Stewart Maiden—and he wasn't there.

George Adair was one of those who stopped by to congratulate Bobby. He seemed to think Bobby was going. He brought a newcomer to East Lake with him, a young man named Watts Gunn.

"Mind if he stays?" Adair asked Bobby as he glanced at the young man.

Bobby smiled. "Of course not."

"You're going into a whole new world when you travel across the ocean, Bobby," Adair started. "No matter what I can tell you about your upcoming trip, I know it will not be enough. This is the kind of thing you have to experience for yourself first-hand before it can be said that you know your way around." Adair settled into his chair while Camellia brought in refreshments.

Adair wet his lips and continued. "The people back in England and Scotland love their game and they're very proud to be sharing golf with us over here in the States." Then Adair broke into a broad grin and squinted his right eye. "But make no mistake about it. Despite the cuteness of their accents and the coziness of their public bars, they are out to beat you. Even though they aren't as outgoing with their feelings as we boisterous Americans are, they have their own ways to show how badly they want to win and defend their turf."

Adair spent hours telling Bobby what the foreign courses were like in general and how to get around, how money exchanged, and every tiny facet of information he could think of or that Bobby could ask.

Finally, they broke up. Bobby, in his now dry voice, asked Gunn, "What did you score today?"

Gunn grinned back. "Got my 80." In fact, Gunn had been waiting to announce it.

Bobby smiled.

"Isn't he about the same age that you were when you got your 80," Adair asked.

Bobby looked at Gunn and nodded. "He sure is."

"Your 80 was on the old design, which was about six strokes tougher," Adair thoughtfully added.

Bobby looked at Gunn. "But the strength of his game is in the long irons which would have served him better on the old course design more so than the new one."

The next day Bobby heard from the man he longed to speak to. "You dae well, Laddie. Juist tak yer time an git tae knaw thee lay o thee laund." Maiden proved how well he knew Bobby. "An don' be puttin a lot o pressure on yersel this first voaige ower." Maiden paused. "Tak time for yersel tae experience thee wey they leeve an play ower thar."

✶

Bobby had supporters who helped pay for his trip; Keeler wasn't so lucky.

"Look, this one trip would cost a lot of money. Right now, our budgets are overdrawn. What you need is the equivalent of what two other departments need for half a year," Cohen tried to explain to Keeler. "Boat trips across the Atlantic aren't cheap these days."

"But you said . . . no, you promised," Keeler tried in his own way to convince his editor.

"I said, come with us and we'll get you the money you need to travel with this young golfer all over the country," Cohen remembered.

Keeler nodded regretfully. He knew what was coming.

"Well, this trip is out of the country," Cohen explained. "And normally, I would understand, and we could still get you what you need, but right now, money is just in short supply."

Hat in hand, Keeler walked sadly back to his desk. He had some spring baseball games to cover.

The American amateur team of Chick Evans, Francis Ouimet, Captain W.C. Fownes, Fred Wright, Jesse Guilford, Fred Hunter, Paul Hunter, and nineteen-year-old Bobby Jones sailed from New York on May 9th on the Caronia, the recently refurbished luxury steamship of the Cunard Lines.

One important player was missing. Robert Gardner, the only American amateur who had played in the previous year's British Open and almost won, could not afford to come.

Standing on the deck of the Caronia, looking over the side at the dock below, gave Bobby shivers. The ship was so high that it stood a few floors above the dock as it rested in the water. Bobby looked over the side of the ship and straight down, and his fear of heights hit him with a rush. He quickly stepped away from the edge. It was a very unsettling start to his trip.

It was the kind of trip that a person like Walter Hagen would have liked; it was a glamorous trip. But Bobby was not like Hagen. He valued friendship over glamour.

To pass the time, the American players hit balls off the back of the ship and practiced their swings to stay in shape. To Bobby, hitting balls into the ocean off the back of a ship seemed strange.

And the noise! The slight drone of the ship's engines disturbed Bobby's sensitivities, and the lovely beat that had been instilled in him in his youth was no longer there. It was being drowned out by the sound of the ship's engines.

The American/British amateur team match began on a course they were visiting for the first time, Hoylake, in Liverpool, England. Bobby seemed to be on his game as he won both his singles match and his foursomes match with Chick Evans as his partner.

But reality where Bobby Jones was concerned wasn't always seen with the eye. In truth, Bobby wasn't on his game. He was playing with sizeable luck. Something was eating away at his psyche, and he reacted to it by acting out on the course—and the British reporters took note.

This trip was the farthest Bobby had ever been away from home. He didn't have his favorite people—Big Bob, O.B. Keeler, or Perry and George Adair—to talk to. Bobby's life seemed to be full of strange voices, unusual food, and new golf experiences. Everything was old and while everyone else was lauding the old architecture, Bobby was set off by it. A numbed feeling began to come over him.

What Bobby Jones did, in the end, didn't matter to the American team effort. The Americans won by a surprisingly successful score of 9 to 3.

Ⅰ

The players stayed to play in the British Amateur, which the British were determined to win. That trophy wasn't leaving their shores again!

Bobby was picked "most likely to win" by odds of 5 to 1. Normally, that would not have meant much to Bobby. He was getting used to being favored in the States, but a lot of things were beginning to sink in. He was in Europe, alone. No one was along to help him with his swing if something went wrong with it.

Bobby also sensed how hard it would be to win a British Amateur, which had all its matches at 18 holes except for the 36-hole final.

The tournament was being held at Hoylake, and the first round went well for the visiting Americans. All eight players won their first matches. The British tabloids took this as further proof that the Americans were too strong for the Brits.

Then reality set in. During the second round, top American golfers Chick Evans, Francis Ouimet, and Jesse Guilford were beaten. Bobby was the lone, top-rated American amateur left in the field to protect the American adventure.

In his third round, Bobby barely got by a Brit who shot an 87. Bobby shot 85, and it was in this round that Bobby's anger came to the fore. He swore vehemently, kicked bushes and golf bags, and pounded his putter into the ground. Staid British spectators were shocked.

Bobby was 2-down at the 15th hole—but then he won when his opponent, E.A. Hamlet, collapsed from the strain of the three finishing holes.

Now the reporters were all over Bobby. Bobby felt like blowing his top. He was a marked man.

Fighting to hold himself together, Bobby lost conspicuously 6 and 5 to Allan Graham. The last American player had lost—and the Americans found themselves watching the remaining matches as spectators.

The Americans bemoaned their losses in British newspaper reports as being due to the bad conditions of the Hoylake links. They complained about the coarse British setup and conditioning of the links, and to top it all off, Bobby complained about the relentless danger of the 18-hole matches when one player could win by merely getting a hot round. In print he said, "I'll come back over when they play 36-hole matches."

Both Bobby and Chick Evans had to be talked into staying to play in the Open.

The Open that year was being played at St. Andrews. Hoylake was one very old and revered course; St. Andrews was another. Older golfers spoke of these two courses in hushed voices, showing the honor they deserved.

But the nineteen-year-old Bobby Jones wasn't caught up in nostalgia or homages. He just wanted to play golf and go home.

Bobby's introduction to the old course was painful. He plotted out the bunkers. They were very strange, strewn about the course instead of along the fairway or near the green as he was used to. They were deep, more like pits than bunkers. Their sides were vertical, like a wall, and sometimes golfers could get out only by hitting backwards; they couldn't advance their balls. The wind coming off the bay played havoc with Bobby's game, but the large double greens and the unusual bunkers really affected his mind. It was not a good first meeting. More and more, Bobby simply wanted this trip to be over.

The Scots let God be in charge of watering the greens at St. Andrews, and the greens wouldn't hold Bobby's shots—not even the good ones. Bobby's clubs seemed to have different traveling distances than he remembered.

Despite these challenges, Bobby qualified for the British Open. He shot a 78 in his first round, just five strokes behind the leader, Jock Hutchinson, a Scot from St. Andrews who had just moved to the States.

The second round found Bobby really trying his best as he created a 74, but he lost a little more ground to the leader.

On the final morning of the tournament, Bobby tried a little too hard. He topped his first tee shot of his third round and then struggled to a front nine score of 46 which he sensed put him out of the running for the tournament.

A very frustrated Bobby then double bogied the short 379-yard 10th hole and stood on the tee of the par-three 11th hole feeling like an alien. The wind waffled in his face as he wrapped his arms around his shoulders and pulled his sweater tighter. He looked out towards the sea and thought of his upcoming boat trip home.

Bobby took the mid-iron out of his bag and settled himself for his shot. But something wasn't right, and he sensed it. He backed away from the shot once, and then he backed away a second time.

The shot started out to the right of the flag, started turning left, and fell quickly and bounced and ran into Hill Bunker. Bobby almost threw his club, but in a tense moment, held himself back. He had heard enough comments about his temper.

As Bobby entered the deep-faced bunker, rage and torment came along with him. His niblick shot would have to be exact for him to finish anywhere near the hole.

It was not to be. As Bobby looked down at his feet, there lay his ball—after he had already hit it. His second shot would have to do it, but that didn't happen either. The bunker was winning.

Bobby gave out a long, low, very aggravated breath. He was facing his fourth shot to the green. He produced a shot that just cleared the edge of the green and barely rolled onto the putting surface. He now faced a thirty-five-foot putt with which he felt no connection.

He numbly recounted his strokes. He counted four strokes and realized again that now he probably had no chance in this tournament. He carefully lined up his long putt and completed his stroke. The ball glided past the hole and settled six feet beyond. Bobby rested the putter on his shoulder and sulked.

Bobby looked at the line of his putt again and again. Each time he thought he had a line, his mind went blank, and he had to start over. "What's the use?" ran through his mind and his heart.

Bobby leaned over and picked up his ball. He was out of the tournament, and he simply wanted to go home. He had never suffered such a letdown on a golf course.

After teeing off last on the 12th hole, Bobby looked over to his fellow competitor and acknowledged what the situation was. "I want my card. I'm withdrawing from the tournament."

He played his last round as a marker for his fellow competitor. He had scored a 72. This trip was over.

The Scottish and British press both teed off on Bobby. They called him a quitter. A few acknowledged his youth, but all of them said that he was going to have to learn to control his violent temper.

On the way home, Hagen tried, in his own way, to console Bobby. They were traveling on the same ship, the Aquitania.

"Pretty rough over there, hey kid," Hagen spoke to him as they wandered around the deck of the luxury liner.

Bobby shook his head. "I thought I was ready for it, but it was all so damned unnerving to me." Bobby looked out at the ocean.

"I almost did that my first trip over. I think I finished tied for 80th or something like that." Hagen shook his head. "When I do my autobiography, that first trip over isn't even going to make it into print," Hagen chuckled. "Not even a mention."

"Your autobiography?"

Walter smiled. "Evans did his last year. Don't know how much he made on it, but I got to figure that mine will be worth a lot more."

✗

Keeler was shocked when he found out what Bobby had done at the British Open. "Wish I could have been over there with you," Keeler said. He still wanted to be of help to the youngster.

"Me too," Bobby said sadly.

"Do you think you'll do better next time?"

Bobby shrugged.

"I read where their press pretty much hung you out to dry after what you did," Keeler said.

Bobby nodded. "I thought I was just withdrawing. I had no chance to tell anyone that. The tournament was over." Bobby shrugged again. "I guess I ended my participation the wrong way."

"But do you think you'll do better next time?"

"If I don't get overwhelmed with what is going on," Bobby thought. "No, I guess I'll have to do better. Too many people think of me as just a hothead who plays well." Bobby looked at Keeler, really focusing. "I'll have to do better if I ever go back. I'll have to do something to show them that I'm not a poor sport."

Bobby's demeanor struck Keeler. He sensed the boy would right the story. "Well, maybe the right opportunity will present itself."

CHAPTER
11

Was 1922 the right opportunity? The National Amateur and National Open championships held that year posed an advantage to Bobby. The National Open was being played at the Columbia Country Club in Chevy Chase, Maryland. That was directly on the train route to and from Atlanta. No stops, no layovers, no oceans. The National Amateur was being played at the St. Louis Country Club where Stewart Maiden now worked.

Bobby arrived in Chevy Chase, Maryland, for the National Open with his dad and O.B. Keeler five days before qualifying was to take place, on July 15th, and he stepped into a hailstorm of protest.

"They've got to be kidding themselves." Walter Hagen shook his head while he walked. The USGA had just decided to hold one 18-hole qualifying round. "Everyone knows that it takes more than eighteen holes to be able to tell who the better golfers are."

"Everyone doesn't include the white shirts who run our ruling body," Gene Sarazen added sarcastically.

"Why is it that ruling bodies wind up being run by people who don't seem capable of applying the rules?" Hagen stopped and rubbed his chin as if he were about to solve something very important.

Sarazen watched as Hagen stood mired in thought. He decided Hagen needed his help. "Because they have to show that they have the power to do something."

Hagen looked at Sarazen. "You know, you're right. Now why didn't I think of that?"

Sarazen thought of something caustic to retort, but he let Hagen's comment pass. He was beginning to figure out Hagen's facade and he didn't want to let his own hand show.

Golf was growing, and it seemed as though all the powerful people had discovered it. President Warren G. Harding and Vice President Calvin Coolidge were at the match. Military bands played while visiting Senators and Congressmen strolled among the golf fans.

Bobby didn't like 18-hole qualifiers at important events. To him, they were just as bad as the 18-hole matches in Britain. He managed to qualify by just one stroke, and his poor feeling about his qualifying score stayed with him as he teed off on the first hole of the tournament. His drive went left on the right- hand dogleg and into a heavily wooded area.

"I thought you had bought the farm with that opening drive," Keeler said to Bobby as they discussed the round later.

Bobby shook his head in exasperation. "It was that first shot out of the woods that made me think I was finished," Bobby added. Bobby's shot out of the woods had hit a long, low log and actually just missed Bobby as it ricocheted back over his head and behind him.

"To come back and get a six from where you were, well, it was a thing to behold," Keeler encouraged.

Bobby shook his head. "One more stroke on that hole and you and dad and I would be back on the train right now."

"But you came back. That's what separates you from the rest of the field, Bobby." Bobby shook his head as he watched Keeler pay the bill. Bobby always had someone around to show him a kindness.

Bobby's first round score of 78 was nine strokes higher than the leader, Jim Barnes, one of the tallest players of his day. Bobby's second round 71 cut four strokes into Barnes's lead.

But it was the third and fourth rounds that finished off Bobby's chances. Playing with Gene Sarazen the first time in a national event, they both shot 77's in their third and fourth rounds, which meant that they both lost nine more strokes to the eventual winner. Bobby came in tied for fifth and Sarazen came in alone in seventeenth place.

Walking off the 18th green after his final round, Bobby's face crimson, he signed his card, handed it in, and walked right past his father and Keeler.

"Hey!" Big Bob called to his son. "What's the big damn hurry?"

Bobby quickly stopped. "I damn well don't know what to do. Forty damn putts. Did you see them?" Bobby looked off and shook his head. "Until I can putt worth the effort, I'll never ever have a chance to win one of these damn events!"

"Tee to green, you have them all beat. Putting is the only thing that you have to do better," Big Bob tried to reason with Bobby.

"The only way the rest of them can keep up with you is with their putting," Keeler stepped in.

Bobby looked starkly at Keeler. "Don't you mean that it's my putting that allows them to keep up?"

Big Bob packed his things with a grumble. "I'm wondering if I should even come to another of these. I think you'd do better without me."

Bobby didn't even want to think of such a thing, and so he avoided the remark. Britain was still on his mind. "At least the next one won't take thirteen days of traveling," Bobby let out.

"I should hope not," Big Bob smiled at Bobby and put his arm around his shoulder. He wished with all his heart that he had gone to Europe with his son.

As they came out of the hotel and waited for a cab, Big Bob and Keeler went to check out while Bobby stood on the curb. He had his back to a pack of reporters.

"That Jones kid may be the best shot-maker out here, but he can't win because he doesn't have the heart." Bobby turned around slowly to see who made the remark. He saw that it was a reporter he had just spoken to a few days ago. He quietly turned back around unnoticed, but enlightened.

"Hagen gave me an insight into what he thinks of Bobby's chances." Bobby was back on the train in familiar company, with his father and O.B. Keeler.

"Oh?" Big Bob said, wondering what Hagen had to offer.

"He said he thought Bobby would win an Open before he won an Amateur and that he thought Bobby needed a bit of philosophy." No one had any idea what Hagen meant about philosophy. "Maybe he thinks the National Open is an easier event to win," Keeler suggested.

"Or that Bobby is a better medal player than he is a match player?" Big Bob questioned.

Bobby hadn't heard a word they said. His mind was still back on the reporter's comment at the hotel.

"Stewart's always approved of my putting stroke," Bobby said to Keeler. They were pulling into the Cleveland train station, on their way to the Oakwood Country Club to play the Western Open. It was a tournament Bobby and his father had squeezed in—in between the National Open and the National Amateur.

"Well, maybe you need to learn a better putting stroke from someone else," Keeler cautioned. He didn't know what Maiden could have been thinking. Bobby's putting continually let him down and frustrated him.

"Yeah, like that Hagen. He's damn terrific inside of twenty feet." Bobby shook his head. "They say Hagen may be the best and boldest putter who plays in the big-time tournaments." Bobby thought for a minute. "There are times when I know I am losing strokes because of my putting, but I'm doing what I know to do, die the ball at the cup."

"Well, it must be something else then," Keeler said and looked off.

The Western Open had a field full of leading professionals. Bobby easily qualified and was so pumped up he led the whole field. He played 36 holes on the first day with a score of 139.

"Great scoring. Now can you just relax?" Keeler said to Bobby as they met up with Big Bob after the second round.

"I don't see why not," Bobby grinned.

They went to their suite at their hotel. Bobby jumped into the tub. His dad brought him a small shot of corn whiskey.

"Me, too," Keeler walked over to Big Bob's bottle. "When did you start this?" Keeler nodded toward the whiskey.

"Oh, Dad introduced me to corn about two years ago. I've been drinking it at home. Dad suggested I might take some on the road with me to make me feel more at home."

"Well, maybe it'll help with your putting stroke," Big Bob jumped in on one of the favorite recent topics.

"I made everything I needed today."

Keeler nodded. "That you did, that you did."

"Except that four-footer on eight in your morning round." Big Bob quickly came back to the issue of putting.

Bobby took another sip and remembered the missed putt. "Wish I could have done that damn one over."

Keeler felt the storm coming before the others did. "My knee's acting up. Must be a front coming through. Maybe off the lake."

"Hope it's not like it was at Inverness," Big Bob remembered.

"Vardon's not here for it to bother," Keeler said, and they all chuckled. The Englishman had fared poorly under American rough weather, while the Brits bragged about their ability to play in inclement weather.

But this time it was Bobby who was fated to score higher.

The howling wind did something to him. His third-round score was a horrendous 83. Hagen jumped into the lead with a 73, and then took the crown with a final round of 71 to win by five strokes over Hutchinson and eight over a tired Bobby.

It was not an auspicious start to the year.

"Now I really want to see Stewart," Bobby bristled on the train ride to Cleveland and the National Amateur.

Big Bob's mood wasn't much better. "I think I'm just jinxing you."

Bobby looked over at his dad. "I never even thought of you out there, so I don't know how you could have done that."

"Well, on your third round, I could almost feel every bad shot before you hit it," Big Bob reasoned.

"Well, I felt every bad shot after I hit it. I still don't think that you had any effect on me."

"Just the same. I think I better start staying home while you go off to win one of these things. What do you say, O.B.?"

Keeler looked at both of them. "I'm still trying to understand what the mind and the heart has to do with the final score," Keeler let his thinking out.

"Oh, it has a hell of a lot to do with the game, a hell of a lot," Big Bob sighed. He sat back in one of his favorite positions, with his legs straight out and his upper trunk turned over into the corner of the seat.

"What do you want to see Stewart about?" Keeler asked Bobby.

"Everything." Bobby shook his head. "Damn everything." Then Bobby added as he got up and stretched. "Wish he could fix my legs." Bobby's legs were painful at times.

As soon as Bobby saw Maiden, he began to feel better. "Hou's hit gaun, laddie?" Maiden grinned economically, which was his custom.

Bobby hugged him. "Could be a lot better. I can't seem to get through a whole tournament without a bad round." Bobby shook his head. "Or when I play someone else, he seems to have his best day yet against me.

"Ye canna help thee seicont wan but ye can chynge thee first wan."

Maiden signaled two caddies to get ready for a round of golf. "A'll shaw ye all A knaw aboot this coorse," Maiden smiled at his pupil. "Hou are Perry an Alexa daein?"

"They're both doing fine. Alexa met a very nice guy from Ottawa."

"A am nae sarprised aboot tha. She' s quite ah leddy."

Maiden looked at Bobby's game hole after hole. He waited until they were finished before commenting. He wanted to see Bobby's whole game, including his last putt.

"A can see why awbody is picking ye oot tae win this wan," Maiden offered.

"But they pick on my putting all the time."

"Till ye dae whit thay think yer capable o, thay're goin tae pyke on something. Yer gemme thro thee green tis so guide, thay figure tha yer problem haes tae be yer puttin."

Bobby had yet to win at the top level, but more than a few sports journalists picked Bobby as one of their top choices to win the Amateur. Grantland Rice, known as the Dean of Sports Writers, picked Bobby as one of his top four choices.

Bobby felt the pressure, and he insisted that his putting was the problem. He still used the old Schenectady putter that Walter Travis had made famous. At times, though, he looked at the putters being used by some of the other players and wondered. Bobby could do no better than thirty-three putts in a round, while other players were consistently down around twenty-seven to twenty-nine putts.

In the National Amateur, despite Maiden's lessons, Bobby shot a 151 to qualify. This was seven strokes behind the medalist, Francis Ouimet.

Bobby won his first two matches with surprising ease, but it was the third round match that he was really looking forward to. His opponent would be Willie Hunter, the reigning British

Amateur Champion. If Bobby could win over Hunter, it would be a victory of note, and Bobby felt that it would make up for some of his poor scoring at Hoylake in his British Amateur debut.

To give more meaning to this round, which had such an international flavor, forecaddies were used. Forecaddies marked the spot of their player's ball with a flag. Spectators had been known to pick up a player's ball not knowing that it was in play. For this tournament, they used flags from a player's country. Bobby's was Old Glory; Hunter's was the Union Jack.

After the morning round, Bobby led Hunter 2-up—and it was a hard-fought lead. Bobby accomplished it mostly by out-driving Hunter. He could easily out-drive him, and he needed to because Hunter was so good with his approach shots and putting. The course was wet from early-week rain and their shots got little or no roll.

The afternoon round started off where the morning round finished, with a struggle. At the 8th tee, Bobby still stood 2-up. But the 8th hole at St. Louis was a great match play hole and it was here that Bobby, in the lead, might have made his biggest mistake.

The drive at the 8th hole was off a good-sized hill. It was possible, for a long driver, to go over the trees, cut the slight dogleg and possibly drive the green. During practice rounds with Maiden, Bobby had done this successfully. So, to take a commanding lead into the final ten holes, Bobby decided to do it again. He figured that a three-hole lead with ten holes to go would put him in a very commanding spot.

"Not sure I like this," Big Bob mouthed quietly to Keeler as they both watched what Bobby was obviously attempting with interest.

"I understand his thinking. I just hope to hell I like his results," Keeler offered back, watching Bobby take bead on the tip of the tree in line with the green.

"That's my boy, though, hell-bent for success," Big Bob

threw in. He had seen Bobby pull off shots like this countless times.

Bobby's effort looked great. But as all hopeful golfers know, looks can be deceiving. As the ball started its decline, it grazed the very top of the only tree that could cause a problem and it fell deeply into the ravine that lay below. Bobby now had a major problem on his hands. His ball had come straight down and it was buried in the grass on the side of an embankment.

His first effort at a recovery was futile. His second was not much better, and the loss of the hole started Hunter onto his third-round victory. Bobby had yet to learn that, sometimes, self-limitations produced remarkable results. That lesson would be fully learned down the road, but this occasion was the start.

As they played the 35th hole with Bobby now 2-down, the pressure was on. He had two holes to go and had to win this one.

As usual, Bobby out-drove Hunter, but Hunter put his second shot close to the flag, and Bobby couldn't match him. It was now going to rest entirely on Bobby's chip. It was not a hard chip, but with Hunter already near the flag, Bobby knew that his approach shot had been crucial. It had also been a mishap of another sort. Walking past his caddy, Bobby had disgustedly flipped his iron onto his bag. It was just a flip of the club. There might have been some feeling in it, but if there were, it wasn't much. Bobby already had his mind on his next shot—that very necessary chip shot.

But, a woman walking past Bobby's bag at the exact time Bobby flipped his club was struck slightly in the ankle by the grip end of the club. It didn't hurt her, and no one thought anything of it—at least, not then. Bobby checked on the woman, and she shrugged off the incident.

Bobby's chip was close, but Hunter two-putted and the third round was over. Bobby was out of that edition of the National Amateur. He had been closed-out on the 35th hole, 2-up and one to go.

"Congratulations. Damn fine match," Big Bob said to Hunter as soon as he could make it across the green after Bobby shook Hunter's hand.

"A well-fought victory," Keeler offered Hunter.

Keeler asked Bobby the question that was in his heart once they got near the clubhouse. "Was that tee shot on eight the right choice with you being 2-up?"

Bobby stopped. His dad listened. "I have to play every shot for all that I can. I want to win matches, not lose them." Bobby started again for the clubhouse. "That's the only way I know to play this game."

As they walked, Keeler had more to say. "I'm just wondering, though, if the right shot is the one to play at times." Keeler was now kind of stumping along with his left knee bothering him again. "That tee shot on eight keeps wanting to tell me something, and I think we ought to talk about it."

Keeler was learning more and more about tournament golf and his participation as a fan gave him a different vantage point than Bobby had. Bobby ignored him, but Keeler had been working on something to say to the young man, and he felt now was the time. "Bobby, you will win championships just as soon as you come to believe that when you step out on the first tee with any golfer in the world, you are better than he is."

Keeler's words rang in Bobby's ears.

As the train pulled its way back to Atlanta, Keeler advanced one of his pet theories about Bobby's golf game. "That tee shot on eight continues to bother me. I keep on thinking that with the two-hole lead you had, maybe you should have played it down the middle and made Hunter be the one that was forced into taking the all-or-nothing shot."

"If I had made it," Bobby shot back, "your thoughts would be how I had made the shot that ended the tournament right then and there."

"But maybe, the right choice was to put the pressure on him by having your ball in play and not down in some ravine. Think how you would have thought had you been in his shoes," Keeler pushed.

Bobby got up and walked around some. The slight jostle of the train's movements beckoned him. "I'll be back," he threw over his shoulder, and he walked slowly down the aisle deep in thought.

When he returned to his seat, Bobby had a smile on his face. "Tell you what. Next time I am in that spot again, I'll try it your way. I'll get the lead, and if any interesting shot challenges come along, I'll put the onus on my opponent to have to force the match rather than taking the action to do it myself."

Keeler smiled. He felt that he had come up with something to help Bobby's game and that he was now a contributor to it.

"Are you going to put that in one of your columns?" Bobby asked sitting back down.

Keeler smiled. "Not if you give me something more interesting to talk about."

Bobby rarely ever read Keeler's columns. He had much more interesting things to do than to read what was written about him. He got busy with the life he preferred, going back to the Georgia Institute of Technology and playing golf with his dad and their friends.

"You got a letter from the United States Golf Association." Big Bob brought it to the clubhouse one Saturday while Bobby and Perry were playing golf.

Bobby simply nodded. He thought that it probably had to do with a tournament, so he stuffed it into his pocket. He opened it when he got home for dinner.

Mr. Robert Tyre Jones, Junior
East Lake, Georgia

Dear Bobby,

Recently it has come to our attention that, during play at the St. Louis Country Club, a lady in the gallery was hurt because of an action on your part. We understand that it happened during play on the 17th hole of the second round of your match with Mr. Willie Hunter.

Although this lady wasn't hurt enough to make a claim either against us or against you, we feel happenings like this cannot be allowed to go on at a United States Golf Association event.

Incidents like this, if allowed to continue, would have a negative effect on the progress we are making in present-ing our game as a healthy family affair that is free of bad behavior or untoward activities.

I can tell you that unless you learn to control your temper, and never again exhibit behavior such as this, you will never again be allowed to play in a USGA sponsored event.

Sincerely,
George Walker
President
United States Golf Association
New York, New York, USA

Bobby sat down in a chair and read the letter again and again. He was shocked.

"Dad," Bobby approached his father. "Look what I got in the mail." Bobby handed the letter to his father.

Big Bob read the letter slowly and then glanced at Bobby and read it slowly again. "How do you feel about this?"

Bobby let a breath out and walked around with his hands in his pockets. "I saw what happened. The lady didn't make a sound and I don't think my club hit her so much as grazed her.

She never even seemed to wince. It might have surprised her, but didn't seem to hurt her."

Bobby paused and looked at his dad. Because his dad was deep in thought and didn't say anything, Bobby thought his dad might have wanted more. "This whole year has been what Stewart would call a real learning experience for me. I'm glad it is over."

Big Bob remembered the situation himself. He knew the lady wasn't hurt, and for that he was grateful.

"What do you want to do about this letter?" Big Bob paused. "You cannot let something like this go without a response."

Bobby nodded, "I know that, Dad." Bobby shook his head again. "I've been trying for almost four years now to control my temper. Ever since I played in the Red Cross matches with Alexa."

Big Bob handed the letter back to Bobby. "You write up what you want to say and I'll look it over and have my office do the letter for you. We'll make it look nice."

The next day, Bobby got to work on his response. He apologized to Mr. Walker and also offered to apologize to the lady, if that was necessary. He told Walker of his attempts to control his temper and promised to do better. He vowed that Walker, nor anyone else with the USGA, would have to call him on his behavior or any other action.

Bobby then talked with Perry, Perry's father, O.B. Keeler, and anyone else would who listen about ways to control his temper. Everyone had a suggestion.

Eventually, Bobby would learn to control his temper in the bigger tournaments by giving himself permission to enjoy the freedom to do what he wished in private play. There were times during the course of private play when he would hit a shot that he felt so poorly about that he just didn't feel comfortable standing there with the club still in his hands. But never again in public play would anyone ever see poor behavior on Bobby's part. And never again would the USGA have to remark about Bobby's actions other than the results of his play.

CHAPTER 12

"Bobby, my dad died." The call came just after Bobby signed out for the Thanksgiving holidays from Georgia Tech. It was Perry.

"When, how?" finally came out of Bobby's mouth.

"They say it was a heart attack," Perry said in a voice that had no tone to it.

"I'll be over," Bobby said. George Adair had been in Bobby's life ever since he could remember. Bobby felt as if he had lost a member of his own family. This couldn't be happening.

But as Bobby arrived at the Adair house, the black crepe bow hanging on the front door gave the truth away. There was a death in this house.

"How fast did he die?" Bobby asked his friend. He glanced up the stairs as a man in a black suit descended. It was the doctor.

"It was right away." Perry mumbled.

Bobby broke down when he gave Keeler the news.

"I'm going to do a column about him as a special tribute for what he did for Atlanta and golf," Keeler told Bobby. "What can you tell me about him?" He knew losing George Adair was not going to be easy on Bobby. Adair had done a lot more for Bobby's game than anyone knew.

Keeler's column was in the Atlanta Journal the next day.

Atlanta Golf Has Lost a Very Special Friend

George Adair, the man who was responsible for the first golf course in Atlanta, and who educated a special class of people on how to play the game, died at his home a few days ago.

The flags at East Lake and Druid Hills and a few other special golf courses were all lowered to half staff in tribute to Mr. Adair, who will always be remembered whenever an Atlanta golfer picks up a club or puts on his golf shoes, for it was Mr. George Adair who did the most to introduce Atlanta to this wonderful old Scottish game.

Bobby Jones was asked what Mr. Adair meant to him and he replied. "Mr. Adair was very important to my formative years in the game. Without having what he did for me when I was growing into the sport, I don't know where I'd be today."

Bobby's youth was now officially over. It wasn't just Adair's death that did it, though that had a huge impact on how Bobby felt. He took stock of his life. He was nineteen years old. He had a gift for golf, that was certain, but he had played in nine national tournaments without a win. He began to wonder if he should compete in national tournaments.

Big Bob had no doubts about Bobby's prospects in golf. He knew tournament successes would follow, and O.B. Keeler was squarely in Bobby's camp too. Keeler wanted Bobby to continue in the big tournaments—and win. He was making friends all over the world by traveling with Bobby and he was becoming a big name in Atlanta due to his inside coverage of the Bobby Jones story.

But Bobby was not happy on the road. He loved the South, and he never wanted to leave it. He missed his little village of East Lake, his parents, his new girlfriend, Mary Malone, and, of course, his weekend golf buddies.

The problem with his leg veins looked as though it would settle the question for him once and for all.

"How's it going?" Keeler was visiting Bobby in a hospital, of all places.

"Pretty good, now that it's all over. Thank God they put

you to sleep and you don't have to bite a bullet like you used to have to do."

"Four operations! Do you have any veins left in that leg?"

Bobby laughed. "I hope so. They tell me the veins left behind will make up for the bad ones they took out."

Keeler nodded. "I came over to see you because I'm working on a column about golf and wondered if I could get some insights from you."

Bobby nodded. "From this position?" Bobby joked, talking about his in-bed pose, then added, "Like what?"

"The Southern Amateur is coming up, and as you know, it will be played at East Lake." Keeler looked off, forming his thoughts. "I was wondering if you thought you were going to be able to play in it."

It was Bobby's turn to think. "I'm not sure that I'll be in shape in time. Plus, I'm finishing up at Tech and thinking of going up North and taking a literature course at Harvard." Bobby looked off. "I'm not sure I want to play in too many more regional tournaments."

It was time for Keeler to make his move. "Did you hear that the committee running the Southern Amateur has renamed their trophy to honor George Adair?"

Bobby looked at him; his face showing his surprise. "Really? So they're calling it the George Adair Trophy?"

"The George W. Adair Trophy." Keeler smiled. He knew that he had motivated Bobby, and now, he waited while Bobby's mind did the rest.

"Well, the George W. Adair Trophy. How about that?" Bobby thought. "And appropriately played first at East Lake where he put the deal together to found the course." Bobby smiled and nodded. "You know it would really be an honor to have your name on that trophy. It really would."

A few days later, another visitor brought Bobby another indication of what he should do.

"Ow's thee leg comin, laddie?"

"Stewart! How the hell are you?" Bobby grinned and quickly sat up.

"Great nou tha A'm comin back tae East Lake."

"You're coming back? When?"

Maiden smiled. "Richt efter A walk oot o here, a walk ower thare."

Bobby took a big breath. "Welcome back, Stewart. We missed you."

"Whaur's yer gowfin freend?"

"Perry was here a little while ago. Since his dad died, he had to drop out of school to learn the family business. But he's still a member out at the course."

"Guide, guide. A hear A better git thee coorse in shape for thee Southern Amateur." Then Maiden smiled gently at Bobby. "Ye gaun play in it?"

Bobby thought. "I'm gonna try."

"You have to go slowly, Mr. Jones," Bobby's doctors said when he checked out of the hospital early. "You cannot force your body to get well. It has to heal slowly, on its own. Do not force your body to do things that it is not ready for or you will be right back in the hospital for a longer stay." Medicine had no antibiotics in 1922 and any operation could easily head in the wrong direction with just one wrong step or an allergic reaction to something. Bobby's medical chart showed lots of allergies from his youth, including listings to a number of normal food items. His doctors and his family were alarmed.

But Bobby's body was ready. Despite only four hours of real practice and one nine-hole practice round, Bobby qualified for the Southern Amateur in a tie with two other players for medalist—one of them being Perry, who also wanted his name on the trophy named for his father.

Bobby played like he had never played before.

"Wonder if it's because you had your leg fixed?" Keeler grinned.

Keeler wrote the story of Bobby's victory, and many local people began to believe that this was Bobby's year.

East Lake had its first 2000-visitor day when two of Bobby's professional friends, Jim Barnes and Jock Hutchinson, came to play a best-ball competition. A lot of the top pros wanted to know what kind of special course had produced a wunderkind like Bobby Jones. They also wanted to meet Bobby's teacher, Stewart Maiden, who had taught Alexa Stirling, known for her fine golf in the top women's tournaments.

The pros faced a blistering round from Bobby. Perry partnered with Bobby, but he wasn't much of a factor. The team of Jones and Adair won 3-up and one to go. Keeler wrote the story of a warm and humid Altanta day that had terrific golf in it.

Next up for Bobby was the National Open to be played at Skokie Country Club in Glencoe, Illinois. This time, Bobby wanted his teacher with him.

"Can you come with me to the Open?" Bobby asked Maiden as they played a long-overdue round together.

"Dae nae see why nae," Maiden said in his normal abbreviated response.

This National Open was different. The USGA had decided to start charging patrons $1 per round or $5 per week to gain entrance to the tournament. Despite the change, the USGA had very few complaints.

On their train ride to Skokie, the main topic was Bobby's putting—still his sore spot.

"Juist dee thee bawl at thee hole," Maiden preached. "Gif it goes in, great. Gif nae, yer neist putt shoud be ah shuir thing," he reasoned. "The main pynt tis ye hav tae avite ony three putts acause tha's whit loses ye strokes tae thee field."

Bobby qualified with scores of 72 and 76 and played his first rounds with Walter Hagen who had just returned from winning his first Open in Britain. As was the current custom, 36 holes would be played Friday and Saturday.

Hagen led all through the morning and closed the first round with a 68. After a light lunch, overseen by Keeler, Bobby came alive and almost caught Hagen in the second round.

After the first two rounds, it was John Black, a transplanted Scotsman, who led the tournament with 142, just two over par. Hagen was at 145 and tied for third place with Gene Sarazen. Bobby stood alone in fifth place at 146.

Keeler and Bobby discussed Bobby's rounds in their shared room that night. "Stewart must have done you some good. I have you down for thirty-two putts in the first round and only twenty-eight in the second."

Bobby nodded. "And I left four putts in both rounds on the edge of the cup. If they had fallen, I'd be tied for the lead right now."

"Well, how do you like your position—4 behind?"

"We'll see if I can take advantage of it."

Keeler didn't tell Bobby this, but he had spoken to other sports writers who were picking Bobby to finally break through and win. He also didn't tell Bobby that he was now helping a lot of the sports writers write their stories about Bobby, so Bobby would be free after his round and not have to answer so many questions.

"Let's have a little one," Bobby said to Keeler as Bobby slid into the bathtub.

Keeler got the bottle of corn whiskey and poured the first of what he knew would be half of what Bobby wanted.

"It's good to see your putting coming around."

Bobby took a drink and exhaled loudly. "It's about damn time." Then Bobby grinned at Keeler.

The next morning, Bobby had his first par round of 70 and pulled into a tie for the lead with Bill Melhorn, who was known as Wild Bill Melhorn for his sometimes extravagantly inconsistent shots. Sarazen was four strokes back with one more round to go that afternoon.

As Bobby was starting lunch, Sarazen was teeing off.

"Going great," Keeler rewarded Bobby. "Just eat a light lunch so you won't have to take three or four holes to get going."

Bobby smiled at Keeler. "This is my best opportunity so far. If I can get a 68, I might just win this thing."

Keeler nodded. "Just play within yourself and hit all-out, hell-for-leather shots."

Bobby was champing to get going on his last round.

After nine holes where he had shot a 36, Bobby thought he was in the lead. Keeler brought him the truth.

"Sarazen just finished with a 68."

Bobby was now facing a formidable task. The score he had to either match or beat was posted and secure—for someone else. He was going to have to post a par round of 36 on the final nine holes to tie Sarazen.

With the pressure on, Bobby lost a stroke on the 10th. Then, trying to get that stroke back, he lost another on the 12th. A thirty-five foot putt for birdie fell as he regrouped.

"Mair o thae, Robin," Maiden encouraged.

Then at both the 15th and 16th holes, something happened which made Bobby wonder for years about the role of fate.

At the 15th, Bobby had a putt of fifteen feet for a birdie, which would go a long way toward making up his deficit. Bobby carefully lined up the putt and stroked the ball only to watch the ball come to a rigid halt right on the front lip.

On the par-four 16th, after two great shots, a putt of five feet rolled directly at the cup, only to also pause on the front lip.

He remembered forever those two putts that just would not fall.

Bobby played consistently for that stroke he needed in his mind. He approached the 17th, which was a long par-four before the finishing par-five 18th. Here Bobby hoped he could par and then birdie the 18th for a tying position.

But Bobby's drive on the long 17th took a wicked bounce left and wound up under a tree. Bobby punched the ball out and to the front of the green, but he couldn't convert the up and down for par. Now, his only hope was to eagle the 18th hole.

Bobby's drive on eighteen was a long booming drive right up the middle which left him in a good spot to go all out for the green. He had reached the green during practice rounds.

His approach, however, was a little too strong and the ball went over the back edge of the green. After Bobby missed his chip, his tournament was over. He sunk the birdie putt but finished up in a second place tie with Black.

"Great effort," Keeler offered as he followed Bobby to the scorer's tent.

Bobby barely acknowledged the remark. He was so worn out.

"Ye duin guide, laddie," Maiden added. Maiden's own best finish in the 1908 Open was a tie for forty-second place. He reached up and patted Bobby on the back and walked along with him to the hotel.

Keeler got Bobby a drink of corn whiskey while Bobby headed for the tub.

"Do you mind if I ask you a few questions about your play today? Ten other sports writers are outside waiting for a story to make their deadlines."

Bobby smiled. "I'll be okay in a minute or two. Just get me another drink."

Keeler got Bobby another drink and sat on the toilet waiting for Bobby to recoup his strength.

"Shoot," Bobby smiled. Then he looked at Keeler. "I like doing it this way rather than having a whole bunch of reporters all asking different questions. Do you think we could do this more in the future?"

Keeler nodded. He was making a list of questions to go with the questions that he had gotten from the reporters outside who wanted their own stories.

"What was the hardest thing out there for you today?"

Bobby thought. "I guess knowing that Sarazen had his score and I was either going to have to match it or beat it," Bobby smiled, his head resting on the back of the bathtub. "His score was in the books, and he worked hard to get it, believe me. Sarazen deserved his victory."

"Well, on nine when you heard about his score, what were your first thoughts?

Bobby kept his head back. "At first, I thought I could beat it. All I needed was another 36 on the back nine. But as I played and my putter didn't handle the pressure I was putting on it, I started to realize just how good his score was. On the 17th, I guess it was, I figured out that this was going to be Sarazen's day."

Bobby sat and relaxed while Keeler fed him question after question until they were all done. Then Keeler went down to the bar where the other sports journalists were waiting. The one question that Keeler neglected to ask was the one that the other reporters were most interested in. What was Bobby's condition?

When Keeler returned to the room, Bobby was already in bed and almost asleep. "Did you phone my parents and tell them that I was okay?"

Keeler smiled. "Sure I did. And your dad passed his congratulations on to you."

The next day, on the train ride back home, Keeler let Bobby know what he had heard from a member of the USGA. "He said you had more people following you than both Hagen and Sarazen combined."

Bobby nodded. "Wish that would win me one of these tournaments."

Keeler remembered something he wanted to ask Bobby. "I saw you ask your caddy to walk alongside you a few times out there. What was that about?"

Bobby looked at him. "To help me keep some people away,

so I could think and not have to answer so many damn crazy questions."

"Why haven't you asked me to do that?" Keeler looked at Bobby.

"Because you have that game leg. If I thought you could keep up with me, I'd have you walking beside me all the time."

"Well, I could keep up with you unless you break into a trot."

Bobby laughed again. "If just now and then you could make it so I feel protected from the fans, I would appreciate it."

Keeler nodded. "I thought it was just the reporters who were bothering you."

"Well, I hate to complain. I love the fact that the fans love golf as I do and will follow me all over the place day after day. But some of them just have to ask me questions, I think, to hear me talk. And I need to keep my mind on the game and not have people chuckling at my accent."

♉

Bobby graduated from the Georgia Institute of Technology as a mechanical engineer, which he had already decided he would not become. He applied to Harvard to take his B.S. degree in literature. In doing so, he had no idea that he was partially fulfilling Hagen's prediction about what he needed to do to able to win a National Open.

He was going to have to take time off from school again to play in the Walker Cup matches and then in the National Amateur in Brookline, Massachusetts. In the meantime, he was doing his best to improve his Latin and French. For English literature, he was already reading Shakespeare.

The Walker Cup matches were held at the National Links on Long Island, designed by Charles Blair McDonald. There was a lot of media coverage.

Surprisingly for Bobby, who had his head in the books for

almost three straight weeks, his game was very good.

First Bobby faced and beat one of England's top amateur players, Roger Wethered, 3-2. Then, teamed with Jess Sweetser, he won in foursomes play by the same amount. The Americans took the cup.

Right after the Walker Cup, the amateurs all traveled together to Brookline for the National Amateur.

National rankings came out and Bobby was listed as the number two amateur in the country. Chick Evans, of Chicago, was ranked number three. Jess Sweetser was number eight. Jesse Guilford, the Amateur Champion of the year before, was ranked number one.

The first day of qualifying dawned crisp and clear. Scores ran below what had been expected, but the second day, the skies poured forth a deluge and the rain continued straight through the round.

Bobby shot 73, 72 and was runner-up to Guilford who scored 74, 70.

"Great round under the circumstances," Keeler said to Bobby as they met at the clubhouse where Keeler stayed to keep dry.

"Yes it was. I'm happy to have qualified."

"Stewart sends his best wishes and your parents said to give you their love."

Bobby smiled.

"So, how's the game?"

"So far, so good. I'm not showing signs yet of the rust I know is under there."

"You looked good out there."

Bobby nodded. "All wet and sloshy."

Keeler laughed. "I was thinking I should have brought a boat with me."

Bobby closed out his first match against an unknown by the score of 3-up and one to go. He met Robert Gardner again and won 3 and 2 in another rainstorm. Then he beat Leo McPhail 4 and 3.

The last match had him playing against Jess Sweetser, his partner from the Walker Cup.

Both players bogied the first hole with matching fives; Sweetser then sunk his spade-mashie from a distance of about 90 yards, uphill on the par-four 2nd hole. The roar that went up from the large gallery stunned Bobby.

Bobby almost matched him by leaving his mashie shot of 80 yards a foot from the hole. In a way, that small 2nd hole was the story of the match.

Sweetser shot a 34 on the front nine while Bobby struggled to a 40. He was 6-down. But Bobby wasn't through yet. He came onto his game and played the second nine in 34 strokes, although his play was only good enough to gain back one hole. They went into lunch with Bobby 5-down. Sweetser had set a new course record at Brookline of 69.

"Sorry," Keeler greeted Bobby.

"Oh, I deserve what I got. You can't shoot a big score against a top-rated player and expect to get away with it."

"You can come back."

"Only if he lets me and, if I were him, I wouldn't do that." Bobby paused. "It seems at times that my opponents come on their games just as I get to play them."

It was as if Bobby could see into the future. Sweetser could do no worse than par that second round and Bobby lost 8-up and seven to play. It would be Bobby's worse drubbing in his National Amateur play history.

"Thanks for the education, Jess," Bobby said in a sportsman-like way as they started back towards the clubhouse.

"Is that what my best golf ever in an amateur was, an education?" Sweetser teased.

"And a great and thorough one at that."

They paused. "You know Bobby Jones, I had to play my best golf today and I knew it. I was up against the best player in the whole tournament."

Bobby looked at Sweetser. "Thanks, Jess."

Keeler had overheard the conversation, limping alongside the young men. "Quite a compliment."

Bobby slowed to be with his friend.

"I guess I'll be seeing you at Thanksgiving," Keeler said, thinking Bobby was going back to school.

"Think I need a trip back home," Bobby threw out. "I just want to touch base with everyone."

"How about if I get some copy from you on the way back?"

Bobby laughed. "Don't know why you even ask that. You'd get it out of whatever we'd talk about anyway."

It was Keeler's turn to laugh.

Unbeknownst to Keeler, and almost anyone else, was the fact that Bobby was going back to Atlanta to visit with the Malone family. Bobby was falling in love.

While at home, Bobby gave Keeler enough copy to carry him almost to spring. Bobby shot a 63 at East Lake and Keeler trumpeted the news for weeks. One of Keeler's columns even went over the new course record stroke by stroke. From what Keeler said in his column, you would have thought that Bobby's round was the best round in the whole history of the game of golf.

Ironically, Bobby was upset by the great round and expressed his feelings when Keeler interviewed him.

"The place I should have shot that damn round was either Skokie or Brookline," Bobby shook his head disgustedly. "Damn."

"But you did have a great round," Keeler countered.

Bobby nodded. "I just hope that next year I'll have one in front of an audience."

Bobby couldn't play golf for the Harvard team because all of his undergraduate credits had been used up at the Georgia Institute of Technology. But Bobby wanted to be part of the

Harvard scene, and he had it in his heart to get one of the big, red Harvard H's. So Bobby did the next best thing. He served as an assistant team manager, and with that, Bobby got himself the school letter he coveted.

The Harvard golf team got something very special from Bobby, too.

"How about a match, you against the team?" the golf coach asked Bobby one day.

The game was on. Bobby against all six members of the Harvard golf team, match play, 18 holes.

For a while, it was a good game. Bobby was only 1-up after four holes, but then they came into a tough stretch of holes and Bobby stepped up his game while the team had to count on someone getting lucky. Their luck ran out on the 14th hole, as Bobby won 5 and 4.

Bobby went on to set a new record at the course and also played a few exhibitions to help raise money for some special causes.

But Bobby missed East Lake, and he was grateful for the break.

"Are ye ony smarter, laddie?" Maiden asked, working away in his shop as Bobby walked in.

"Now, that's a relative thought that can be answered in diverse ways." Bobby smiled.

Maiden stopped and looked strangely at him. "Tha gaed richt ower ma heid. A howp tha ye don hae ta talk tha wey aw thee time nou."

"Me, too," Bobby laughed.

Of those who missed Bobby the most, Mary Malone was at the top of the list. She and Bobby had been writing letters back and forth, and it was obvious to those around that they were heading in a very serious direction.

Bobby's days at East Lake were spent getting ready for the National Open, which was going to be played at Inwood Country Club, at Inwood, New York.

"Yer goin tae hiv tae relax mair ower yer puttin, laddie,"

Maiden coached. "Tha weel allou yer intueetion tae play ah bigger pairt in yer distance straik."

"I'm trying. I just wish that we were playing on greens as fast as the ones at the Open are going to be."

"But awl ye hiv tae do tis tak thee faster green speed intae consideration whan ye putt up thare," Maiden reasoned.

"Maybe you can do that, but it took me days to get used to the greens at Merion and Oakmont and Skokie and Brookline."

"Weel, hou aboot gif we gae ah bit early an allou ye thee time ye need tae mak thee ajusmens."

Bobby's eyes grew wide. "That's a great idea! I hope that they'll let me on the course early."

Stewart laughed. "Personally ah howp tha thay don't."

Bobby looked at Maiden. "Now, why's that?"

Maiden laughed. "Cause in goin early ah wis hopin tae stop aff in Nassau an see ma guid-brither, Jimmy. His coorse is juist a wee bit doun thee road frae Inwood."

"And Jimmy has bent greens at his course?"

"We'll git him tae cut thee greens doun juist lak ye'll hiv tae play at Inwood."

"Are you Bobby Jones?" Bobby suddenly looked up to see two men standing before him.

"An wha tis daein thee inquirin?" Maiden stepped up as all those around Bobby were learning to do.

"Me and him," the man said, pointing to his companion.

Maiden looked at the man. "Are ye awaur tha yer are trespassing on private property?"

The men looked at each other and back at Maiden. "We just wanted to meet the golfer that Keeler has been writing about in his columns."

"Than A suggest ye write tae Maister Keeler. But richt nou, ye better git aff this property or based on ma authority, A'll be duty boound tae caw thee polis an hiv ye areestit."

Bobby and Maiden watched as the men quickly headed off the property.

"That's thee thrid time this month tha A've hae fowk come ontae thee coorse lookin for som big gowfer person."

Bobby laughed.

"We need tae git thee coorse tae pit up a fence. Ah lot o fowk juist leuk at ah coorse lak this as parkland, e'en wi thee flags an bunkers vera apparent." Maiden shook his head. "It's juist tha thee gemme is sae new ower here."

Before leaving for the Open, Bobby accompanied Mary Malone on a trip back to Augusta to be introduced to a few of her relatives. Mary's family roots were in Augusta.

After a day and a half visiting, Bobby asked, "Do you mind if I take a few minutes out and go over to Augusta Country Club. I just want to be around Mother Nature for a bit."

Mary nodded. "Take your time."

Bobby arrived at Augusta Country Club and went in to see the club professional. But as Bobby went into the men's room, he was surprised to see who was walking out.

"Mr. Travis!"

Walter Travis quickly looked up. "Hello, Bobby Jones."

"Good to see you, Mr. Travis. I didn't know that you came down South."

"Sure I do, Bobby. I'm on my way back from Florida where I'm working on a few new course designs." Travis smiled at the young man. "So, I hear that you're close to winning now and again."

Bobby sighed dramatically. "I've been close a couple of times, but as you know, there's a big difference between winning and not doing so."

Travis nodded. "I think I remember some of that." He smiled. "What about your putting. Did you ever decide to do anything different with it?"

Bobby shook his head. "Nobody seems to see the need for me to do anything different—other than you."

Travis looked off. "Well, you're an excellent through-the-green player, maybe even the best, but from my experience, your putting should be helped."

Bobby got brave. "Do you have time now? Is there some place you have to be?"

Travis smiled. "As a matter of fact, I have no place I'd rather be than here, and yes, I have the time to tell you what I know."

Travis went to the pro shop and got a few balls and a putter. He decided to hold the lesson in the men's locker room to avoid accumulating a crowd wanting to watch Travis teach Bobby Jones, a huge hero to the state of Georgia.

"Take your normal stance."

Bobby did as instructed and took a stance aiming at an ash-tray they put down at the end of the carpet.

"Now, as you start back, which hands are doing what?"

Bobby explained how both of his hands worked together.

"What about how you bring the putter to a stop and start the forward swing?" Travis continued gathering information.

"I guess I just do that naturally because I don't pay any attention to stopping the backswing."

Travis noted that.

"And, of course, your grip."

Bobby held the putter up so Travis could see the under part of his hands on the putter.

"And your stance," Travis noted again, as if taking inventory. "Why so wide?"

Bobby hunched his shoulders. "Just the way I've always done it." Bobby looked at Travis. "I sometimes have some great rounds with only twenty-eight putts or so. And I've also had some rounds where I've dropped some long important putts. But, I have yet to notice what I'm doing differently."

Travis looked at Bobby and invited him to sit down. "You should never have more than thirty putts in a round, ever." Travis watched as Bobby followed his every word.

"I know that some of what I'm going to show you will not seem to be right, but as you probably know, changes in golf take time. You learn something one day and it may take a week or two before that lesson starts to pay off. Putting is like that, too."

Then Travis smiled. "I learned golf at an advanced age. I was a little over thirty. But I fell in love with the game, and knowing that I was a late starter, I had to do some quick learning." Travis stroked his beard. "To make the quickest advances, I figured that putting was where I could make the quickest progress."

He continued. "I spent weeks and weeks on putting greens whenever I could. I practiced and practiced and measured anything and everything for results." Travis looked at Bobby. "I did feel like I was sleeping with my putter." Travis paused very perceptively. Bobby grinned, remembering a couple nights he slept with one or another club.

"What I'm showing you has proven itself over twenty years of tournament play," Travis went on. "The putting stroke should be called a rap, because that is what works best. People think stroke and they get too casual. They need to learn to give the ball a tiny rap on the back that will help it hold its line better. So, I'm recommending that you shorten your back stroke and come into the ball with a brisk knock or, as I said, rap."

Bobby listened intently.

"I also recommend that you use what I call a reverse Vardon grip on your putter." Travis took the putter out of Bobby's hands and showed Bobby his grip; the index finger of his left hand over his little finger on his right hand.

Bobby took the putter back and tried the reverse Vardon grip with the putter.

"That's it," Travis said when Bobby held the putter up where Travis could see his new putter finger grip.

"It felt funny," Bobby said as he sat back down.

"Now, about how you take your putter back," Travis looked at Bobby, "this is what I call the hard part."

Bobby waited.

"The putter is taken back with the left hand." Travis took a breath. "Being right-handed, your right hand has to be your master hand, and you won't understand completely until you try it for a while. You take the putter back with your left hand and somewhere close to when you start back, your right hand takes over and you give the ball a nice firm rap."

"Enough to make the ball die at the cup." Bobby added what he had been taught.

"Or enough to get the ball just past the cup. Whatever your desire is." Travis was very serious. "But your right hand is your master hand. The one that you pull the trigger with. The one that you do very important things with, like leading your putter."

Travis started to stand up. "Want to try it all together?"

Bobby smiled. He stood up and took a narrow stance and worked to get the correct grip and, using the few balls they had, rapped the balls toward the ashtray. The first ball went past the ashtray but the second went just to the left of its target.

Travis had one more thing to say. "Narrow that stance!" he almost barked. "A narrow stance helps you make your internal sensitivities work better."

Bobby narrowed his stance. His next putt came to a halt just as it touched the front of the ashtray.

"That's it, Bobby Jones."

Bobby retrieved the balls and tried again.

"Time will make you the master of the technique. But having mastered it, you will improve your putting and it may even help the rest of your game, if that is possible." Travis grinned.

"My thanks, Mr. Travis." Bobby smiled and they shook hands goodbye.

"Good luck to you, Bobby. You have a fine game."

Bobby and Maiden worked on getting Bobby used to his new putting technique. Maiden even tried it, but it was Bobby who came up with something else that helped his game—and it came from Travis's technique.

"You know, now that I'm more conscious of taking the putter back with my left hand, I seem to be able to take the other clubs back farther, too. It's as if I have better extension, now."

"A don want ye messin wi yer irons or yer lang clubs," Maiden responded. "We hiv tae get ye ready for this season whilk is comin real fast."

Bobby and Maiden arrived in Nassau, New York. They stayed with Jimmy Maiden in his house there. For the first time, Bobby played with both Maiden brothers. They challenged him to beat their best ball. What Stewart and Jimmy really wanted was to put pressure on Bobby's game to see how he performed.

Surprisingly, it was Bobby's putting that seemed to cause him to loose the match between the three of them.

"See, it's the damn greens," Bobby said walking off the course and not very happy with himself. "I hope I learn to cope with the speed of these things."

Jimmy Maiden looked at Bobby. "A mallet lak thee Schnectady yer usin is great on thee slaw greens ye hiv doun sooth, but up here ye micht want tae switch tae something lichter."

"Like what?"

"Let's see wha A hiv." Jimmy Maiden walked over to his shop. He came back with a light putter. "This wis brocht back tae me by a couple tha juist returned frae thee Adirondacks." Jimmy watched as Bobby took it from his hands.

"Calamity Jane," Bobby grinned as he saw the name on the bottom back of the club. "Is that why they got rid of it?" The name of the club had been punched into the bottom of the back edge of the club along with the club maker's name, Condie.

Jimmy Maiden laughed.

Bobby put the club down and stroked it a few times. "It's light, that's for sure." He brought the putter back, mainly with his left hand, switching control over to his right hand, shortened his back stroke, and rapped the ball firmly and watched as the ball headed towards its target—practicing Walter Travis's lesson.

"Plop." The ball dropped over the edge and into the cup.

"Nae too licht, A tak it," Maiden dryly kidded, watching.

"That's the longest putt I've made since I got up here." Bobby smiled at the brothers. Then Bobby looked at Jimmy Maiden. "How much?" He asked referring to the putter.

Jimmy Maiden shook his head.

"I'll take it," Bobby grinned.

Jimmy Maiden left to tend to business but Stewart watched Bobby fall in love over the next two hours on the practice green. At one point, Bobby sank twenty out of twenty-five putts from ten feet.

Bobby was ecstatic. The love affair was on!

"I thought I would be using that old Schenectady forever," Bobby remarked to Maiden as they finished for the day.

"A thoct ye wad too. Yer thee vera leal kynd, laddie."

Bobby took his new love, Calamity Jane, to Inwood. There, another unusual development was waiting for him.

"It's from my grandfather," Bobby said as he opened a telegram at the front desk of their hotel.

Bobby's eyes misted as he read it.

"Is awthing okay, lad?" Maiden asked.

Bobby held the telegram out for Maiden to read. "It's from my grandfather. He says, if you have to play on the Sabbath, hit them straight and make all the putts go down."

A large dark wall had come down in the Jones family.

The USGA had 360 golfers that wanted to play in this, the 1923 National Open, so they qualified players over four days. Each golfer had to qualify over 36 holes on one of the four days. The low eighteen and ties from each day's results would qualify. The Open itself would be played on 36 holes each day, on Friday and Saturday.

Bobby shot 77, 79 to qualify, six strokes back of the medalist leader. Walter Hagen shot the same score. Hagen had just returned from Britain where he failed to defend his British Open Crown. Hagen was a favorite at the National Open because the newly-formed PGA Championship Tournament had been held at Inwood just two years before. He had experience on this course.

"If I wasn't putting great, I don't know where I'd be," Bobby admitted to Keeler and Maiden. "This is not an easy course."

"Wan straik at ah time, laddie," Maiden offered.

"No one is doing well," Keeler threw in. "The course is winning."

Bobby played with Hagen for the first two rounds. Play on the course was still hard and scores were running high. For the first two rounds, Bobby shot 71, 73 to Hagen's 77, 75.

Bobby was two strokes back at the start of the third round. Bobby Cruickshank, was third at 73, 72. Jock Hutchinson had the lead with scores of 70, 72.

In his third round on Saturday morning, Bobby hung on to fire a 76, which he thought had pushed him down the ranks of the top players. In fact, it had pushed him into the lead by three strokes over Cruickshank who had scored a 78.

Hutchinson now stood one stroke behind Cruickshank.

"Eat light," Keeler instructed after telling Bobby where he stood.

"This is not an easy course. Do you know who designed it?" Bobby asked.

"Dr. William Exton and Mr. Arthur Thatcher," Maiden joined in.

"They did one damn fine job. There's not an easy hole out there," Bobby moaned. "It's so easy to get yourself into a real predicament."

"Yer in thee leid, laddie. Awbody is struglin mair than ye," Maiden said.

"Do you think a 73 will win it for me?" Bobby asked.

Keeler wasn't sure what to say, but Maiden did. "Juist pit thee best nummer yee can up thare an howp tae hell tha yer law mon."

Despite everything, Bobby only managed a 39 on the outgoing nine which was two over par. Bobby had his scoring sights on the incoming nine where he had never been over 35. If he got a 35 on the second nine, he felt his 74 would win.

By the 14th hole, Bobby was two under on his inward play. He felt good. Calamity Jane was hot.

Bobby parred the 15th and now faced the last three holes, which were all par-four holes. They were the same holes he had played at two under in the first three rounds.

"He's in guide shape," Maiden offered, watching.

"He's in excellent shape. I've waited forever to see him in this spot," Keeler countered.

"Did ye send ah telegram tae Big Bob?" Maiden continued.

"You bet. I want him here in spirit, even if he thinks he's a jinx."

Then Bobby got into trouble. First he bogied sixteen, then he bogied seventeen and finally, struggling, he double bogied eighteen.

"I think you still won it," Keeler said to Bobby as he came off the last green.

Bobby looked sideways at Keeler, his eyes glazed and sunken into the back of his head. "But I didn't finish like a champion; I finished like an old yellow dog."

Bobby and Sarazen turned in their scores, and Keeler took Bobby up to a private room that had been provided for him.

"All week long, I finished strong on the last three holes, but not today." Bobby huffed. "Not when it's really important."

"I just heard that Cruickshank has to birdie eighteen to tie you."

"If I had played well, he wouldn't have had that chance. He'll probably do it." Bobby shook his head.

The knock on the door brought the news. "Hello, Bobby."

It was Grantland Rice.

"Mr. Rice."

"Cruickshank caught you. He hit two good shots to get to the 18th green and sunk his ten foot putt to get his birdie."

It looked like Bobby had had it. He was physically worn down and emotionally spent. The last thing he wanted was another eighteen holes to play in a tense playoff.

"You were low amateur by eight strokes," Rice told Bobby. "Second was Reekie. Evans was at 309 to your 296. Ouimet was at 317."

Bobby nodded, but he didn't hear him. He was already thinking about the playoff. "If I had finished 4, 4, 4, I would have shot 72 and we would be going home," he said.

Francis Ouimet had roomed with Bobby during the tournament. Keeler was in with Maiden. The good thing about the arrangement was that it enabled Keeler to stand guard over Bobby's room, and even Maiden at times. Too many people wanted a piece of Bobby—a handkerchief, a piece of hair, or some other trinket to be able to brag about.

So, it was Ouimet who spent hours talking to Bobby as he bemoaned his finish. "I almost gave the damn thing away," Bobby said to Ouimet.

"But you didn't." Ouimet was trying to think of something positive to say. "You played two rounds each with Hagen and Sarazen and beat them both." Ouimet laughed. "That's playing some serious golf." He continued, "And I'll bet that fact was noticed by Hagen."

But to Bobby, the only thing that mattered was the last three holes where he felt he let himself down.

Playoff day bloomed gray and cloudy. Lightning could be seen in the distance. It was typical National Open weather.

Rice's Sunday morning column was a calling card to all the golfers in the New York area, and the USGA estimated that somewhat over 10,000 turned up to see play.

At two o'clock they teed off. At the nine-hole turn, Rice had the perfect descriptive line. "It's a ding-dong, nip and tuck battle."

Keeler looked at him and smiled. "Sounds like a column header."

Out of the first seventeen holes played, only three holes were tied. Both men—both named Bobby—took turns getting the lead.

Keeler, Rice, and Maiden were dragged along by the drama being played out before them. At times, Keeler tried to walk along with Bobby, but he fell out of step because of his arthritic leg. Rice and Maiden were there to protect Bobby, and so was his caddy, Luke Ross.

On the 18th tee, a long par-four of 425 yards with the last 170 yards over water, the match was even. A tie here meant another 18 holes that Bobby could ill afford to play.

Cruickshank hit his drive very poorly and the ball only traveled 150 yards down the left side, finishing behind a tree.

Bobby, wanting to take advantage of this opportunity, hit his drive 235 yards down the right hand side but it faded into the wave of spectators gathered there.

Neither player was performing very well.

Cruickshank had to lay up before the big lake that fronted the green. He was left with a third shot of 180 yards.

It took a few minutes for the official to get the fans to give Bobby room for his shot. His ball lie cleanly on a sand-dirt combination. He had to drive 170 yards over water to the green, into a slight headwind.

Bobby looked at the situation that faced him, looked again, and again, grabbed his driving iron, took his stance and swung.

The ball bore through the gusting air only rising at the end of its flight. It plopped down on the green and the fans let out a roar. Fumbling, Bobby gave his club back to his caddy and tried to see where the ball wound up.

"It's six feet from the hole, Mr. Jones," his caddy said to him, reinforcing what Bobby thought he saw. "It almost hit the flag."

"Great shot," Rice said, but Bobby never heard that.

Cruickshank played his third shot into a greenside bunker, and then pitched out and two putted for a double bogie.

With the outcome no longer in doubt, Bobby two putted for his par—and his first ever—National Open title.

Before Bobby knew it, he was hoisted up on someone's shoulders and paraded around the green while a bagpipe played in the distance.

CHAPTER
13

Bobby's train was greeted by one of the biggest homecomings in Atlanta seen since the Civil War.

On the train, Keeler had asked Maiden, "Did you arrange for that bagpipe?" Maiden had merely snorted a smile.

A parade ushered Bobby into downtown Atlanta. The Georgia Governor made an announcement and a dinner of over 500 of Atlanta's elite was held at East Lake. Bobby said a few choked words. The dinner was not what Bobby wanted, but everyone else wanted it, so he obliged.

He received an expensive sterling silver service for his house and Keeler got a gold watch for his part in telling the story of Bobby Jones.

Shotguns, grandfather clocks, watches, and lifetime memberships to courses followed, all given to golf's top amateur and the South's new hero. The USGA did not impose a top dollar ceiling on these "gifts."

"Got another gift for you." Keeler gave Bobby a large package he was carrying.

Bobby carefully took the wrappings off the package. "Newspaper stories?" Bobby asked, as he flipped through the package of clippings.

"The real article. I had the other reporters send me their actual stories." Keeler looked proudly at the package. "Some from Britain, too." Keeler chuckled. "Wanted to see if the other guys used the stories I gave them."

Bobby looked at the full package again.

"You need to put all your telegrams in with them, too.

They'll be nice to look back on years from now." If Bobby had done what Keeler suggested, he'd have had several scrapbooks full of mementos from this one tournament alone.

Keeler sat down as Camellia brought them both drinks. "You know, someone made a lot of money on your Open win." Keeler spilled the beans.

"Money?" Bobby said. "Oh, you mean that calcutta pool thing."

"Oh, so you know about it," Keeler noted. "I understand the pool was $150,000."

Bobby didn't say anything.

"Someone bought you for about $50,000," Keeler said again.

"Do you know who?" Bobby grimaced.

Keeler shook his head. "I think it was someone from Atlanta," Keeler said. "But no, I don't really know who." Then Keeler kidded. "Maybe you'll hear from them when they want to thank you."

Bobby's face turned beet red. Keeler didn't let up.

"I hear things are getting pretty serious between you and Mary."

Bobby smiled. "I think we're about to set a date."

"Now, that's serious." The men were both lost in thought for a few minutes.

Suddenly, Keeler chuckled. "Marriage is like golf in many ways, so I'm sure you two will be good at it."

Bobby commented, "Well, your marriage is good even though you don't have a great golf game."

Keeler looked straight at Bobby. "My marriage used to be good. Right now is not the time for me to be talking about my good marriage."

"I'm sorry," Bobby quietly emoted.

Keeler nodded. "Thanks. Maybe it'll get better."

"I hope so."

"See, just like golf," Keeler ribbed. "There's a lot of hoping in golf too."

"But hopefully not so much time apart," Bobby added.

"Not for a good marriage, I guess." Keeler started thinking of what might have been. He knew a divorce was on the horizon for him.

"Say, you've put weight back on," Keeler exclaimed.

"Camellia is one damn fine cook," Bobby said.

"How much weight do you think you lost last time?" Keeler asked, giving the young man a critical once-over.

"About twelve pounds," Bobby replied.

That wasn't news Keeler was about to report, and he hoped Bobby's parents didn't know about it.

The date for Bobby's wedding to Mary was set for June 17, 1924. Keeler reported the news in one of his columns.

Bobby spent a little time at Harvard that spring to finish his degree, and he also used the time to set up exhibitions for Perry and him to play. He wanted to get Perry back into golf after the hardship of losing his father.

The exhibitions also allowed Bobby to try out the new golf technique he was working on.

"So, is it working?" Perry asked Bobby as they met for an exhibition.

"Anything would work better than what I was using." Bobby grinned as he drew Calamity Jane out of his bag.

"This game has so many facets to it," Perry remarked thoughtfully.

Bobby nodded. "I've changed the way I look at match play now," he said. "It would be hell for many to think that when you play match, you're playing against par just as you would in medal play where you're counting strokes against par."

And hell it was. Bobby's new system of looking at a match as a battle against old man par gave him and Perry the match over two club pros 6-up and five holes to go. Bobby was the low scorer by five strokes.

On May 21st, Bobby won the Alabama-Georgia Open, which was played at Druid Hills, the course not far from East Lake. This was a course George Adair had helped start, and Bobby loved it and played it regularly.

The Atlanta Constitution sports writer wrote that Bobby performed like a golfing machine, running away with the tournament with a victory by 14 strokes over the runner-up.

"Hou's yer putting, laddie?" Maiden asked.

"I hate to say it, but even with a good win, I can remember eight to ten putts that could have come my way over the course of the tournament."

"Tha's gowf," Maiden chuckled.

Then Maiden asked for a rare favor. "Hou aboot doin somethin for me?"

Bobby looked at Maiden. "Name it, friend."

"A hiv this new young member wha needs tae spend som time wi his putting, an for some uncannie reason thinks verra highly o ye," Maiden continued. "A wis wonderin gif ye wad spen som time puttin wi him?"

"Which member?" Bobby wondered.

"His name is Watts Gunn," Maiden said working on a club as he talked. "Ye micht hiv seen him aboot."

"I've seen Gunn play. He has a wonderful iron and long club game."

Maiden nodded.

Suddenly, Bobby realized that what he had just said about Gunn was what people used to say about him. "I'd love to help him with anything that I know."

From there, Bobby took the lead. He asked Watts Gunn to play in his weekend group.

Soon, Bobby was off to Detroit—home of the Oakland Hills Country Club and the 1924 National Open. The USGA announced that Bobby wouldn't have to go through qualifying rounds because he was the reigning champion.

"All set?" Keeler asked Bobby as a way of striking up a conversation when they arrived at Oakland Hills. Keeler had talked his paper into allowing him to arrive earlier than usual, so he could get more copy on Bobby's early rounds.

"As set as I need to be," Bobby grinned.

"How's your weight?"

"Good for now. Maybe staying right at the club will allow me more alone time to refresh myself during the tournament."

"Think that'll do it?"

Bobby smiled and then shook his head. "If I knew that would do it, I would have done it before." Bobby looked out the window at the beautiful scene of the club, which was green and rich with a view of Mother Nature. "You know, I wonder if, somehow, I can make this Open into fun instead of so full of pressure like they usually are."

"Sounds good," Keeler reasoned. Anything that would help his favorite golfer would win Keeler's approval.

Not having to qualify took some pressure off Bobby, as did a practice round with Walter Hagen.

"You ready, kid?" Hagen joked as they got ready to play a practice round.

"As ready as I'll ever be." Bobby had heard a lot of stories about Hagen, but he had never seen anything unusual himself. As he watched Hagen get ready to tee off, though, he did notice something. Instead of having his caddy make a little sand tee for his drive, Hagen flourished a little white peg in his hand. Bobby wondered if the ball would stay on the peg long enough for Hagen to hit his shot.

Hagen's drive was a good one, right down the middle with just a hint of fade on the end.

"Nice drive," Bobby offered, moving into position to hit his drive.

"You might want to try one of these," Hagen said, flipping a peg to Bobby.

Bobby caught the peg and looked at it. Hagen came over chuckling. "It's a tee, a 'Ready Tee.'"

Bobby watched as Hagen demonstrated how the peg was used. He positioned the ball over the tee between his first two fingers. Then he pushed the peg into the ground, leaving the ball on top.

"Is it legal?" Bobby asked.

"They said it's okay," Hagen said, flipping his thumb over his shoulder at some officials of the USGA that were behind him. "Of course, I'm being paid fifteen hundred dollars to use this gimmick. For that kind of money, anything can get approved," Hagen bragged.

Bobby hit his shot, picked up his tee, and looked at it.

"Here, kid. Here's some more. I want you to leave the used tees in the ground for the kids as souvenirs." Hagen watched Bobby peruse the little wooden peg.

"Are they really paying you that much just to use these things?" Bobby questioned.

"Sure are," Hagen grinned. "Of course, they knew I'd be the best one to get them the most exposure. That's why I leave the tees in the ground."

All that day and the next, Bobby tried to remember to leave the tees in the ground, but he already had fans chasing his divots, and now the fans wanted his little tees too.

"I like these things," Bobby said to Hagen, as Hagen questioned Bobby about the tees.

"I like them best when I break them in two," Hagen chuckled.

Hagen noticed the way the fans and reporters hung on every nuance of Bobby's game. It bothered him, and he tried not to let that show, but it did. It showed in his game.

"What do you think of the course?" Keeler asked Bobby between practice rounds.

"Tough. It has very large, undulating, fast greens."

"But with the greens being so large, they must be easy to hit."

Bobby chuckled. "I'd rather have a thirty-yard pitch than a thirty-yard putt."

Keeler looked off and Bobby watched his eyes squint with more questions.

"Take it from me," Bobby continued. "Large greens are easier to hit, but they're hard as hell to putt on if your ball is a long way from the cup." Bobby watched Keeler still try to grasp what he was saying. "Just ask Stewart. He'll tell you that the big thing in putting is avoiding the three-putt greens. The bigger the green, the more likely you will be far enough away to cause a three-putt." Bobby shook his head. "Especially in one of these big events where the speed of the greens is so fast compared to what we normally play."

Keeler left to tell the other reporters what Bobby had said, and Bobby crawled into bed with a book about Shakespeare. The next day he faced his opening round in the National Open as the defending champion.

Bobby shot 74, 73 his first two days and tied for the lead with "Wild Bill "Melhorn. The fans were a problem for him during his rounds, and he was hot under the collar about it. The officials moved them away and out of range as much as possible, but it was not enough. Five times, Bobby had to sit down while the officials cleared the fans out of range.

Cyril Walker was in third place. He shot 148 for the first two rounds. Hagen was in fourth place, with two 75's.

For his third round, Bobby teed off with Gene Sarazen. They had become a familiar pairing, and they got along famously.

Bobby came in with 75 and Walker posted 74, which put them in a tie for the lead. Third-day positioning was causing everyone to tighten up. The third round average for the field was 80.

The wind picked up in the afternoon, but Bobby was okay until the 10th hole when he double-bogied the 450-yard par-four hole for the second time in the tournament and had to birdie the par-five 18th for a final round score of 78. This gave him a four-round total of 300, the outright tournament lead.

"All right," Keeler told a very tired Bobby. "Melhorn finished with a 78. That gives you the lead."

Bobby nodded, looking around. "Whew, that wind was something else again."

But there was more news. "Walker still has a chance," Keeler reported.

Bobby nodded. He knew.

Walker had heard how Bobby finished. He knew that a score of 77 or less would do it for him. He pared the last four holes to take the title by three strokes.

Bobby and Mary were married in a beautiful ceremony on the large back lawn of Mary's home. An hour before the ceremony, the lawn, the porches, the gazebo, and even the front lawn were overflowing with guests. Only 350 people had been invited, but a head count would have been twice that. Bobby didn't mind. They were all friends of his in one form or another.

O.B. Keeler stood in the third row. Standing on his toes to survey the crowd, Keeler spotted Stewart Maiden tucked down on the front row, not far from where Bobby and Mary were holding hands.

Later, after the ceremony was over, Keeler kissed Mary and wished Bobby great and good luck. "I so want you two to be happy."

Bobby smiled and Mary kissed Keeler on the left cheek.

"I'll not wash that cheek until Bobby wins his Amateur," Keeler kidded.

The local Atlanta papers covered the special occasion, and

the person in Atlanta who did not know about the Jones and Malone wedding was rare indeed.

Bobby and Mary honeymooned in Asheville, North Carolina. Bobby did not take his golf clubs with him, but as they drove to Asheville, they passed through a little town called Highlands. There, Bobby saw a golf course being built by Donald Ross. He made note to come back and play it.

While on their honeymoon, Bobby read about Hagen winning the British Open again. Bobby got a good chuckle reading Hagen's words after he won. Hagen had come within two strokes of winning the past three British Opens and he was the first golfer to repeat his victories in both the American and British Opens.

Upon their return, Robert Tyre Jones, Jr., and his wife, Mary, moved in with the groom's parents until they could afford their own home, as was the custom of the day.

It took the couple two full days to open the gifts that were awaiting them.

Bobby was happily married to the woman of his dreams, but golf had a way of calling him in such a way that he had to turn away from the people and things he loved.

The Walker Cup was played on Long Island in 1924, not far from where Bobby won his first Open title. The British were not expected to field a strong team, and they didn't. America retained the cup by the score of 9-3.

Merion, the site of Bobby's first entry into a national event, played host to the National Amateur.

Bobby was accompanied by his caddy, Luke Ross, and O.B. Keeler, who shared a room with Bobby at the Greenhill Farms Hotel.

"I'll bet you're going to like it here better this time," Keeler said to Bobby over breakfast.

"If I do myself proud, I will," Bobby grinned back. Bobby's expectations of himself were always so high. It was the thing that gave Keeler his award-winning columns.

"Wish I had been here the first time," Keeler added.

"You wouldn't have liked it. I lost hard," Bobby countered.

"But I might have protected you from those dirty pants remarks."

Bobby laughed. "Then I wish you had been here, too."

The Philadelphia papers got a lot of their information about Bobby from Keeler. A multi-page, multi-picture spread showed the comparison of Bobby's two different visits to Philadelphia and Merion. It was the story of the evolution of the South's great golfer.

"This is where it all started for me, O.B.," Bobby said, looking out the window as the taxi brought them to Merion.

Keeler nodded, looking out.

"It happened so fast and unexpectedly that I almost forgot to be excited." Bobby looked around. "I was following Perry around most of the time." He laughed. "You should have seen me that first afternoon when all of a sudden I had thousands of people watching me." Bobby paused. "I'm afraid my 89 that afternoon let them all down."

This time was different. Bobby shot a qualifying round of 72, then matched it by a second 72. He was in the tournament.

In his first round eighteen-hole match against the Canadian Amateur Champion, W.J. Thompson, Bobby won 6 and 5 in a real rout.

In his next match, Bobby played Ducky Cochran who had won the qualifying medal. That didn't faze Bobby at all. He won 3 and 2.

But what almost got to Bobby in this match was the run Cochran threw at him after Bobby got to dormie, 5-up with five to go. Suddenly, Cochran went birdie, birdie. With three holes to go, Bobby began to worry about how long Cochran would keep this up, but the streak ended on the 16th green with par-fours for both competitors. They halved the hole, and the match was over.

Next, Bobby beat Rudy Keppler 6 and 4 in another rout. Bobby had picked up steam. His game was rhythmical and smooth, and people kept gathering to watch.

Bobby moved into heavier competition as he played the winner of the 1914 Amateur, Francis Ouimet.

"I don't really want to play Ouimet," Bobby moaned to Keeler the night before.

Keeler sympathized with Bobby. "But you're not playing Ouimet," he countered. "Remember, you're playing old man par." It was a comment that carried quite a gift in it for Bobby. Bobby and Ouimet had become friends. To Bobby, friends were a big part of his life.

"I discovered something special out there today, O.B." As usual, Keeler was all ears.

"If you can just keep on shooting pars at them, eventually, your opponent will have to crack." Bobby hadn't gotten many birdies in his match against Keppler. So, he settled for pars.

More and more people flooded onto Merion hoping to either see Bobby or, incredibly, to get one of his divots or a piece of his hair or a tee he had used. They seemed to know that this was going to be the tournament where golf's number one amateur finally stepped into his crown. But Bobby didn't feel the same way.

"I'm not sure that I really want to beat Francis," Bobby pleaded again over breakfast.

"He plays against par and you do too," Keeler prodded.

Bobby nodded sadly. "But Francis is a dear friend."

"Try to forget you're playing Francis. Do your best to play against the card," Keeler threw in. "The only way to win one of these amateur events is to win all the matches, no matter who your opponent is."

Bobby and Ouimet met outside the club and strolled together to the first tee. Neither man wanted this match to take place.

"Good luck, Francis," Bobby murmured as they shook hands. He bowed just slightly to his opponent.

"Same to you, Bobby Jones," Ouimet grinned.

Sometimes a match is over before it even starts. This match was like that. Ouimet couldn't get his game going and won only the 18th hole in the morning round. Bobby took an eight-hole lead into lunch.

"Looks like your technique of playing old man par is working," Keeler smiled at Bobby from across the small grillroom table.

Bobby merely shook his head from side to side. He was still sad about beating one of his best friends in the game.

That afternoon, Bobby continued playing well, while Ouimet had already played his best. The match concluded on the 26th hole, with Bobby 11-up and ten holes to play.

"Thank you for the lessons," Ouimet grinned as they shook hands.

Bobby shook Ouimet's hand, but couldn't think of anything to say. Bobby was now in the final.

In their room that night, Keeler brought Bobby his first shot of corn whiskey as Bobby sank into the tub.

"You did a great job today playing against par. You did just as you said you wanted to."

Bobby sank further into the tub. "It was real hard with Francis as my competitor, believe me." Bobby let out a deep breath. "I only hope I do as well tomorrow."

"From my vantage point, you're playing the best golf that I've ever seen you play." Keeler paused, thinking. "I think part of it has to do with your age. At twenty-two, you're now a fully grown man."

Keeler told Bobby about George Von Elm, who was going to be Bobby's opponent in the final the next day.

"He's from Salt Lake City and has a number of victories in the Pacific Northwest and also in a Trans-Mississippi tournament. He lost in the final in the Western Amateur to Chick

Evans." Keeler looked satisfied. "Should be a good match between you two."

Bobby nodded. "Only one thing bothering me about this year's tournament."

Keeler listened. "What's that?"

"No one's gone crazy against me yet, and Von Elm has the last chance for that to happen." Bobby looked off.

As Keeler watched Bobby step up to the tee the next morning, he was amazed at how Bobby had grown to handle himself. He easily walked around the tee in front of over 10,000 fans, spoke to officials, and even talked occasionally with a sports writer or fan. A rope was up over the back of the tee, but some people worked their way over to Bobby to touch him or his clubs.

The announcements were made, the applause died down, and the game was on.

Bobby had prepared himself for a steady challenge, but after he lost the first hole by giving it away, the challenge came from within Bobby alone, playing against par.

Bobby outplayed Von Elm from tee to green, and at the end of the first 18 holes, stood 4-up.

"So, how's it really going?" Keeler asked Bobby as they met at a small table in the dining room away from everyone. During a round, Bobby and Keeler often walked side-by-side but they did so silently, hardly ever talking but always passing messages through eye contact.

"I love the course. I'm in my game, the fans are great, and I'd like to stay 4-up for the next fifteen holes."

Keeler grinned. "Well, all right!" Keeler made sure Bobby had only a light lunch.

The afternoon round was an even better version of the morning round. Bobby won every other hole and lost none of the front nine holes. That put Bobby 9-up. After that, the match ended on the 10th hole—but it ended in a very unusual way.

Von Elm was on the green with his second shot, as was Bobby. But Bobby was inside Von Elm and only six feet from the hole. Von Elm putted and missed.

For a second, Von Elm hesitated. Then, he walked over to Bobby and said, "Don't putt that one. I've had enough." Von Elm had conceded the birdie putt and the match to Bobby, 10 and 8. It was the largest winning score in a final since the very first National Amateur was played.

With his win in the National Amateur, the trophies in both American national tournaments had traveled south of the Mason Dixon Line for the first time.

In this National Amateur, Bobby had beaten five opponents by a total of 36 holes up, or an average of 7-up in each match. He had been down in his first match just once, and then only briefly. After that small deficit, he had taken command in his matches.

"You know O.B., if I had played against par in my other tournaments, I might have a few more of these big trophies." Bobby grinned as he looked at the trophy that sat on the train seat across from him.

"I'm sure you would have," Keeler smiled, making notes for one of his columns. "What was the deal on that last green with Von Elm?"

Bobby shook his head. "I'm not sure. All I know is that he gave me the putt which, to me, conceded the win. He was still putting for a par while my conceded putt gave me a bird, a win by 10 and 8."

"I heard some official say the final score might be 9 and 8."

Bobby shook his head. "It's all the same to me." Bobby looked down at his feet for a second or two. "You know, I really didn't do anything different this time. It was just that no one got hot on me like they have in the past."

Keeler looked at Bobby. "That's seemingly true."

Bobby grinned. "It's as though my time had come." Bobby looked off. "What was it that the pros used to say about a tournament winner?"

Keeler looked at Bobby. "They used to say that it was his tournament to win."

Bobby looked at Keeler and smiled. "I can see why they said that now." Bobby looked out the window at the passing scenery. "Nothing happened in this damn tournament that was of any surprise to me. Nope. Nothing at all."

Thousands of his fellow citizens met his train as it arrived at the Brookwood station in Atlanta. A shy Bobby managed to speak a few words while sneaking peeks at his new bride. A thousand cars were parked alongside the parade route, creating the biggest traffic jam Atlanta had ever seen.

Newspapers all over the land took the position that it had only been a matter of time until Bobby laid claim to what he was due. Everyone, they said, knew that this temperamental Southern golfer would win all the titles he wanted to win. At the age of twenty-two, Bobby had won both national titles. He was considered by most to be the top golfer in the land.

But none of the papers picked up on what Keeler really thought. He felt that Bobby's marriage had settled him down, resulting in a more relaxed player who easily accepted his fate and approached matches with a calm, quiet demeanor. Keeler didn't say it, but he also thought Bobby had won a victory over some of his inner demons.

Back in Atlanta, Bobby was feted. He had brought an uncommon success to the South which only fifty-seven terrible years before had suffered an ignominious fate at the hands of the Union forces. The South had its pride back, and it showered Bobby with gifts to show how much it appreciated that. Bobby turned down the monetary gifts that would endanger his amateur status, but all the other gifts were accepted even if they were duplicates. The gift Mary liked best was the sterling silver plates for twelve that matched the silver service they had received the year before.

Over 300 special guests arrived at the East Lake Club for a dinner on Bobby's behalf. Keeler started off the night reading telegrams to Bobby from Walter Travis, Jerry Travers, Grantland Rice, and Charles Blair McDonald, one of the founders of the USGA and the first winner of the National Amateur.

All of Bobby's favorite people were there—Perry and Alexa, Stewart Maiden, his wife, Mary, of course, his mother and father, Big Bob and Clara, and, for the first time, Robert Tyre Jones, Sr., his grandfather.

An hour into the dinner, the lights were dimmed and a screen was put up. Pictures of Bobby, Perry, and Alexa appeared on the screen as they were years ago, playing the East Lake Golf Course. Bobby and Perry appeared in motion picture shots obviously taken at Merion eight years before. With the appearance of these Merion scenes, it was obvious to both Bobby and Perry who had taken them. It had been George Adair.

Out in the mists of the universe, where important things are decided, a question was growing about who the number one player in the golfing community really was—Bobby Jones or Walter Hagen. As Bobby was being lauded for his amateur win, Hagen was being lauded for his professional win of the British Open. Which was more important? Hagen had no problem answering the question.

"Mr. Jones is an excellent amateur golfer. That I know very well," Hagen pontificated. "However, he has not the national wins that I have, nor does he have the regional or Open wins that I possess."

The new golf magazines, American Golfer, the Southern Golfer, Golf Illustrated, the Western Golfer, the Transmississippi Golfer, and newspapers all over the country got into the debate.

They picked either Hagen or Bobby as the best golfer in the world, setting up a discussion that began to grow in disproportionate ways.

The USGA received 450 entries for the 1925 National Open, and so, it decided to qualify the field regionally to help golfers save travel expenses and to make it easy for other golfers to enter.

Bobby picked the Eastern qualification site at Lido Golf Club in Lido, New York. He made the field easily, despite the first day's downpour, scoring 72 and 71.

The Open was held at the Worcester Country Club, in Worcester, Massachusetts, just west of Boston.

During Monday's practice round, Bobby set a new scoring record of 66. Bobby's playing partner was Walter Hagen, who scored his first hole-in-one but could only score a 72—even with the hole-in-one to help him.

The rumor going around the Open was that there was not a professional that could beat Bobby. The calcutta that followed that rumor was a run-away for Bobby. A number of gamblers even combined their resources to bet on Bobby.

The professionals badly wanted to win the Open because being the Open winner would trigger a flood of requests for exhibitions that could bring $30,000 to $40,000 in income opportunities.

Some newspapers were openly asking why the professionals couldn't beat this part-time golfer who simply played for the love of the game.

"If nothing else, I simply want to beat Jones," Hagen said to Gene Sarazen as they played a practice round. "And if I don't do that, I want you to beat him." Hagen looked strongly at Sarazen.

"I'll do my best," Sarazen smiled with a grin on his face. "I could use the coin that comes with the Open title." Sarazen smiled again. "Mary wants to buy a farm in upstate New York and let me travel on my own while she runs the farm."

Hagen snickered. "I wish my wife wanted to stay home." Hagen dreamed for a minute. "That would be perfect for me."

"I'll bet," Sarazen grinned. But then Sarazen got back to the topic at hand. "Why do you think that Jones is so good?"

"Has to be what he's learning from that old Scottish pro that's at his course. There's nothing of value he can learn from another damn amateur."

The East coast was in the midst of a heat wave and afternoon temperatures ran into the mid-nineties in Worcester.

Hagen played with Bobby the first day, which meant that they were going to play two rounds together. Hagen had a lead over Bobby as they played the 11th hole of the morning round. Bobby's approach shot was off to the right about thirty feet off the green in some tall grass when the unthinkable happened.

"I need to add a penalty stroke to my score for this hole as I caused my ball to move," Bobby called across to an official.

The official walked slowly over to Bobby and Hagen came over from the other side. "I didn't see it move," the official stated.

"It moved as I was addressing the ball," Bobby said, "It moved a couple of inches." He looked around for Keeler but didn't see him.

"Did you see his ball move?" the official asked Hagen, who had arrived at the spot.

Hagen shook his head, first looking at Bobby's ball. "I didn't see it move and I wonder how it could have moved."

The official looked back at Bobby. "No one else saw your ball move and I wonder if you just thought it may have moved but it didn't move."

Bobby looked at the shot he still had. "I know my ball moved." Then he looked at both the official and Hagen. "I know what I have to do, thanks."

The official wandered back to the side.

Hagen shot 72 to Bobby's 76 in that morning round. Neither man was really on his game. Hagen's round was saved by an abnormal number of saving putts and a chip-in from off the green.

Keeler knew that Bobby's off-track performance was partly due to the upsetting loss of a stroke that he had to call on himself on the 11th hole.

"Are you sure you saw it move?" another official asked Bobby as he turned in his card.

"For sure," Bobby looked at the man. "Right when I was addressing the ball with my club and getting ready to hit the shot, the ball moved a couple of inches." Bobby hated that it happened, but he knew that it did.

"Were there any other witnesses?" the official pursued.

Bobby couldn't believe the trouble he was going through to report the rules violation. "None that I know of, no."

"Who was your playing partner?"

Bobby turned around and saw Hagen coming towards them. "Hagen."

"Did you see his ball move on eleven?" the official asked Hagen as he came to the table to turn in his scorecard.

Hagen shook his head, which preceded his answer. "No, and I told the official there at the time that I didn't." Hagen signed his card and handed it in.

Then Henry Fownes, Vice-President of the USGA, looked at Bobby. "Well, Bobby, it seems a matter for you to decide. Do you think you caused your ball to move?"

Bobby looked at Fownes. "I know I did." Bobby handed his card in and it had the extra stroke added on for the 11th hole.

"You okay?" Keeler said to Bobby as they sat down to lunch with only forty-five minutes to spare before he had to go out again.

"As well as someone who just threw a damn stroke away," Bobby huffed. "I should have been more careful."

"Those things are hard to tell, aren't they?"

"I sometimes think a golf ball has a mind of its own."

A group of reporters wanted to talk about Bobby's rules infraction and came to their lunch table, but Keeler indicated that he'd tell them about it after Bobby teed off on his afternoon round.

"Seems peculiar that so much seems to want to be made out of a simple scoring penalty," Keeler said.

That afternoon, Bobby shot a 1-under 70 and moved into a tie for 10th place, while Hagen ballooned to a 77.

Sarazen tried to approach Hagen after his round but Hagen was so upset he stalked angrily past him. Sarazen had shot rounds of 72, 72 and wanted Hagen to know.

When Bobby got the media's attention for his afternoon round, Hagen got more upset. "Damn amateur," Hagen huffed under his breath, seeing all the reporters gathered around Bobby.

"Do you think Hagen would have turned himself in if his ball had moved and no one else saw it?" one reporter asked.

"I like to think that he would," Bobby said knowing that the reporter wanted a different answer.

"But golfers don't usually report something like you just did." The reporter looked at Bobby. "What you did is very admirable."

Keeler was listening very closely.

It was obviously a crucible event. "You'd as well praise me for not breaking into banks," Bobby shook his head and continued his statement, the first part of which became famous. "There is only one way to play this game."

Keeler glowed, and his mind worked at creating the copy he would use as a column header.

Bobby's partner for the last day of thirty-six-hole play was Tommy Armour, who was known as the "Black Scot" for his pitch dark hair and very dark eyes.

Bobby's third round was another hard-fought 70, which moved him into 4th place, tied with Joe Espinosa and four strokes behind the leader, Willie MacFarlane, who was the club pro at Oak Ridge in Tuckahoe, New York, and who had hardly played golf the previous eight months.

Bobby teed off for his last round right behind Johnny Farrell, twenty minutes before MacFarlane and an hour before Francis Ouimet.

"Even par should win this damn thing," Bobby said to Keeler as they stood by the first tee of the 375-yard par-four hole. Keeler was protecting him from intrusion by fans.

As the last round developed, steady, encompassing pressure enveloped Bobby and he could not score the way he wanted to. Time and opportunities passed him by and he came in with a 74, which was good for a score of 291, seven over par.

"Do you think now that you should have turned yourself in for that penalty of the moving ball?" Bobby was asked by a reporter.

Keeler grabbed Bobby and pulled him over to the side. "Let's go up to the room and get away from all this."

As they left, Keeler spoke to Bobby. "The only one who has a chance to catch you is MacFarlane, and I understand that his twosome is five holes behind and he's struggling."

"I felt as though I was both looking over my shoulder and trying to see ahead out there. It was hard for me to keep my mind on my game. I guess I've just about had it." Bobby stopped and looked at Keeler. "For some reason, I kept on thinking about what luck meant."

Bobby had just fallen asleep when Keeler awoke him later with the news. "MacFarlane finished bogie, birdie, par and tied you at seven over. Do you just want to sleep to get rested up for tomorrow's playoff?"

Bobby nodded and turned back over and fell deeply asleep.

The first nine holes of the playoff, MacFarlane shot a 37 to take a one stroke lead, which Bobby made up for on the incoming nine when he shot a 37 to MacFarlane's 38. These two golfers had played 90 holes and the total score was still all square.

On the second eighteen, Bobby shot a 35 on the outgoing nine to MacFarlane's 39. He looked like he was going to take the tournament when MacFarlane started grinding away, playing catch up. After they both parred the 16th hole, they teed off on the 17th tied.

"This thing is getting humorous," Bobby said to Keeler as they stood waiting for MacFarlane to hit his second shot at the green. "106 holes and still tied."

"Looks like a third playoff," Keeler mumbled.

Bobby's face turned hard. "No," he grated. "There won't be another playoff. I'll settle it one way or another in this round."

The two golfers both birdied the par-five 17th hole and moved to the 18th tee still tied. Keeler watched as Bobby hit another blistering drive past his opponent. It was very obvious to Keeler that Bobby was determined to win on this last hole.

The par-four 18th hole was only 335 yards long, but it played uphill to a little green that sat on a ledge on the side of a hill. As usual, Bobby out-drove MacFarlane and stood aside while MacFarlane hit his approach onto the back of the green about forty feet away from the flag.

As Keeler watched Bobby line up his shot, he sensed that, just like a few years ago at St. Louis, Bobby was going to go for it.

Bobby's mashie-niblick shot hit the very top edge of the bunker only about twelve feet from the hole. The ball bounced up in the air and seemed to pause as both Keeler and Bobby, and countless others, held their breaths. But then the pause stopped and Bobby's ball came straight down and into the bunker.

Keeler's crooked footsteps followed his young hero as Bobby played under pressure. He watched as Bobby popped his ball out of the bunker and onto the green, eight feet from the hole.

MacFarlane put his long treacherous putt very close to the hole and Bobby missed his last effort to tie—and the 1925 Open was over. After 108 holes, Bobby had come out one stroke too many and was the runner-up for the third time in four years.

Keeler's column didn't mention the loss. It and countless other newspapers across the country mentioned the rules violation Bobby had called on himself. Keeler's headline read: **There Are Some Things in Life Finer than Winning a Golf Trophy.**

CHAPTER
14

"You're going to have to play your best today," Bobby's opponent said. Bobby was playing in the all-day Sunday matches at East Lake which were followed by one of Camellia's great meals. "Wattsie shot himself a 2-under the other day. I heard Stewart talking about his score all afternoon." They were talking about Watts Gunn, the newest golf star to come out of the East Lake petrie dish.

"Well, maybe we shouldn't give him two a side anymore," Bobby grinned.

"Are you going to come to Oakmont and try your game out against the big boys?" Bobby asked Watts as they finished play.

"A'd love tae see ye twa gae up thare thegither," Maiden always seemed to be around when he needed to encourage his boys.

"I don't think my father would permit me to go," Watts answered. His father was a judge for the city.

"I'll take care of that," Bobby said. And, as promised, he went to see Judge Gunn.

"Now what in tarnation brings you here on such a pleasant day when you could be honing your game to bring another fine trophy home from the North?" Judge Gunn said in greeting Bobby.

Bobby reached across Judge Gunn's desk and shook his hand. "I have come on behalf of your son, Judge Gunn. I think he would be a fine representative of our course and the South in the country's National Amateur."

Judge Gunn stroked his chin in thought. "I don't think that

Watts is ready to be facing the competition he would meet at our nation's top amateur tournament," he said. "He doesn't have your demeanor. He is kind of young for his age."

Bobby took it all in. "Judge Gunn, I've played in the National Amateur for seven years and I've played with Watts over a similar period of time. I can tell you that he is the equal of more than half of the players I've gone against. I believe he would comport himself very well." Before the Judge could say anything, Bobby added. "I would personally look after Watts, Judge."

"If I can have your word on that, I'll let him go with you." Judge Gunn stood up.

Bobby shook his hand. "You have that, sir."

The USGA decided to change its format again. For the first time, they were going to play the tournament over six days. There would be sixteen qualifiers for the tournament which would be played in match play. All the matches would be 36 holes; there would be no 18-hole matches.

Bobby qualified second in the field at 147 while Gunn qualified at 154. The big news was about who did not make it into the match play rounds. Five previous winners of the National Amateur did not make it through qualification, and that started the week off on an unusual note.

In his first-round match, Watts won 15 holes in a row from his opponent and won the match 12 and 10. In his second match, Watts met the worthy opponent and big tournament winner, Jess Sweetser of New York. Watts beat him by the score of 10 and 9. Watts had played Oakmont for one stretch of 52 holes in even par, and he became the big news of the day.

That took a lot of pressure off Bobby. The sports writers asked Bobby a lot of questions, but most of the questions were about Watts.

"Are you ever going to cool off?" Bobby teased Watts as they met for dinner with Keeler who was trying to file stories about his two golf stars to send back to Atlanta.

"I hope not. I sure love this golf course," Watts smiled back. "Even the shots I miss seem to want to go at the hole."

And Watts did not cool off. He won all of his matches easily and carried himself to the final.

Bobby was doing his own good playing. He had run through his side of the field with his lowest win margin—6-up and 5 to go.

"Tomorrow, we meet on the first tee for one of the most important golf tournaments we will ever play in our lives," Bobby said to Watts as they ate dinner. "I want you to get a good night's rest, so you'll be ready to give a good accounting for yourself out there."

Watts grinned across the table. "I'm sure glad you talked my dad into letting me come to this tournament."

Bobby was proud of Watts. "Well, let's see what you're made of tomorrow."

"I guess I ought to phone my dad and let him know I'm in the final."

Bobby laughed. "Don't worry about that. Your dad knew about that before you did."

"I have a funny feeling Watts is up to something," Keeler told Bobby as they watched Watts walk off after their meal was over.

Bobby decided to follow up on Keeler's hunch and paused down the hall from Watt's room before entering his own.

Sure enough, about an hour later, Watts came out of his room, all dressed up and heading out for a date.

"Where the hell do you think you're going?" Bobby came at Watts.

"Well, there was this girl in the gallery the past two days and I...."

"Nope. No. Nothing doing." Bobby grabbed the lead. "I made a promise to your father that we're going to keep." He had a hold on Gunn's shoulder and was turning him back into his room.

"But I don't want to let her down," Watts pleaded.

"If she's really worth it, she'll be available after tomorrow."

Two very good players, both from East Lake, were playing the final in the National Amateur. Some fans mumbled the question. "Why didn't they just hold this down at East Lake and save them the train fare?"

As they met on the first tee, their smiles of appreciation for each other were obvious. "Are you going to give me my regular three strokes?" Watts asked Bobby.

"I'm going to give you hell to pay today," Bobby grinned, but he was greeted with a brand-new Watts that day. Watts had learned Oakmont's secrets.

Bobby played the first 11 holes at one under par and found himself 1-down.

They came to the par-five 12th hole, which had been renamed the "Ghost Hole" for the two little girls who had supposedly caused an official to use his megaphone right at the top of Bobby's backswing in 1919. That maneuver caused Bobby to top his shot and lose the hole in the match play final.

This time, there were no little girls, and Bobby didn't lose the match either. With Watts on in three, Bobby was in a green-side bunker in three. He popped his ball out of the bunker to within ten feet of the flag and just barely made the putt to halve the hole with Watts.

A hot run began—and it was Bobby's. He won his second National Amateur, 8-up and seven to go.

He was gracious in his victory speech. He praised every-thing about the tournament, and when word got out that Watts played only because Bobby intervened with his father, the press put another feather in Bobby's hat.

As their train pulled out of the Pittsburgh station, Bobby leaned across at Keeler. "If I could be a national champion of the United States six years in succession, either Open or Amateur, I'd feel I could hang up the old clubs."

Keeler smiled. "Well, that looks possible to me."

"How about just you and me having a go at each other at your course and mine?" Hagen proposed to Bobby. Hagen had seen the newspaper stories that said both were evenly ranked in the world of golf. Bobby was the reigning amateur champ, while Hagen was the PGA champion—again.

Over the next couple of months, arrangements were made. The match was set at 36 holes at both courses. Hagen took the match seriously, but to Bobby, it was just some off-season fun.

Hagen decided to charge spectators, a thought that didn't gain much support. But Hagen prevailed, as he usually did, and a charge of $3.30 a head was set for the match. That was three times the fee the USGA was charging for spectators to attend the Open.

The match was advertised as the "Battle of the Century." The advertising was intense. Everyone took sides, which made it more interesting.

Over the first nine holes of the match, Hagen scratched out a 2-up lead, despite the fact that he was also busy trying to count the heads of the fans that showed up. Hagen was good at estimating income.

After the morning 18 were over, Hagen had a 3-up lead. They were playing at Whitfield Estates, one of the Adair Realty holdings. Bobby was having problems with his irons, while Hagen's putter was hot. Hagen sank some very long putts, especially on holes that others had thought Bobby was about to win.

The afternoon round went no easier for Bobby. His irons didn't come off right while Hagen's putter did some great work.

At the end of 27 holes, Hagen was 3-up, but in the last nine holes, Hagen got hot as Bobby cooled off. Hagen stood at 8-up going to Hagen's home course.

At the Pasadena course, Hagen got right back into his game

while Bobby still struggled. Hagen was on his favorite greens with his well-known excellent short game.

He walked slowly and surely away from Bobby and won by the large score of 12-up and eleven to go. It was a rout.

Bobby's iron play was poor, but it was his putting that cost him the match. He had eight more putts than Hagen in the first two rounds at Whitfield Estates. At Hagen's home course, on greens Hagen knew well, over a round and a half, Hagen had twelve fewer putts than Bobby.

"I'd like to give something to the amateur for his efforts," Hagen announced at the dinner in their honor. "Here, kid. Something for your efforts." He held out a package that Bobby took and opened slowly. It was a pair of diamond and platinum cuff links. They had cost Hagen almost $900. Hagen could afford it after what he made with his share of gate receipts.

Keeler got Bobby on the phone that night. "How'd it go?" he asked.

"Lots of Hagen lessons," Bobby huffed. "His game was on; my game wasn't. He had lots of help from me, maybe even too much."

"You know why?" Keeler asked.

"No, do you have any ideas?"

"You know after last week with you being 8-down, I started to wonder. You lost one hole for every four-and-a-half holes you played, right?"

"That's about it."

"Well, let me say something here," Keeler's grin came right through the lines. "First, both you and Hagen love the game and are good at it." Keeler said. "Right?"

"Right," Bobby answered.

"And lots of people mill around both of you, but Hagen thrives on people while you like small doses of people, and if you have too many people around, they wear you down."

"That sounds right."

"Now, hear the rest." Keeler paused. "Two weeks before the

match, Hagen started working on the match while you were working to get to know his course."

Bobby grunted.

"He worked to get you off your thinking game. He knew that anything he could do to move you away from your game would help him." Keeler stopped and listened. Hearing nothing, he continued. "And, of course, you're used to a certain setup for tournaments. You have help to keep people away from you while you play." Keeler took a breath. "On top of that, you've been away from home for a while and your wife is pregnant." Keeler paused again. "These special events are not as important to you as they are to some, like Hagen." Keeler then nailed the real problem for Bobby. "Then, last but not least, there's what you discovered about match play. Did you play against old man par like you found out you needed to do?"

Keeler didn't want Bobby to feel bad, but he knew Bobby needed to hear what he had to say. "For golfers like you, real champions, the match starts on the first tee. But with golfers like Hagen, the match starts as soon as he can start it."

Keeler couldn't see Bobby, but if he had, he would have seen him sit straight up.

⚘

"You all packed yet?" Keeler teased Bobby.

"I'm taking a little detour before I get on the boat," Bobby responded. They were headed to England for the British Open.

Keeler waited.

"I'm going to go and visit J. Victor East up in Massachusetts. He works for Spalding, but he said he'd be glad to test all my shafts and make sure they match up for me."

"Well, I hope he's as good as they say he is," Keeler cautioned. "Playing around with your golf clubs before you play in two of your biggest events of the year is treading into some deep water." Keeler worked out the details. "I'll bring Wattsie up and we can meet on the dock."

Bobby's entry into the Spalding Company's plant was kept quiet.

"I've been working on shafts now for seven years," East told him. "Besides the load test we do on them, we also do a new test using a doctor's stethoscope which helps them line up even more."

Bobby nodded, watching as East took his favorite mashie out of his bag. Turning the club around, East sighted down the shaft as he would a gun.

"Pretty good. Who did it?" East asked.

"The old professional that I learned the game from, Stewart Maiden."

"One of the best I've seen in a while."

East thumbed through Bobby's clubs, taking out one or another and looking closely at them. He took out Bobby's famous putter, sighted down the shaft, and looked closely at the face. "See this?" East asked as he held the face of the club to show some sheen from a nearby light.

"What do you see?" Bobby asked.

"Your club has some high and low spots probably from the caddies rubbing the faces with emery paper to get it clean." Something struck East. "C'mere." He led Bobby to a table that looked like a small billiard table. "This is where I test putters for accuracy."

Bobby nodded.

"We brace your putter in the moving arms, put a ball in place where you would normally strike it, and watch to see how straight it comes off the club." East smiled. "Then, because the perfect spot is so hard to hit on a regular basis, we move the ball around a little to see how the different parts of the face make the ball react."

Bobby watched as East tested his favorite putter. Ball after ball was struck lightly in an imitation of a putter's swing as

Calamity Jane told its story.

Amazingly, one ball or another went off line from its target.

"Not surprising that you have a problem with your putting," East said. "Your face is worn in certain places causing high spots that cost you an extra stroke now and again."

"Should we just smooth the whole face down?" Bobby asked.

"You're going to cause the club to be a lot lighter. It would be easier for me if we make you another just like it."

"You can duplicate it?"

East nodded. "We'll make an exact mold of your club and go from there."

Bobby thought. "How about making two?"

East smiled. "Once we have the mold, we can make whatever you want."

Bobby thought very earnestly. "Make me six."

"Done."

♀

"I'm so excited," Watts said as he met Bobby on the ship. For both Watts and Keeler, it would be their first trip overseas. Bobby was the married man, with a new baby girl, but Keeler and Watts were bachelors looking forward to a good time. Keeler had just gotten his divorce.

The boat whistle went off signaling final boarding and Watts almost went crazy.

Originally, Bobby had hoped to play in the British Amateur, the Walker Cup matches, and then the British Open. But that would mean almost three months away from home. The more Bobby thought about it, the more inclined he was to skip the British Open and cut his visit to England short, leaving right after the Walker Cup matches.

"This is the one that matters," Keeler remarked at the start of the British Amateur. That got Bobby pumped.

"Don't I just know it!" Bobby agreed. "Until they change the format away from all these 18-hole matches, this one will always be the hardest one to win."

Bobby went out and won his first match, after he had received a bye, a free pass, for his first round. His second day found him winning his next two matches. Bobby was surprised; he didn't think he was on his game.

The next day, he won two more matches, including a tough one against Robert Harris who was the defending champion of the British Amateur. Bobby was riding a high, but he was still homesick..

"I'm thinking of going home right after the Walker Cup matches," Bobby finally told Keeler.

"If you're going, I'll go too," Keeler responded. "But don't go before you let these people see your real game. You'll feel as if you let them down if you do."

Bobby looked at him questioningly.

"The golf fans over here remember you from your last trip over. This is your opportunity to set the record straight," Keeler explained. "You'll be playing St. Andrews in the Walker Cup, a course they consider so sacred over here."

He had one more point to add. "I mean, you'll have a chance to make up for what you did back in 1921."

That night Bobby must have slept a troubled sleep because he woke up with a very stiff neck. Every time he tried to turn his head, a shooting pain ran down his side. He thought of pulling out of the tournament but remembered what others might think. So, he went on with his match.

By tee time, Bobby felt better, but not entirely better. His worst-yet round produced a licking by an unknown, Andrew Jamieson, by the score of 4-down with three to go. Jamieson had finished his 14 holes 2-under while Bobby had been 2-over par.

Bobby's caddy actually wept. "Tisn't fair when the best golfer doesn't win. Tisn't fair."

"It's okay," Bobby soothed. "It's just a game."

"Mr. Jones, if I go down to St. Anne's for the Open, can I have your bag?"

Bobby smiled at the young man. "I'd be proud to have you on my bag again."

Jess Sweetser from New York was the only American left in the tournament, which no American had won since Walter Travis and his Schenectady putter had done the job back in 1904. Bobby, Watts, Keeler, and all the American amateurs stayed around to support Sweetser in the finals as he became the first American-born player to win the British Amateur by beating Alfred Simpson 6 and 5.

"I'm going home right after the Walker Cup matches are over," Sweetser remarked to Bobby as they mingled after the awards ceremony.

"Well, damn, Jess. If you're going, I'm going," Bobby said, and he made his statement good by booking passage back to the states on the Aquitania, which was sailing right after the cup matches were over. "I just damn want to go home. I miss it."

But the following morning at breakfast, Bobby had changed his mind. "I guess I'll stay."

Keeler grinned. "I think you made the right decision."

Bobby couldn't have known it, but his decision would set into motion a series of events that would take the Dixie Boy Wonder to the top pinnacle of the game.

☙

Right away, Bobby felt better about his decision to stay. The whole town of St. Andrews seemed to want to make the Americans feel welcome by flying the American flag above their shops and houses.

The outcome of the Cup came down to the last match between George Von Elm of California and Major Hezlett, which was halved. The Americans retained the cup, with a 6-and-a-half to 5-and-a-half victory.

Doing his part, Bobby won his singles match over the great British amateur Cyril Tolley by a whopping 12 and 11 and teamed with his East Lake golfing buddy, Watts Gunn, to win their foursomes match 4 and 3. Bobby's game was coming around fast.

Watts had sunk a birdie putt from 120 feet from one side of a double-green onto another—one of the only courses to use double greens—and the roar from the appreciative crowd on the 13th hole was heard all the way inside the old Royal and Ancient clubhouse. After that, all Watts could talk about was the Old Course and its intricacies.

Keeler and Watts left for Paris to have a bit of fun. Bobby went up to St. Anne's to see the course and the kind of shots he was going to have to hit. He then traveled to the Sunningdale Golf Club in Surrey, near London, to qualify for the British Open.

In Surrey, Bobby visited the golf shop owned by Jack White, the professional at Sunningdale, who was much respected for the golf clubs he made, especially his persimmon drivers. There, Bobby fell in love with a beautiful Jack White driver.

When he held it in his hands, his breath was in short supply.

"I call it Jeanie Deans," White said as Bobby almost fondled the club.

Bobby looked at the club. "Jeanie Deans?"

"Jeanie Deans is an old name in Scotland for something heroic or beloved."

Bobby took the club with him, and the next day, a special journey began with Bobby, Jeanie Deans, and his now-famous putter, Calamity Jane.

The competitive course record at Sunningdale was 70. Out of the six holes Bobby played, he birdied the first three holes and parred the others. Then he parred the last three of the front nine and birdied the first two holes of the back nine.

A whisper ran through the crowd at the 12th hole that a 69 was posted by Archie Compston, the English professional.

Bobby birded one more of his last six holes, and he was in with a bogie-free, six-birdie round of 66. He had beaten the course record by a 4-stroke margin, and the crowd was lit.

Keeler was back, and just in time. The media gathered around Bobby after he left the scorer's table, treating him like the media back in the States—they crowded him.

"I'm going back to our room," Bobby finally tensed out, his nerves shot from the round.

Keeler nodded. "I'm really proud of you," Keeler said, and he turned to take care of his fellow press.

"They're calling your round spectacular," Keeler told him later that evening. "One of the best, if not the best, ever in qualifying history."

Bobby sat up. He had been lying in bed, resting.

"You had 33 front, 33 back, 33 putts, 33 other shots," Keeler grabbed a breath. "You had only three's and four's on your card, and…," Keeler laughed, "you had twelve pars, six birdies, and no bogies." Keeler's grin lit up the room. "They're saying this round was so perfectly balanced, it will go down as being the best of all time."

Bobby ran his hand through his hair. "None of that means that much to me. It surprises me what people look for in a round." Bobby looked out the window. "I just need some rest."

The following morning, Keeler said something to Bobby that lessened his tension. "The other reporters have a bet on that you won't break 70 today. They think you came onto your game a week early."

"I know people bet on me all the time," Bobby flared. "But I'll be damned if I'll let them think they know what I can and can't do."

"Damn," was all Keeler could say as they walked toward the scorer's table. "You threw them all off," Keeler snorted.

"A fine 68."

Bobby's 134 for the two rounds was a new scoring record for qualifying for a British Open. The bookmakers went crazy. Gambling was legal in England. Bobby was listed as the favorite at 6 to 1. Hagen was down the list at 12 to1.

As the British Open began, the odds on Bobby changed to 3 to 1.

CHAPTER
15

St. Anne's was not as hard a course as Sunningdale, but the fact that the British Open was being played there had its own impact on the course's playability.

Bobby had to fight for his first round score. It was made better by the one-putts he magically produced that finished off his last four holes. The twenty-foot putt he sank on the final green was a roll of beauty—up, over left, down, around, and in.

Never the less, Bobby's position was behind Hagen, who had the low on opening day—a 68.

Hagen was in rare Hagen form as he approached the group of foreign sports writers. "My kind of course, boys." Hagen grinned, and he worked on his hair.

Bobby's second round 72 took him past Hagen, who suddenly started struggling, and into a tie for the lead with "Wild Bill" Melhorn. The press started calling Bobby's play "spectacularly steady." Hagen noticeably winced when he was asked by sports writers why his play wasn't as steady as Bobby's.

On the morning of the final 36 holes, Bobby and Al Watrous met on the practice area. They were going to be playing together. They'd been friends for a while.

"How about coming across the street with me while I get something to eat?" Watrous asked Bobby as they finished their practice session.

Bobby instructed his caddy to meet him on the first tee in an hour, and Bobby and Watrous walked off the course through the gate and into the village.

Watrous obtained what he wanted at a little village store,

and he and Bobby started their walk back to the course. Watrous walked through the gate, and Bobby followed. But he was stopped.

"You need a ticket to get back onto the grounds, sir," a gate attendant said to Bobby.

Bobby's hand immediately went to a vacant spot over his heart where he normally wore his contestant's pin. "Ah, I'm in the tournament," Bobby said to the attendant.

The attendant shook his head. "You may be, sir, but you need either a contestant's badge or an entry ticket."

Bobby looked at Watrous who stood there, stunned. "That's Bobby Jones," he said. "He's playing with me in the group at ten o'clock."

The attendant looked at Watrous's badge but repeated his mantra. "That may be, sir, but the gentleman needs either a contestant's badge or an entry ticket to get past the gate."

"Uh, how much is a ticket?" Bobby inquired, holding out his hand with a bunch of British coins in it.

"This'll do," the man said, taking a few coins and giving Bobby a ticket.

In the third round, Bobby's morning 73 took him up to 2nd place behind Watrous who had shot a blistering 69 and was two strokes in front of Bobby. Hagen and George Von Elm were a few strokes behind the two leaders.

Going back out for the afternoon round, Bobby addressed Watrous. "The winner and runner-up are in our group. I'm sure of it. But, we can't afford to play match play and let others pass us." Bobby looked out on the course. "It's going to be an hour or more after we finish before Hagen finishes." Hagen was playing in a later group. "That should make our wait time more interesting."

The pressure began to mount as they turned onto the back nine because both Watrous and Bobby had scored even par 36's on the front nine. Watrous's two-stroke lead was intact.

When they got to the 13th hole, Watrous showed the strain.

He three-putted, reducing his lead to one stroke. He three-putted the 15th hole and he and Bobby were even. On the 17th hole, Bobby hooked his drive into a long sand bunker, 190 yards from the hole, while Watrous was down the middle and onto the green in two.

Despite the blind shot due to high grass and a hill, Bobby nipped his mid-iron shot perfectly, sending the ball onto the green six feet from the flag.

Watrous, stung by Bobby's shot, promptly three-putted, giving up the lead.

After Watrous three-putted the 18th hole, Bobby had the lead by two. He had finished 4,3,4,4,4, perfect par. It was Bobby's strongest finish in a medal play event.

Watrous grabbed Bobby around the shoulders, and the two men walked like brothers off the last green.

Now they had to wait for Hagen to finish.

Keeler was already on top of that. "I heard that Hagen's thrown his chance away out at the 14th hole," he anxiously reported.

But Keeler was wrong. The news was that Hagen still had a chance if he were to eagle the last hole. Hagen, strutting, measured off his approach shot to the hole.

"Take the flag away," Hagen shouted at his caddy. He had his mashie iron in hand and was attempting to hole a 160-yard shot which would tie Bobby for the lead.

The crowd watched Hagen's perfectly-struck shot impact just beside the hole and bounce over the back of the green.

"Congratulations!" Watrous quickly shook Bobby's hand.

Keeler slid next to Bobby. "You did it. You're the only American amateur to win the oldest golf tournament in the world." With that, Bobby's shoulders noticeably dropped. He could now relax. Or so he thought.

"I want to thank the Royal and Ancient, the St. Anne's course, and everyone who has attended this Open tournament," Bobby said as he accepted his trophy. "I also want to congratulate Al for such a fine effort and thank him for being my playing partner over the last two rounds."

Bobby had always thought that Adair would be around to see him challenge for an Open, and that thought prevented him from saying more.

News got around that Bobby had to pay to get back into the tournament to win it.

"Hagen would never do that," one sports writer wrote. "His cap doesn't fit his head now."

Another sports writer tied Bobby's penalty stroke from the previous year's National Open with his payment of an entry fee for this British Open. "A golf champion worth cheering for," he wrote.

Bobby didn't come out of his cabin for three days. He was totally spent. He was on the Aquitania headed for New York where he would take a train to Columbus, Ohio, for play in the National Open. What Bobby would have preferred would have been to go home to East Lake, but that wasn't possible for him.

"Something special is being lined up for you in New York," Keeler said to Bobby as they crossed the four-and-a-half day halfway point of their journey back to the States.

"Like what?" Bobby responded, still exhausted.

"Like a ticker tape parade."

"We don't have any extra time to spend in New York." Then Bobby realized what Keeler had said. "A ticker tape parade for me, a golfer?" Bobby shook his head. "I thought that those things were just for Army generals or admirals or explorers."

"Hagen is going to be just so pissed." Keeler smiled and rubbed his hands together. "I wish I could be there when he hears about it."

Bobby started laughing.

Keeler was keeping a secret from Bobby. Bobby's wife, Mary, and his parents were coming to New York to meet Bobby before they all headed to the National Open together.

"There's something, a thought if you will, that I would like to express to you," Keeler began.

Bobby sat up on his bed. "Why so serious?"

Keeler looked at his shoes for a second. "You know how, at times, I seem to see things?"

Bobby broke into a full but twisted, tired smile. "What was it that we called it?"

Keeler smiled. "My historical point of view?"

"Well?" Bobby asked, as Keeler sat there quietly.

"I'm not sure that what I'm about to say is going to be very well received by you."

Bobby frowned. "After all this time together, you don't know me?"

"Oh, I know you alright," Keeler grinned. "That's why what I'm about to say worries me."

Bobby nodded slowly.

"I know you're thinking of retiring, which you have yet to say to me openly."

Bobby acknowledged it. "I am," he said. "With real good reason." Bobby looked sheepishly at Keeler. "What more can I do to have a better year? Besides, my family is worried about how long it takes me to recuperate from tournaments and trips." Just then, a smile crossed his face.

"Were you just now thinking of East Lake?"

Bobby nodded and laughed. "I'm not surprised that you come close to reading my mind."

Keeler chuckled. "I'm a newspaper snoop, for Christ's sake. I'm trained to look into what people say to get at what they mean. And you are my prime target."

"And you're good at it."

"Thanks." Keeler grinned. "Coming from the best golfer and gentleman on the face of the earth, that means an awful lot to me."

Bobby looked at him. "So, back to the beginning. What's so serious?"

Keeler looked right at Bobby. "Our home is Atlanta, the capital of Georgia, the heart of the South."

Bobby nodded.

"Well, since the Civil War, which was about sixty years ago, who from the South could really be called a national hero?"

Bobby scrunched his shoulders up. "How about George Adair?"

Keeler shook his head. "Not everyone knows of Mr. Adair. Unless I miss my guess, and even you said my views about things like this are pretty accurate, you're about to get elevated to the first true hero to come out of the South since the war."

Bobby's face glazed over. "You really mean that, don't you?"

Keeler nodded. "I'm very serious about this. With what you have done now, on top of what you've already done, you're about to be treated as the first true hero of the South since Reconstruction."

Bobby sat there in shock. "All for hitting a little white ball around?" Bobby paused and it took Keeler to add the obvious part.

"Better than anyone else." Keeler sat there in silence.

Four hours out at sea from New York, another ship met Bobby's and transferred fifty newsmen who were anxious to get the whole story. Keeler took charge.

When their ship docked, Bobby and Keeler were greeted by representatives of the mayor of New York. They were driven to City Hall where they met Bobby's wife, his parents, and, surprisingly, Bobby's namesake grandfather, as well as a hundred or so of Atlanta's elite citizens, including the Mayor of Atlanta and the publishers of Atlanta's three largest newspapers, the Journal, the Constitution, and the Georgian.

"You checking up on me?" Keeler said to his editor.

"Just came up to congratulate you two. You have no idea how many papers your stories about Bobby and Gunn are selling for us."

"Oh, yes I do." Keeler grinned, letting his eyes travel to his old boss from the Atlanta Georgian.

Before Bobby knew it, he was the subject of Mayor Jimmie Walker's welcoming speech, which included a comment about Bobby's famous birthday date, St. Patrick's Day, and a trip down Broadway where all kinds of confetti rained down upon them. Bobby had never seen anything like this in his entire life.

Bobby watched as his grandfather was interviewed at the big dinner that night.

"I just happened to be here on business," Bobby's grandfather responded.

♣

"I hate to say goodbye to you again." Bobby and Mary faced a very tearful good-bye. Mary was pregnant with their second child.

"You come home safe, you hear?" Mary said kissing Bobby on the side of the cheek. "We all miss you."

"I'm proud of you and so is all of Atlanta," Big Bob said to Bobby. "Your mother and I are coming along with you to Columbus, if it won't jinx you."

Bobby had tears in his eyes. He truly wanted to be going home rather than on to Columbus.

The Scioto golf course in Columbus, Ohio, was waiting for its first real test by a national tournament. Designed and built by leading architect Donald Ross in 1916, the course had a healthy growth of rough. The USGA set up a new three-day tournament format with 18 holes the first two days and 36 the final day. Open Saturday had been created, a huge, exciting day of golf that decided it—winner take all.

Again, there was a thirty-six hole cut.

"Take it easy and do as little as you have to," Keeler stressed to Bobby. Bobby had still not recovered fully from his trip to Britain.

Bobby loved being back on a parkland Donald Ross course. It felt comfortable to him. He didn't have to adjust to bunkers in unusual places and fairways and greens that were only watered by God on the links courses in Britain.

Bobby's first round of 70 was two under par. That put him in 2nd place in the field behind "Wild Bill" Melhorn who was on another hot streak with a 68.

"I'm pulling out. I'm plum worn out," Watts said after he had just managed a first round at 84. "I don't know how you do it."

Right now, Bobby was wondering that about himself, too.

"Early to bed?" Keeler asked. He and Bobby had gotten into the habit of ordering room service to avoid the interruptions, and even though Bobby's parents were there, Bobby wanted to keep his winning formula with Keeler. Big Bob was all for it.

Keeler didn't talk about the possibility of Bobby winning the National Open, becoming the first golfer to win both Opens in the same year. He felt that it would just cause Bobby added pressure. Besides, Keeler thought, Bobby was most likely thinking about that on his own.

"Have you heard what the calcutta is?" Bobby surprised Keeler as they ate.

Keeler put his napkin down. "I heard a little bit about it, but not the whole story."

"What did you hear?"

"The pot is around $150,000."

Bobby's eyes grew and he looked at Keeler, questioning.

Keeler nodded and decided to tell Bobby the rest. "I'm told that you were sold for a little over $35,000."

Bobby threw down his napkin. "If those things keep growing, golfers are going to need bodyguards!"

Keeler smiled. "I thought that's what Ridley was doing for

you." Chick Ridley was a member of the East Lake Sunday group. He was an excellent golfer in his own right, but his job on the road with Bobby was to guard and protect him. Keeler and Bobby's caddy took turns walking quietly alongside Bobby to keep people away as well.

Bobby's second round was a horrible 79. Keeler was not surprised. "Why can't I play this damn game?" Bobby huffed as soon as he saw Keeler standing off the 18th green.

"You're still tired from the trip abroad," Keeler surmised. "I thought that a round like this was coming for you."

Bobby's eyes showed rings around them. They seemed to be sunken in his head.

"Go to bed and get as much rest as you can."

Keeler spoke to the other newsmen and gave them the full story of Bobby's round, which included another penalty that he had called on himself on the 15th green. It happened when Bobby lifted his putter while getting ready to stroke his ball. The wind blew the now-unprotected ball a full inch. Bobby again had to argue with others who said that his ball hadn't moved.

The headlines in the papers carried what most people felt: "Jones Shoots 79 and Is Out."

"Do you think he's thinking of retiring because of his nerves?" one reporter asked a shocked Keeler.

Rather than deny the story, Keeler chose to take the higher ground. "If he would retire, it would simply be to go back to playing golf for fun with his group of friends at East Lake."

After Bobby's horrendous second round score, he found himself six strokes behind the lead set by Melhorn. Between Bobby and Melhorn were four other golfers, including Leo Diegel and Joe Turnesa of the famous golfing Turnesa family. The weather was also a big factor; it had been rainy and windy on both previous days.

Bobby awoke Saturday morning with a horrendously sick feeling in his stomach.

"Ask someone in the club where the nearest doctor is," Bobby told Keeler as he held his stomach.

Sensing the worst, Keeler almost ran to the front desk and had them call a local physician who agreed to see Bobby immediately. The physician prescribed paregoric for Bobby's troubled stomach. This worried everyone, remembering Bobby's troubles with his stomach as a youth.

Bobby teed off just twenty minutes behind Turnesa and an hour before Melhorn. He knew his work was cut out for him. He had six strokes to make up on the leader and he had almost no strength left in his system.

The USGA had forecaddies out to make sure a player's balls, especially Bobby's, remained undisturbed.

In the third round, Bobby shot a 71 and got five strokes back from Melhorn who scored a 76 and one stroke from Turnesa who scored a 72.

Turnesa now had the lead at 217, while Melhorn was at 219. Bobby followed at 220.

It was quiet at lunch, but Bobby couldn't eat at all. It seemed as though everyone was feeling the tension. It was very clear that Bobby was near the point of exhaustion.

On the front nine of the last round, Turnesa got a stroke back from Bobby while Melhorn was further back and reported to be struggling. That left Bobby four strokes behind the lead with nine holes to go.

Bobby parred the 10th; Turnesa parred the 11th. The 12th was a long 600-yard par-five. Turnesa bogied it and Bobby birdied it when it was his turn to play. Bobby was now two strokes down and six holes to go.

At the 13th par-four hole, Bobby parred. Turnesa had bogied it. At the 14th hole, Bobby parred. Turnesa had bogied that hole too. At the 17th hole, Bobby parred. The 17th had been another bogie for Turnesa. Bobby was now one stroke ahead going to the 18th hole, a par-five, when he heard that Turnesa had birdied that hole just a few minutes before. Bobby would have to match Turnesa's birdie to keep his lead.

Bobby's drive on the par-five, 480-yard hole was marked off at 310 yards, leaving him a mashie iron into the green that he left twenty feet past the flag.

Bobby's last putt to win the 1926 Open was six inches from the cup. He made it.

When Bobby returned home, there were boxes and boxes of gifts waiting for him. He received four lifetime memberships to courses and another matching set of shotguns and several watches.

"Those memberships are something else," Big Bob said as he looked at the pile of gifts. "First time I have ever seen anyone mount a golf club membership on a card and put a gold base on it."

"I think I know what would keep you at home more." Keeler got Bobby's attention. "How about if we do your biography?"

"I'm only twenty-four years old."

"It's not how old you are that counts. It's what you've done and how many people want to read about you. Chick Evans did his biography six years ago. He was only twenty-six and the book sold real well, especially around Chicago."

"I can't imagine anyone wanting to read my biography."

"You've got to be kidding."

"I'm not, but if you think it will keep me home, I'll do it," Bobby sighed. "I wasn't even home for my own damn anniversary."

They got started on the book just a few weeks later. Keeler thought he was going to have to do most of the work, but Bobby loved being at home writing. It was the first chance he had to use his education from the Georgia Institute of Technology and Harvard.

"I know what I'm going to do," Bobby said at one of their editing sessions. "I'm going to Emory to become a lawyer, just like my dad."

Keeler smiled. "I think I could have told you that."

Bobby smiled. "Well, how come you didn't tell me then? Would have saved me some time."

Bobby sat back. "I'm going to take a trip with a bunch of the boys in a couple of weeks to a town called Highlands in North Carolina where they just finished a golf course." Bobby's breath came out in a rush. "I want to get ready for the Amateur and I want to do a good job defending my title."

Those were the words Keeler had been waiting to hear. Golf wasn't over for Bobby.

"And I have news for you as well," Keeler said. "I'm going to follow you back into marriage."

Bobby gave him his full attention. "I'm glad for you."

Then Bobby paused and slowly looked at Keeler. "I think I have a title for the book." Bobby watched Keeler's face light up. "How about, 'Down the Fairway'?"

"The ball isn't going where I want it to," Bobby complained to Stewart Maiden.

"Are ye shuir yer nae juist playin up tae me. A mean for Christ's sake, ye juist wan the Open."

"C'mon," Bobby gruffed, wanting to prove his point. They walked out to the practice area. Bobby hit one shot and Maiden grunted. Bobby hit another shot and Maiden grunted again.

"Here, muive this back," Maiden instructed with the handle end of an iron on the tip of Bobby's right foot.

Bobby moved to hit the shot and Maiden grunted. "Muive this." Maiden whacked the back of Bobby's left shoe to move it forward. Then he made Bobby turn his shoulders slightly to the right.

"Nou," Maiden mumbled.

"Now what?" Bobby asked.

"Hat 'ell oot of it."

Bobby settled in and focused his aim and hit the ball as hard as he could. The ball landed right on top of his target. Bobby smiled.

"Wish you'd been with me at Scioto," Bobby chuckled.

"Wha for? Ye wan it." After Bobby hit a few more, they walked back to Maiden's shop.

"The whole world wants me to do an interview with you," Keeler told Bobby. "Especially the Associated Press."

"Would that stop all the fan mail and requests that take up so much of my time?"

Keeler waved his head. "Not especially. But it would be a more formal way for people to get to know you rather than through all the bits and pieces I've been writing."

"How do we do an interview?" Bobby asked.

Keeler smiled and made himself comfortable. "Simple. In your own words tell me how you got started in golf."

"Luck," Bobby answered quickly and solidly. "The biggest piece of golfing luck I ever got was when the Atlanta Athletic Club got Stewart Maiden for its professional. I was five years old then and living opposite the gate of the East Lake golf course. The next year, my dad moved our family into a little cottage on the club property, alongside what is now the first fairway. I took up golf with a sawed-off cleek that one of the members had given to me.

"Stewart never gave me any formal lessons as such. I just followed him around the course and watched him play. I wanted to play golf and he was the best player at the course. I imitated his style like a monkey, I suppose. The luck was in the fact that Stewart had the finest and soundest swing I have ever seen. Very orthodox, so to speak."

"What do you mean by orthodox?"

"I should say it was a style which would suit fundamentally any player unless he was anatomically eccentric. There is nothing unusual or odd about Stewart's methods."

Keeler's questions took Bobby through his history in the game, his favorite and worst memories, how he played, even down to his feet being so close to each other, which was not the popular practice at that time. They also talked about some of the special shots he used to win tournaments.

The interview was almost finished when Keeler broached the subject of Bobby's penalty strokes that may have cost him a few tournaments.

Bobby held his hand up to signal Keeler to stop. "There is only one way to play the game," he said.

Keeler's two-column, twenty-inch story ran in hundreds of American newspapers. Keeler for his part in it was awarded an honorary membership in the Associated Press and given another watch.

"If I get one more watch, I'm going to go into the jewelry business," Keeler laughed.

Bobby had something else on his mind. "I've registered at Emory. I'm hoping to complete my law degree in two years."

"No more selling real estate?"

Bobby shook his head. "Not if I can help it. I don't think that I'm cut out for sales."

Keeler knew that with the impending birth of Bobby's next child, Bobby was working hard to bring in income to support his family. Toward that end, Bobby had started talking to some syndicates about doing a daily golf column.

On the East coast train ride to Springfield, New Jersey, to play in the National Amateur at Baltusrol, Bobby and Keeler continued their conversation about Bobby's upcoming book.

"That part of your story about predestination just may shake a few people up."

Bobby looked out the window. "Well, then, I won't feel alone. It's one of the only parts of the game that I cannot really put my finger on. And if you think it'll bother some others, imagine what those thoughts are doing to me. I want to lead my own life, not a life that someone or something is picking out for me."

"And all the time I was thinking that it was plain luck on your side."

Bobby's thoughts drifted. "I just have had so many shots the past two tournaments that you could say were almost given to me by someone or something." Bobby's eyes hadn't moved from the passing scenery even though he didn't see it. "If I didn't know better, I'd swear . . . ." Bobby stopped short.

"You gonna finish that thought?" Keeler nudged.

Bobby quietly shook his head. "Not for now, because I'm fairly sure I couldn't." His eyes traveled to his long-time friend. "I've reasoned out a lot of the mechanical side of this great game and some of the psychological side, but there are a lot of things that have happened over the course of my time in tournament golf that make me wonder who all has a hand in my future."

Keeler looked off. "You know that they've given your last three big wins a name, don't you?"

"You mean that Triple Crown thing?"

Keeler nodded. "People seem to think that having the two Open crowns won by an American amateur has a very special meaning. I can't say that I disagree with that thought."

"I just hope that no matter what some of these things mean, I can defend my amateur crown."

"If you win this one for three in a row, a lot of sports writers are going to go crazy thinking up names for your achievements," Keeler smiled.

"Including or not including the sports writer with the Journal?"

"Oh, him too." Keeler grinned.

The odds on Bobby winning the 1926 National Amateur were phenomenal. It was truly Bobby against the field as far as the sports writers were concerned. Watts Gunn was again with Bobby and Keeler. The threesome got themselves a beautiful suite for the week.

Bobby's father and mother also came along. They wanted to make sure Bobby was being taken care of. They didn't like what the tournaments were doing to his health.

For qualifying, Bobby shot a one over par for the two trips around Baltusrol and won the medal, just missing a record score. Some began calling him a golfing machine. In the calcutta that always followed the qualifying, Bobby was sold for almost half the price of the pool. It was obvious that the gamblers thought the only sure thing was Bobby.

The Associated Press even came out with an amateur golf ranking system. Bobby was number one followed by Jess Sweetser, who was very ill in a sanitarium with tuberculosis, and George Von Elm, Francis Ouimet, Jesse Guilford, and Chick Evans.

The USGA had changed the format of the tournament again. It was now scheduled as two eighteen-hole matches, followed by three matches of 36 holes.

The first match pitted Bobby against a young Dicky Jones who fought Bobby down to the 17th hole, where Bobby held a one-hole lead. Then Dicky birdied the long par-five 18th hole, forcing Bobby to do the same to win the match.

That afternoon, Bobby won his second eighteen-hole match by the score of 4 and 3.

Then it was on to the thirty-six hole affairs, which brought with it competition against better players. Chick Evans was first.

Anyone with an interest and a memory knew that years before Evans had beaten Bobby in their last meeting at the Western Amateur. For followers of the sport, most thought that their rematch could easily be the highlight match of the tournament.

By the second round of their match, both players looked as if they had been through a battle. Whenever Bobby birdied and parred, Evans followed suit. Bobby could get no space between him and his opponent.

They arrived at the 28th tee of the round and suddenly Bobby got a second wind. Evans visually slipped away, and Bobby won the match 3 and 2. His opponent the next day would be Francis Ouimet, his old friend.

"You okay with who you're playing tomorrow?" Keeler asked Bobby at dinner.

Bobby's crooked smile showed that he was okay with the draw.

"Can I offer you a thought?" Keeler pursued. "Think of it as only a game."

Bobby laughed. Keeler had made a good point.

A lot of people had remembered Bobby's drubbing of Ouimet a few years back. They wondered if vengeance might be a factor. Ouimet was playing great golf.

But Bobby took control of the match right from the start by finishing the first nine holes with three birdies and parring the rest. He never looked better as he won, walking away from Ouimet 6-up and five to play.

Bobby's opponent in the finals was a man he had beaten twice before, George Von Elm. Everyone said Bobby had Von Elm's number because Bobby's wins over the man had been by 9-8 and 7-6.

In one of the hardest and closest matches of the tournament, Von Elm pulled off what a lot of other golfers could not. Over 35 holes, Bobby was only one over par but he lost to a strong Von Elm who had come into his game by the score of 2-up and one to go.

Win or not, the gifts kept coming.

Bobby's second child was not far from arriving when the

Atlanta Athletic Club announced that it wanted to do something special for Bobby in honor of what he had done for East Lake, Atlanta, the State of Georgia, and the South.

Keeler served as Master of Ceremonies. He held fort by telling Bobby-stories that he knew had not been written. Then he motioned for Bobby to join him on the stage.

"C'mon up here, Mr. Triple Crown," Keeler motioned to Bobby.

Bobby almost stumbled as he climbed up onto the temporary stage.

"We've been traveling together a long time," Keeler grinned at Bobby. "I tell people that Bobby and I spend more time together than we do with our wives."

Bobby, loosening up, pointed his finger at Keeler. "He snores. A lot." The audience howled.

Keeler addressed his friend. "But believe me when I say that I have no idea what it is that the Atlanta Athletic Club has for you in this little box." He gave the little square box to Bobby Jones who faced the audience and bowed just slightly to everyone.

"You can open it and share it with us, if you like." Keeler hinted.

Bobby opened the top of the box with his right hand. He drew out a little wooden house with a note and a check stuck inside the door of the house. Keeler shrugged his shoulders to tell Bobby he truly had no idea what the gift was.

Bobby took out the note and the check and read the note.

"We of the Atlanta Athletic Club would like to tell you how much we have appreciated what you have done for our city and our club by giving you this physical tribute of our appreciation." The eleven names of the board members followed.

Bobby looked at the check. It was for $50,000. This put him into a state of shock. Evidently, someone knew that Bobby had been looking at a house for almost precisely that amount.

The applause of appreciation that followed Bobby's recognition of the gift only added to the emotional feelings that were welling up inside of him.

Bobby looked out at the audience. "I am truly overwhelmed." Bobby reached into his back pocket, grabbed his handkerchief, blew his nose, and slightly wiped his eyes. "I never expected or thought that something like this was even possible." Bobby shook his head. "You all and golf have been so kind to me in giving me the friends that I have and wholeheartedly appreciate." He let out a big breath. "I cannot believe that I have done anything that would warrant this." With that, the whole audience stood and applauded.

Later that evening, Bobby asked Keeler what he knew about the gift.

"Nary a thing," Keeler replied. "About two weeks ago, though, the president of your club called me and asked me what most of all you were worried about."

Bobby looked at him.

"I told him that you wanted to have a place of your own for your family and that you felt that it was time for you to make your own way in the world, especially with your new child coming." Keeler smiled. "I might even have told him about the place that you were looking at."

A few weeks later, Bobby was playing golf with Stewart Maiden when the topic of Bobby's amateur status came up.

"Sae, haes the USGA said onything tae ye aboot hiving ony problem wi gettin thee hoose as a giftie?"

Bobby was silent for a long minute. "Not as yet. I'm not sure they are even aware of it, though news like that seems to travel quickly at times."

To be on the safe side, Bobby wrote a letter to the USGA, inquiring as to whether they knew of his gift of the house on Tuxedo Road. He asked if they had any problem with it under the rules of amateur status.

Two days later, Bobby got a letter back from the President of the USGA. Yes, they knew about the gift and because of the size of it, they were probably going to have a problem approving it.

Bobby wasted no time. He went to see Big Bob. "I'm not sure what the USGA may do about my getting the house as a gift, but in a nicely informal way, they led me to believe that my receiving the house may affect my amateur standing."

Big Bob sat back in his chair. "Is there any dollar amount that they deem to be too much?"

Bobby shook his head. "Not that I'm aware of. But they've been known to just take someone's amateur status away if they feel that it's best for the game." Bobby hung his head. He was worried. "Remember what they did to Ouimet and Travis?"

"We could try to fight it if they have no stated dollar amount."

Bobby shook his head. "That sounds to me like we'd be going against the very organization that I want to support."

"Disagreements are a part of life, even for people who live together."

Bobby nodded. "I wonder if I should just apply for a mortgage."

That afternoon, the matter was taken out of his hands. Bobby's grandfather, Robert Tyre Jones, Sr., arrived for a visit on his way back from business deals in Jacksonville for his big mill back in Canton.

The three Jones men were suddenly under one roof, and the topic of discussion turned to Bobby's problem.

"So, the only problem then is money?" Robert Tyre Jones, Sr., asked, after he heard the account from the other two Jones men.

Big Bob nodded. "Bobby wants to make his own way."

Robert Tyre Jones, Sr., smiled. "I should hope that we all do. It's the righteous thing to do." He looked intently at Bobby. "I've told your father many times that life is about work, not play. Every extra day that you can give to our Lord in honest work is an extra day that your soul will spend in heaven."

Bobby had heard it before.

"But to make amends in our family for how hard I've pushed my ideas at my son, I am willing to do something different."

Both Big Bob and Bobby looked questioningly at the grandfather. "I am willing to loan my grandson the $50,000 that he so suddenly needs, but with one proviso."

They all waited.

"If my grandson will sign a loan agreement with me and pay me back at the rate of $1.00 per year, I will bring forth the $50,000."

Bobby was shocked, and he was even more shocked when his father began crying. The Jones women all rushed into the room to see what the ruckus was about.

The following day Bobby wrote a letter to the USGA. He told them he would be returning the money to the Atlanta Athletic Club and to please consider the matter closed.

Bobby's decision echoed through the halls of the USGA. To them, it was further proof that Bobby was truly a great amateur.

Newspapers all over the world told the story of the great amateur who turned down a large sum of money to keep his simon-pure amateur status. Bobby was elevated even further in the minds of those who considered themselves protectors of the game of golf.

Because the National Open was going back to Oakmont, the site of Bobby's National Amateur win two years before, a lot of people believed Bobby was going to just walk away from the field. But it was not to be.

Bobby had just finished his first year at Emory. The finals had been very rigorous and had taken a lot out of him, besides severely limiting his practice time.

So, Bobby's rounds of 76, 77, 79, and 77 brought him in at 309 and he wound up in eleventh place.

CHAPTER
16

"So, why the change of heart?" Keeler wanted to know. Bobby had decided not to go to England to defend his British Open crown and then he had changed his mind.

"Oh, a bunch of reasons." Bobby answered. "Stewart gave me an impassioned plea, and he was right. It's important that I should defend my win last year at Lytham and it's a chance for me to show them that the young man who quit the last time he was at St. Andrews is apologetic for that." Bobby grimaced at the uncomfortable memory. "Plus, Dad wants to go and see the golf villages over here just like Mr. Adair did so many years ago."

Bobby continued thoughtfully. "And, I have a very special debt to pay to someone and I thought that this would be the best time to do it because I may never be back."

Keeler looked at him. "You're just going to leave me hanging with that?"

Bobby smiled. "It's special, very special, and I don't want to spoil the surprise. I know what your big newspaper mouth would let out." Bobby grinned. "You'll find out before anyone else does. It's only about eight days from now."

Keeler's shoulders drooped. "I can't believe you'd keep something from me."

"You're a big guy," Bobby teased. "You can handle the wait time."

In defending his British Open title in 1927, Bobby had a big task in front of him—for no one had successfully defended a British Open crown in over twenty years.

Bobby qualified easily after his second round of 71, and he was in the tournament. He opened his defense with a 68, the first below-70 score he had ever had in twelve rounds of the British Open. He had only twenty-eight putts in the first round and didn't miss a putt less than twelve feet. On the long 5th green, which also served as the 13th green, Bobby sank a putt of 120 feet.

Bobby's second round was a hard-fought 72, and his third round held his tournament high of thirty-six putts. Still, he was starting to leave everyone else behind.

His final round left him worn out. He was out in front by six strokes and past looking back at the field.

It was the first time in history that a golfer had won the Open of either country with an under-par figure. From the 1st to the 72nd hole, Bobby had been totally in charge. It was said to be the finest performance ever by a golfer in a country's Open championship. The newspapers trumpeted that fact to a waiting world.

Stewart Maiden, who had accompanied Bobby on this trip, and Big Bob stood on the 18th green as the crowd came and swept Bobby away on its shoulders. All they could see of Bobby was Calamity Jane held high up in the air. Twenty thousand people had swarmed over the course and onto the green. Sounds of "good boy Bobby" and "Bonnie Bobby" reverberated through the crowd.

Big Bob was worried for his son, but there was nothing he could do except wait in his hotel room for the crowd to return Bobby to him.

Finally, Bobby limped into his hotel room to get ready to accept the old Claret Jug, the trophy of the British Open. His shirt clung to his body and his hands worked nervously to get the knot in the tie undone.

"Here, let me." Keeler tried to undo the knot and, failing that, took out his penknife and cut it free. "There."

Bobby fell into a corner chair, exhausted.

Keeler handed Bobby a glass so he could pour him a drink, but his hand shook so badly, Keeler took the glass out of his hand. When he returned the glass to Bobby, filled, Bobby struggled with one hand to bring it to his mouth. He had to accomplish it using two hands.

The other men in the room disregarded what Bobby was going through; they just couldn't accept what they were seeing.

"Ah score o 285 is wunnerfu, lad," Maiden glowed. "Loest score evir in aither open."

"I wouldn't have believed that scene if I hadn't seen it," Big Bob added.

"Hit wis ah great ettle," Jack McIntyre, Bobby's caddy chimed in.

The call came for Bobby to come down to the 18th green to accept the Claret Jug.

"Knaw wha yer gaun tae say, laddie?" Maiden questioned.

"As little and as quickly as possible."

Maiden smiled. "Ye can dae a lot wi few words efter sic a grand victory." Maiden chuckled. "Yer gemme did a lot of thee communicatin."

Bobby smiled back at his golf teacher. "Thanks, Stewart."

"Ma pleisur, Robin." Maiden hadn't called him that in years.

Bobby stood in the middle of the green with the officials of the Royal and Ancient. He actually looked small compared to some of the larger, older men who stood around him. Nonetheless, it was his aura that was the center of attention.

Bobby shyly smiled as the compliments to both him and his game were made. The applause seemed to resonate across the course and off the old buildings that surrounded them at golf's home. The sound of the sea and the sea birds came into play when the excited crowd settled down to listen.

It was Bobby's turn to speak. "I had rather win a championship at St. Andrews than anything else that could happen to me. You have done so many things for me that I am embarrassed to ask one more, but I will. I want this wonderful old club to accept the custody of the cup for the coming year."

The roar of the appreciative crowd could be heard for miles.

"Yer sin's som special kynd of mon," Maiden told Big Bob as they stood off to the side.

Big Bob only nodded. He was working on controlling his emotions.

Bobby didn't venture out from his room for several days. He was so tired and he was deathly afraid of getting swarmed over again by his adoring fans.

"Can you tell me what the secret is now?" Keeler begged.

Bobby shook his head. "No, but it won't be long now before you see it." He added, "Do me a favor and find out how we get to Carnoustie from here."

That got Keeler's attention. "That's not on our route home."

"Maybe not ours, but it's someone else's route home."

Keeler crinkled his eyebrows and headed out to get the information.

Their party left the following morning.

"Wha ship are we gaun back on?" Maiden asked Bobby.

"I think we're going back on the Transylvania." Bobby smiled. "But that's not for a few days yet."

"Och?" Maiden quizzed.

"We have one more stop to make over here."

A taxi pulled up and loaded their bags. It headed away from the train station. Maiden brightened up. He sensed where they were headed.

"Are we gaun tae thee ferry ower thee Tay?" Maiden asked.

"Yes, we are, Stewart," Bobby grinned.

"The ferry haeds tae my auld toun."

"Yes, it does." Bobby's grin grew even wider.

"We're gaun tae Carnoustie than?"

Bobby nodded.

"To play the course?" Keeler asked.

"Probably, unless it rains or something."

Maiden sat glued to the window. Finally getting bold, he asked. "Sae, we're gaun tae stop aff in Carnoustie?"

Bobby's grin broke out again. "I've heard so much about that village for so many years, I just had to see it. I might never come over again."

Maiden began to realize what this was all about. "Yer doin this for me?"

"Yes, but I figure we're all going to get something out of this." Maiden's face seemed to take on a glaze.

"Ye knaw, A din think A wad iver be back." Maiden had a hard time talking. "A niver did."

On the ferry going across the Tay, a piper in full battle-dress played. It was like a welcome-home salute for the old Scot.

The ferry station at the foot of the village was exactly the same as when Maiden had left it twenty-six years before. "Stewart, yer back?" came the call from the old stationmaster.

"Aye Wullie, but only tae leuk aroond."

"Yer mither is gaun tae be so gled tae see ye."

"And A her." Bobby had learned that Maiden's mother was going on eighty-one and wanted to see her son before she passed on.

Two open cars sent by the provost of Carnoustie greeted them. The cars took them to city hall for a presentation of a key to the city and a luncheon. Then, it was off to the golf course for an exhibition by the newly crowned defending British Open champion. Six thousand local citizens followed them step-by-step across the village. Keeler's headline which ran a few days later read: **The Pied Piper of Golf.**

Bobby played with three local amateurs. Maiden was in a group right behind.

Stopping at his ball on the 2nd hole, Bobby looked at his approach shot and motioned for Stewart to come to his side. He was conferring with his great teacher.

On the 3rd hole, Bobby did it again. He conferred with his teacher before proceeding to hit his shot.

Keeler could stand it no more. "Is this course extra hard or are you just tired?"

Bobby laughed. "I want these people to realize how important Stewart has been to me and my golf. There's no way I can show them history, but I can do this for him."

As the round wore on, Bobby used Maiden less and less. The need for the lesson was over.

In August, Bobby's book, "Down the Fairway," was published to glowing reviews. The foreword was by Grantland Rice, the leading sports writer of the time. Most reviews said it was the finest piece of golf literature ever written. None of the reviewers noticed Bobby's remarks about predestination.

Also in August, Bobby, Keeler, Big Bob, and Watts Gunn traveled to Minneapolis for the National Amateur being held at the Minikahda Country Club, another Donald Ross course. Chick Evans won the Open there in 1916, he still held the course record, and he was a natural favorite. But because of his defense of his British Open crown, and because everyone knew the National Amateur was Bobby's preferred event, Bobby was far and away the betting favorite.

No matter what others think, however, it always comes down to individual performance, and Bobby was in a struggling frame of mind. He was having such a hard time, in fact, he was worried about even qualifying.

Bobby shot a 75 for his first qualifying round. Qualifying was led by a few newcomers to the national scene, Phil Finlay and Gene Homans.

"How about coming out with me this next round?" Bobby asked Keeler.

"Sure," Keeler responded. "What's up?"

"I need to try to take the medal on this thing. My first round was that bad. I'm going to have to shoot the works and I want a friendly face to help me along."

"How about this?" Keeler tilted his head and gave Bobby a crooked smile.

"That'll do," Bobby laughed.

By the 5th hole of his second qualifying round, Bobby stood at 3-under. "Thanks," he acknowledged to Keeler.

Bobby had his 31 on the front nine, then shot an even par 36 on the back, which won him the qualifying medal and set a new course record. Watts Gunn was the player who didn't qualify.

In his first round, an 18-hole affair, Bobby just squeaked by Maurice McCarthy 2-up, but he had to win the last three holes to do it. He got by Homans, 3 and 2. Then it was on to the thirty-six-hole events, which brought out the best in Bobby. He beat Harrison Johnson by 10-9, and Ouimet 11-10. He faced Chick Evans in the finals.

Bobby took control. In the first nine holes, Bobby took a commanding lead of 5-up. He had scored seven three's in the first eleven holes, and he played the front 4-under while Evans shot 3-over. The match was over, and yet, it went onto the 29th hole where Bobby secured his win 8 and 7.

Bobby now had National titles in five straight years. He had mentioned to O.B. Keeler years ago, almost halfheartedly, that he wanted to win six in a row. He was almost there.

"Do you know which hole won the Evans match for you?" Keeler asked Bobby on the train ride back home.

Bobby waited.

"It was your spoon second shot on the par-five 9th. Your ball traveled 250 yards uphill to a small green and wound up two inches from the cup. It was a ridiculously easy eagle that really bothered your opponent." Keeler smiled. "I watched Evans's face change when the shot came off. It looked like he was thrown into a state of shock."

Bobby just sat there. "But did you hear that fan who was no more than ten feet from me?"

Keeler shook his head.

"As I stood and looked at the shot, then pulled my club, he said, 'I've heard that you're a good long-club player, so let's see what you do with this.'"

The sour look on Bobby's face said it all. "As soon as I hit it, I knew I had caught every bit of it." Bobby looked coldly at Keeler. "As the ball came to a stop and the fans up around the green set up a roar, this guy says, 'But you didn't put the ball in the cup.'"

Bobby and Keeler were both too tired for another parade, but it happened anyway.

In the fall of 1927, Bobby started his second year of law studies at Emory.

"You going over to Britain this year?" Keeler asked as they sat for lunch. Keeler was writing a column, so his expense account took over.

"I need to finish my studies and help dad with his law prac-tice." Bobby looked out over the lunch crowd. "Dad's firm is doing a lot of work for the Coca Cola Company and he's been keeping me apprised of it for when I come in."

"Sounds smart."

Bobby nodded. "They're just going to have to understand why I can't be there this year."

"I'm sure they'll understand," Keeler offered, and he made a motion to leave. As he was paying the check, the last words of Bobby's book, "Down the Fairway," came to mind:

Tournament golf! It's different from just golf in other ways, especially when it leads, at last, into the cage of championship. I read a line somewhere, or a title, "The Cage of Championship." It is something like that. Something like a cage. First you're expected to get into it, and then you're expected to stay there. But, of course, nobody can stay there. Out you go— and then you're trying your hardest to get back in again. Rather silly isn't it, when golf—just golf—is so much fun.

Still, championship has its compensations. There was this sight of New York harbor, in 1926, when I was bringing the British Open championship cup home. New York harbor, and the Macon coming out with the home folks aboard, and the band playing Valencia.

I've been awfully lucky. Maybe I'll win another championship, someday. I love championship competition, after all, win or lose. Sometimes I get to thinking, with a curious little sinking way down deep, how I will feel when my tournament days are over, and I read in the newspapers that the boys are gathering for the national open or the amateur. Maybe at one of the courses I love so well, and where I fought in the old days. It's going to be queer.

But there's always one thing to look forward to— the round with Dad and Chick and Brad: the Sunday morning round at old East Lake, with nothing to worry about, when championships are done.

"When you leave the golf scene, they are going to miss you, Rubber Tire Jones Junyah."

Bobby stopped.

"That's how it sounded in the South when they used to introduce you at the regional events," Keeler grinned. "Now, on the fust tee, from East Lake, Jawja, Mr. Rubber Tire Jones Junyah."

Bobby grinned a crooked little grin. "Leave it to you to notice that."

But Bobby was not the one leaving golf.

"A'm gaun tae hiv a gowf schuil aroond New York," Maiden announced.

"You're leaving again?" Perry asked. Bobby was too crestfallen to utter a word.

Maiden nodded. "Maist likely for guide. A'll be naur me brither, Jimmie, an we mey git tae wirk in thee schuil thegither gif A dae ah guide job."

Perry walked outside. He had tears in his eyes. Maiden motioned for Bobby to go out and help him.

"You going to be okay?" Bobby asked.

Perry shook his head. "I think I'm close to having played my last round."

"What?" Bobby asked.

Perry looked at him. "Well, Dad's company is in serious trouble. We are probably facing bankruptcy."

"Adair Realty?"

Perry nodded. "Remember the Florida boom?" Perry's head fell onto his chest. "Well, as they say, boom to bust. My stepbrother thought he could fix things by going out to the Midwest and selling some great Florida land deals to well off farmers."

Bobby knew the history.

"He not only sold off most if not all of the swampland, he even sold some properties two, maybe even three times, thinking the farmers would never know." Perry shook his head. "Well, a few of the farmers learned what he did." Perry paused. "We have some very large claims against us."

Perry wiped away his tears and blew his nose on his handkerchief. "I'm sorry, Bobby. This just isn't my day," and he walked away.

It was the last time Bobby saw Perry on the course for many years.

"You don't have to finish at Emory to take the bar exam," one of Big Bob's partners instructed Bobby.

"But I don't want to fail it and not be able to take it again."

"That's not the way this works. Most future attorneys take it early just to see what they'll be up against down the road. You can take it again after you graduate."

So Bobby took the law exam and, surprising no one except himself, he passed it.

In 1928, the Walker Cup was played in the States, so Bobby didn't have to contemplate going abroad. He was now the father of two children, and he had never liked leaving his family anyway. Then, there was his new position with his father's law firm. O.B. Keeler had to work harder to get copy for his columns.

"Mind if I come out and watch your Sunday group?" Keeler asked Bobby by phone.

"Not at all, but it may bore you. There are no yelling crowds and very little excitement."

Keeler showed up at an early hour on Sunday morning, but he found Big Bob already singing "Home On the Range" out his back door and Camellia preparing a Sunday morning spread.

"C'mon in, Mr. Keeler." Camellia greeted the newspaperman at the door. "Help yourself to a big healthy breakfast." She pointed at the dining room.

Keeler was hungry, so he was the first to dig into the food.

"All by yourself?" Bobby kidded as he arrived and sat down to eat.

"Your dad has quite a voice," Keeler said between mouthfuls.

"Yes, he does," Bobby smiled. "That's the way that he calls a few of our friends to Sunday morning breakfast."

The food was finished in twenty minutes and, without any undue delay, seven players and one game-legged reporter went out to East Lake where they joined another five men in the locker room.

"You usually have twelve players?" Keeler asked Bobby as they put on their golf shoes.

"Between twelve and twenty. One group of eight guys went off to play in Florida, but Dad and I didn't want to go." Bobby added, "Wattsie usually plays, but he took the trip to Florida, too."

Keeler watched as a deck of cards was used to determine foursomes and then playing order.

"You mean you never know who you're playing with until the cards are dealt?" Keeler asked.

"Right. And we don't know who tees off first or last until we deal them, too."

"How do you work the bets?" Keeler pursued.

Bobby grinned. "With strokes and against everyone. We have individual matches and foursome matches. If you and your group play a great round, you could probably make a whole twenty-five bucks."

Keeler laughed. "No calcutta?"

The players bantered back and forth as they teed off and played hole after hole. After the morning round, they all got back in their cars and headed to Big Bob's place.

"Welcome home." Camellia greeted them at the door.

Twenty-one men filed into the large dining room and quickly took seats around the table, which was piled high with food.

"Well, how'd you do?" Keeler asked Bobby as he pulled out a chair to sit down.

Bobby smiled. "Not too bad. My 67 will win me a few bucks unless a lot of guys were hot. Sixty-eight is about my break-even score. Better than that, I win some, worse than that and I lose some." Bobby paused as he was loading his plate up with food. "But our group did well. We had two eagles and six birdies between us."

Keeler watched the players figure out over lunch who had won what in the morning round. Then, they went through the card process again to pick out partners for the afternoon round. All the while, Clara's favorite German Opera music filtered into the room from the library.

That afternoon, Keeler saw what Bobby had been talking about for years. It was just a simple group of men who got along and loved the game of golf.

"I don't think these guys know who you are," Keeler remarked to Bobby after the afternoon round was over and the tallies were made up in the grillroom at East Lake.

"I like to think that it's they who really see who I am. They don't fawn over me and make all those grandiose speeches for simply playing good golf."

"Stands to reason," Keeler smiled, making notes.

"To me, this is real golf. Golf with friends, without a bunch of people chasing after discarded tees, others gambling large sums of money on you, or constantly having to worry about hitting someone, or having your life put under the microscope so that everything you do winds up being fodder for newspaper copy."

Keeler's head snapped up. "Moi?"

"You aren't too bad. You write the kind of things that, to me, are acceptable. But you know how some of the others stretch things out of proportion." Bobby shook his head. "They just want to create headlines to sell newspapers."

They both sat there quietly. "I like people, but I like them in small doses." Bobby looked off, grasping something. "That last day in 1927, when I successfully defended my British title," Bobby's face showed an ethereal light, "I never felt so alone in my life as when they lifted me up on their shoulders."

For the first time, the USGA automatically qualified the thirty top finishers from the previous year's Open. Bobby could finally skip the nerve-racking process of qualifying.

The 1928 National Open was played at Olympia Fields in Chicago. The favorites were Bobby, of course, Walter Hagen, Gene Sarazen, Horton Smith, and Johnny Farrell.

Bobby's first two rounds would be played with Farrell, a little-known club pro who had scored well on the Olympia Fields course during practice rounds. It was said by many that Olympia Fields didn't favor Bobby because his game was more oriented to longer courses.

Bobby shot 73 and 71 the first two rounds to take a lead of two strokes over George Von Elm and Bill Leach. Hagen was back at 147, while Farrell was at 151.

In his last two rounds, Bobby would be playing with one of his best friends, Gene Sarazen, about a half hour after Farrell and a half hour before Hagen.

Von Elm shot himself out of the tournament with his third round 76 while Hagen stayed close, matching Bobby's 73. Farrell pulled up with a third round 71.

Bobby was having trouble with his driver but was overcoming it with great short-iron play and very accurate putting from Calamity Jane.

His lead in the final round built until, after the 5th hole, he got the message that he was about five strokes in front of his closest competitor. Ironically, he suffered a let-down at the news. Over the next five holes, he went double bogie, double bogie, bogie, bogie, bogie. Now, a number of players were back in the tournament—especially "The Beautiful Irishman," Johnny Farrell, and a young amateur player from Wilmington, North Carolina, Roland Hancock.

First Farrell finished birdie, par to come in at 294. Then twenty-five minutes later, Bobby finished par, birdie to complete a haggard 77—a tying score.

Both Bobby and Farrell waited as Hancock stood on the 17th tee with the knowledge that pars on the last two holes would give him the tournament and change his life forever. He finished bogie, bogie and drifted off into obscurity.

The first thirty-six-hole playoff in National Open history was scheduled for the next day. It was the third playoff Bobby had to play over the past six years.

"Did you hear that fan on the 15th hole?" Bobby asked Keeler as they ate in their room.

"The one who said he had some serious money riding on you?"

Bobby nodded. "You would think he would be smart enough to know that it might be best if I not know."

"You might think that." Keeler smiled. "Then again, you might also consider the source, considering the vagaries of the game and someone willing to gamble money on it."

Keeler chose to change the topic. "The USGA is getting a number of complaints from the pros who think you've been getting some favored tee times and favored partners to play with."

Bobby was shocked. "I'll bet none of that would come up if I was losing."

Keeler chuckled. "Well, for gosh sakes, let's not lose to make them happy!"

Bobby thought. "You can tell anyone who raises the issue with you that I have not pushed anyone for better tee times or my choice of partners. Do you think that will do it?"

Keeler flinched his shoulders. He had been hearing complaints like this for years, but he had chosen not to tell Bobby.

The playoff between Bobby and Farrell began at ten o'clock the following morning. The first round was a real battle over pars for the first 15 holes, then the long-time wear and tear on Bobby showed. He bogied his three closing holes. Morning scores were Farrell 70, Bobby 73.

"Damn," Bobby said walking with Keeler to lunch.

"You can make that up," Keeler offered.

"I shouldn't have fallen down so badly." But Keeler saw Bobby's face, which told him why Bobby faltered.

The afternoon round started. On the first two holes, Bobby shot 4, 4 while Farrell shot 6, 5. They were even again. Bobby double bogied the 3rd hole and Farrell had the lead which he held until he bogied 10, 11, and 12 to give Bobby a one-stroke lead.

Farrell almost aced the 13th hole and the two were even again with five holes to go.

Bobby missed a curvy three-foot putt on the 16th hole and Farrell again held a narrow lead.

On the par-four 17th Bobby hit his drive down the middle while Farrell put his drive in the rough. Farrell hit a gorgeous recovery to three feet and the pressure fell on Bobby. The best Bobby could do was to hit his shot to twenty feet from the cup. Bobby dropped his putt and Farrell matched it and they went to the par-five 18th. Bobby still one down.

Bobby managed to reach the fringe of the 18th hole in two while Farrell miss-hit his tee shot and followed that with a shot into the rough. Farrell hit a brilliant recovery to seven feet from the cup while Bobby just missed his eagle try.

As Farrell got ready to hit his putt, a disturbance rose in the gallery. A few photographers were finally removed by an official. The pressure had mounted for everyone.

Farrell moved to address his putt again and, in just a few seconds, made the putt and won the 1928 National Open. Bobby made his putt just to affirm the records.

Keeler could see that Bobby's eyes reflected a deep, bone-tired weariness.

Bobby became his firm's litigator and was handling case after case. Thankfully, he was able to cut his hours back so he would be ready for the National Amateur to be played at Brae Burn in Boston, and for the coming Walker Cup matches, where he was to serve as captain.

The American Walker Cup squad was loaded with experience and they ran away with the competition by an 11 to 1 score with Bobby winning his singles match against the reigning British Amateur champion, Phil Perkins, by a score of 13 and 12.

It was on to the National Amateur at Brae Burn.

On the way, Keeler went over his notes. If Bobby won at Brae Burn, he would keep his streak of at least one national title a year and he would also tie Jerome Travers with four National Amateur wins and become the first golfer with eight national titles to his name—passing Britishers Harry Vardon and Harold Hilton.

Keeler smiled to himself. He took things like this seriously, but he knew Bobby had other things on his mind right now.

Despite the fact that Bobby had practiced Brae Burn and had actually liked the layout, he shot an opening 77, which put him far down the list and caused him to worry about qualifying again.

"Those first six holes just about killed me," Bobby moaned to Keeler over lunch. "Someone in the gallery kept on saying I wouldn't break 80 and I started to think that way myself."

"Maybe we best cover you front and back in addition to both sides," Keeler mentioned.

"Just keep that person who wants me not to break 80 away from me."

Bobby qualified with a 151 total for the two rounds. Now, two 18-hole matches were next. He easily got by his first match, but then met Ray Gorton, who was the Brae Burn course record holder.

Bobby's driver and long-iron play was off, and he struggled through his first nine holes. Luckily, his opponent was also off his game. Then both of their games caught fire, and they alternated winning holes through the 18th to go into sudden death. Bobby won when his opponent's game collapsed.

Bobby was onto his favored thirty-six-hole matches, which

he won easily, 14-13 and 13-12. In the finals, Bobby faced the British Amateur Champion Phil Perkins, who, the media was saying, wanted another chance at the "Greatest Golfer in the World." Perkins lost to Bobby 10-9, which was the biggest winning score since the first amateur was held in 1895.

Bobby had now won four of the last five National Amateurs and Grantland Rice, in his national sports column, recommended that the trophy be automatically given to Bobby at the start of the year to save a lot of people a whole lot of unnecessary travel and trouble.

He had also met his goal, half-hearted or not, to win at least one national tournament for six years running.

CHAPTER
17

Keeler had columns to write.

"Are you going to do any out-of-country traveling this next year?" Keeler asked hopefully at another lunch paid for by his newspaper.

Bobby finished his pea soup. "I hope not. My wife misses me almost as much as I do her when I'm away from home, and we have two children now," Bobby explained. "Then there's my parents, and I've also noticed the number of kidnappings in the news recently that scare the living hell out of me."

"You mean that little eight-year-old girl that was taken over in Decatur?"

"Her and a couple of others."

"Most of those were for money."

"I don't care what the hell they're for. I have children now, and a lot of people might think they're an easy hit if they know I'm away."

Keeler tried a different angle.

"You fulfilled both of your last golfing goals. I was wondering if you have set any new ones."

"Not that I know of." Bobby continued eating his lunch. "I'd like to build the practice up like my dad and the partners have been proposing."

Keeler tried again. "Well, what, if anything, are you looking forward to in golf for next year?"

Bobby knew what Keeler had been fishing for. "Just our two National events. I really want to play Pebble Beach. I've heard a lot of good things about that course." Bobby smiled his shy little grin. "But that trip's going to be expensive, too, so I better get back to the office soon."

"Is it true you were issued an invitation to play in Japan?"

Bobby said, "Yes, but I'm not going. That's something for the pros to do."

Keeler tried to think of something to say, to prolong the lunch.

Bobby beat him to the punch. "There's something I've been wondering about. Because of your insight, I best ask you."

Keeler managed to stifle a shout for joy.

"What happens if I start not being able to win anymore?" Bobby's face wore a weary look. "They write all these columns calling me the mechanical man and the automatic winner. They don't seem to know just how hard it is to win one of these tournaments or how much work it is or what they take out of you."

"Well, you make it look easy."

"You know, I've often wondered if what I have is a gift, as they used to say. The reporters always make note of the fact that I don't play a lot of golf unless I have something special to get ready for."

"You don't have to defend yourself to me."

"But if I never win another big tournament, would they say I lost my gift? Or would they maybe realize my wins weren't so easy?"

Bobby continued, "I sometimes wonder what would happen if I just couldn't win another time."

Keeler composed his thoughts. "You have become very special to Atlanta, Bobby," he started. "None of the other writers at the paper get the level of mail that I do. People beg me to get you to do something. There are more people interested in you than are interested in any other Southern sports figure."

"But what if I couldn't win anymore? What if this gift just left me?"

Keeler didn't like the road this talk had taken. "Do we have to think like that? Can't we just keep on doing what we've been doing and let the future take care of itself?"

"I've had so many thoughts about 'what if?'" Bobby looked at Keeler. "You know, of course, that I cannot keep doing what I've been doing forever. Or even for much longer."

Keeler nodded. "I know that. That's worried me for a long time."

Bobby sat there. "I've heard stories for a while now about Jefferson Davis and how the people looked down at him in the last years of his life for losing the Civil War."

"But you're not like him. When I spoke to you about being the hero of the South, I didn't mean that in the past tense. We're not about to lose a tournament and, in the run of things, lose the South."

Bobby continued his train of thought. "It's funny. On the one hand, I'm very glad to have brought so much interest in our game to so many people. But I know I cannot keep this going forever, and I guess I'm just looking ahead, trying to figure out how to handle things when it's time to move on with my life." Bobby looked troubled as he said, "Everything has a start and an ending, whether it's a round of golf or a career."

"And do you have any time in mind for that to happen?"

Bobby looked directly at him. "You know, I'm not sure it's up to me to figure that out."

Bobby wasn't fully prepared for the National Open at the Tillinghast designed Winged Foot course. It was probably the only time in his life that he wasn't. Due to his other responsibilities in life, he just had not had the time to pour himself into his game.

"So, what do I tell everyone?" Keeler asked Bobby as they rode north on the new Birmingham Special. Bobby's wife, Mary, was with them. Bobby had refused to leave her behind this time.

"Tell them that I'm not yet on my stride but that I hope to be ready when the tournament starts." Bobby grinned. "Over the next ten days, I'm going to get my game in shape and know everything about Winged Foot that there is to know."

Keeler reported that and more. Bobby had played only ten rounds in the last couple of months, but Keeler didn't tell his readers that. He also didn't tell them that he thought Bobby was testing his gift.

In his final rounds of practice, Bobby showed that he had indeed accomplished his goals, as he shot two 69's. Then, as had become his custom of late, he took the final day before the tournament to rest, practice a little putting, and read.

The start of Bobby's first round of the tournament startled him as he double bogied two of the first three holes. But then he really buckled down and played the last 15 holes in six under par to complete a leading first round of 69.

"You really know how to scare a guy," Keeler said as Bobby turned in his card.

"I hope you couldn't hear my heart pounding after that damn third hole."

Bobby had a one-stroke lead over Al Espinosa and two strokes over Gene Sarazen and two others.

Bobby's second round of 75 left him tied in second place with Denny Shute, two strokes behind the co-leaders Espinosa and Sarazen.

On Open Saturday, Bobby found himself playing aside his friend Al Watrous, teeing off almost an hour behind Espinosa and a half-hour behind Sarazen. The course was hot and dry, giving the ball a boost off the tees.

In the morning round, Bobby shot a 71 and took a three-stroke lead over Sarazen, while Espinosa was another shot back.

In the final round, Sarazen blew himself out of the tournament with a 78. Espinosa was next. He completed a fine 75 for a total of 294, which left Bobby standing on the 15th tee in perfect shape. Finishing with all pars would give Bobby a three-stroke win.

Keeler watched nervously as Bobby threw his lead away on the next hole. He triple bogied the 397-yard 15th hole. Now it would take all pars on the last three holes just to tie Espinosa.

Bobby got his par on the par-five 16th, but he had taken three putts from twenty feet to do it. Working hard, he got his par on the par-four 17th.

Now, Bobby faced the 18th hole which he played at better than par his previous six rounds around the course. This time, however, his second shot was not good enough. He left his approach short on the grassy side slope of a bunker. He had to gently traverse the bunker to get close to the cup for his necessary par putt.

Bobby chipped to twelve feet off the side of the cup and Keeler watched Bobby study the hardest final putt he had ever faced, just to get into a playoff. His putt would have to break about a foot; then, the final line turn downhill would make the ball pick up speed as it raced to its side-sloped target.

Keeler couldn't watch. He turned away and sat down on the bank as he heard the crowd quiet down. Keeler heard the gentle clink of Calamity Jane striking the ball ever so gently. The huge hush of a collective intake of waiting breaths sounded like a giant sucking sound.

Pandemonium! The crowd rose to its feet with a thunderous roar, and Keeler knew Bobby had made the putt. He was now into a thirty-six hole, Sunday playoff with Espinosa.

"What a putt, huh?" Bobby said to Keeler after he signed his card and turned it in.

"I never saw it. I was scared to death after what you did on fifteen and sixteen. I just couldn't watch." Keeler looked forward to getting back to their room for a drink.

Bobby and Espinosa approached the USGA and got a half-hour-later starting time for their Sunday playoff. Bobby wanted to take Mary to church and both Al and his wife wanted to go to church as well.

In the playoff, Espinosa immediately took a two-stroke lead over Bobby by simply parring the first hole. Then Bobby got to work and caught Espinosa by the 12th hole and, after that, started walking away with the play-off and the title.

Bobby shot a 72; Espinosa shot 84.

In the afternoon, Bobby shot a 3-under 69 again. Espinosa could do no better than 80. Bobby won by twenty-three strokes.

In the awards ceremony, USGA President, Findlay Douglas, called Bobby the greatest golfer that ever lived.

"You know, of course, that you only win the Amateur when you haven't won the Open that year," Keeler startled them on the way home.

Bobby stared at him.

"That's been your pattern," Keeler reiterated. "The only wins you have in our Amateur are when you haven't won the Open in that same year."

Bobby slowly nodded his agreement. He didn't tell Keeler that in 1926, he thought that he had been just a few strokes away from winning them all.

Bobby got to work on his game for the upcoming National Amateur.

"I'm taking Mary and our kids," Bobby informed Keeler when they met to discuss their coming trip. "And Dad wants to see Pebble Beach. He heard that the views from the course are even worth a round in the 90's," Bobby smiled.

"I'd like to take my wife, but her parents aren't in very good shape. She's being the dutiful daughter."

"Did you tell your boss you were riding with us in our private train car?"

"I can't tell him things like that," Keeler replied. "He'll get spoiled and cut my travel budget."

Keeler rode with his feet up, viewing the country from the casual seat of the private car. All the while, though, his mind was working on golf and on Bobby's golfing career. Thanks to one of Keeler's foreign friends, O.B. had learned that if Bobby were to win this, his tenth national crown, he would leave his tie with John Ball behind. Ball, the great British Amateur, was the only other man who had ever won nine national events. On his own, Keeler realized that, also with this win, Bobby would match what the Midwestern star Chick Evans had done in 1916 by winning both national events, and that he'd pass the record of Jerome Travers of four National Amateur wins.

The second Bobby got his feet on California soil, he played Pebble Beach. He tied the course record of 73. Thousands of golf fans showed up to watch. They looked like waves flowing over the course.

He played a second round and tied his own new course record. A third round, and he shot an easy 70. Then he shot a 67 which included a run of nine holes on some of the most challenging and scenic holes in America, the 5th through the 13th, where he scored a three on all nine holes except one where he had a four. Keeler was ecstatic. "This is the best shape I have ever seen him in before the start of a tournament," Keeler told the Jones family.

Bobby took his traditional day off to rest and read.

The crowd of fans following Bobby on his qualifying rounds was estimated at close to 9,500. Bobby didn't let them down. Although he didn't set another record, his scores for qualifying totaled 145. He tied with Gene Homans for Medalist Honors.

Bobby's opponent for his first round match was an unknown from Omaha, Nebraska, Johnny Goodman, who was only twenty years of age. He had traveled to Pebble Beach in railroad cattle cars.

"Where were you last night?" Bobby directly addressed Keeler at breakfast the next morning.

"I, ah, went out with a couple of the other sports writers."

Keeler reached for his coffee. "Just stoking the waters, so to speak."

"Where did you go?" Big Bob continued the search.

Keeler decided to act nonchalant. "Just over to one of the big lodges."

Bobby could tell that Keeler was hiding something. "Who were you with?"

"Oh, just Rice and Richardson and Kieran." Keeler mentioned three of the biggest sports writers in the country.

"And?" Big Bob continued. He too now sensed that Keeler was holding onto something.

Keeler put his spoon down and looked at the two men. "There are some things I'm not sure I best bring to words."

"Why not let us be the judge of that?" Big Bob said.

Keeler hesitated. "We went to see the auctioning of players."

"A calcutta?" Bobby asked.

Keeler nodded. "That."

"So, what was it like?" Big Bob asked.

Keeler looked at Bobby wondering if he really should continue. "It was pretty much as usual."

"How much did Bobby go for?" Big Bob looked directly at Keeler.

Keeler tried to figure out a way to get out of answering, but couldn't. "$23,000."

Big Bob's eyes grew wide and Bobby put down his fork.

"Damn," the Jones men said in unison.

"The pot is close to $145,000. The winner gets seventy-five percent when his man wins." Keeler watched the two men.

"How the hell do they make sure the pot is correct?" Big Bob wondered out loud.

"Oh, they collect from the winning bidder right after he wins the bid." Keeler smiled. "No checks."

Big Bob looked at Bobby. "He just told us that someone is walking around with about $150,000 in his pocket." Big Bob calculated. "Whoever bought you stands to get about a

$108,000 when you win this amateur." Big Bob shook his head. "Talk about making money off someone else's work."

"Was this calcutta like the rest of them?" Bobby asked.

Keeler nodded. "Pretty much the same. I understand the winning bidder is from Boston."

"He came all the way out here to place his bet?" Big Bob shook his head.

"Unless I miss my guess, a lot of the big bidders travel to a number of the calcuttas every year." Keeler admitted. "A number of them looked familiar to me from past calcuttas."

After Bobby left to get ready for his first-round match with Johnny Goodman, Big Bob and Keeler talked. "Have you mentioned these calcuttas to Bobby before?" Big Bob asked.

Keeler nodded. "Yes, he knows about them both from me and from others. He also knows that the USGA has been working to put them out of business."

Big Bob looked at Keeler. "I didn't know that they were being played for so much money." Big Bob stopped. "If the gangsters ever find out about them, they may just decide to do something about them on their own."

Bobby quickly managed to lose the first three holes of his match to Johnny Goodman, giving two of those holes away. Goodman really only won the third hole, which he birdied. It was all Bobby could do to catch Goodman by the 12th hole, and he did.

On the 13th hole, Bobby beautifully negotiated a stymie to halve the hole. He just missed the green on the par-five 14th with his second shot while Goodman struggled to get his fourth shot near the cup.

As Bobby bore down on his third shot, hoping to get the ball close for a birdie putt, his mind wandered for just a second. His finely-cut third shot just caught the top edge of the bunker that he was negotiating. Insead of a hole-winning birdie, Bobby got a hole-losing bogie.

One down with four to go.

Goodman played steady golf and Bobby hunted for the one birdie that seemed just out of reach—so Bobby lost for the first time in a first round match, 1-down.

The fans were totally stunned by the unexpected result.

"Done any thinking about next year?" Keeler was always pushing.

Bobby looked tired. "At times. But nothing is certain yet. If our practice continues to grow, I don't know how I'd get the time to go over to the Isles to play." Bobby leaned his head back and thought. "But I'm due to be the Captain of the Walker Cup as you know."

"Well, a long, long time ago, you had a goal of winning one big tournament. After your win at Inwood, you seemed to change your goal to one win a year for six years. Now, you've passed that goal. I was wondering if you had put anything else into place?"

Bobby thought quickly of the lofty goal that had been growing inside him, but he just couldn't bring himself to tell anyone about it. Not even Keeler. At least not yet.

"No, not completely, but I can tell you that this year, I will be in the best shape possible."

In late October, the world paused as the stock market suffered its biggest drop in history. Almost $2,600,000,000 in stock values were lost, a figure most people couldn't even fathom.

There was another kidnapping, again for money.

Money had become a more valued commodity than life.

"They want you to come play in the new Savannah Open," Keeler announced to Bobby. It was good to focus on golf; the other news was just too grim.

"Those pros just want to get me while I'm not warmed up for the season yet," Bobby laughed.

"I'm not talking about the pros." Keeler brought some wadded newspaper pages out of his jacket. "Look at these."

Bobby looked at the sports pages of the Savannah Morning News that Keeler held out to him. There were fifteen display ads on one page and another twelve on another page imploring Bobby to come and play in the coming Savannah Open at the Savannah Golf Club. Some ads were even addressed to Keeler, asking him to talk Bobby into playing. All of them were from important people.

Bobby looked at the ads closely. "Think the pros put them up to this?" he kidded.

"I should think it would be hard to turn down these invites," Keeler said.

"Isn't this something?"

Bobby sat back and was deep in thought. "Let them know I'll be there," he said. It would be his first winter tournament since 1927. His was the last entry into the tournament, and it caught the pros by surprise.

He threw down the glove to the professionals right from the start by shooting a 67 in the first round and setting a new course record.

A new young professional by the name of Horton Smith, the leading money winner the past two years, picked up the glove by shooting his own 66 in the second round. He took the lead from a struggling Bobby who shot a painful 75.

Bobby came back in the third round with another new course record of 65. He tied Smith going into the last round. It was a two-man battle for the title.

Playing just a few foursomes apart in the last round, Bobby and Smith matched stroke for stroke until the 17th when Smith took his final lead. Bobby Cruickshank was third, seven strokes back.

"Hell of an effort," Keeler said as they came off the last green.

"Tell them I'm going to play in the Southeastern Open in Augusta," Bobby said. He knew that Keeler's columns carried weight.

"That's the season-ending tournament for the pros."

Bobby simply nodded.

"The pros are going to be waiting for you after what you did here."

Bobby tilted his head. "Maybe it's time I really test my game and see what I can do."

Keeler couldn't help but ask. "Okay, what's going on? You quickly decided to play in Savannah, and now in Augusta, after telling me that you might be too busy to play much this year."

"You know, I forgot how inspiring it is to have so many people pulling for you," Bobby managed. "Of course, playing against the pros who are constantly working on their games was fun, too."

"But, you're not going to Augusta just to hear the cheers or to play with the pros, if I know you," Keeler queried.

Bobby crooked his head. "I'm going to Augusta to test my game. It helps that Mary's family is there. We'll have a home there and be comfortable, almost like at East Lake." Bobby gazed out the window. "I do want to make sure my game is ready when I captain the Walker Cup team on their soil."

Finally. Keeler knew he would be going abroad for the third time.

Weeks later, Bobby and his family arrived at Augusta for the Southeastern Open. It was being played on two courses: Forest Hills and Augusta Country Club. Keeler was there, of course.

"They tell me they had to get hold of Horton Smith up in North Carolina," Keeler reported to Bobby. "They have to round up a few pros before they think they can beat you."

"There's a whole bunch of people in this tournament besides me, but I appreciate the compliment," Bobby said.

"I hear that the tournament committee is going to pair you and Smith together for the first two rounds." Keeler shook his head. "They were in such a dither to get Smith to play here that he's not going to be able to even practice on the course before the tournament because of prior commitments."

Bobby stood up. "Horton's a nice young man." Bobby looked off and thought. "Should be fun."

In a final tune-up round on the Forest Hills course, playing with Ed Dudley, Gene Sarazen, and Al Espinosa, Bobby missed tying the course record by one stroke. That sent a big message to the pros. Whoever was going to step forward to match steps with Bobby was going to have to take some mighty large steps.

"Betting has you against the field even up," Keeler mentioned to Bobby. "What you did at Savannah is being talked about."

"That's going to rile up a few of the pros," Bobby countered. "I only hope they can still keep their minds on their games." He grinned.

"Bet they can't, even with Hagen not here," Keeler laughed.

"Does anyone know where he is?"

"He's in Indonesia, I think." Keeler added. "Rumor is that he'll finish his traveling in time for the Open at Hoylake."

Bobby and Smith met on the first tee and smiled at each other. They had really enjoyed their competition in Savannah.

Smith bogied the first hole and Bobby birdied the second hole, and he never looked back. Bobby scored 72, 72 for the day and, being at even par after the two rounds, headed two players by two strokes and Smith by four with no one else under 150.

The story centered around the lightning-quick, shiny greens at Augusta Country Club. At least three pros four-putted, and three-putting was common. The course had quick-cut the greens an extra time between the two rounds.

The second day, Bobby was favorably paired with Gene Sarazen and Al Espinosa.

"That's going to stir up more hot water," Keeler said of the pairing.

"I'm not doing anything but following instructions."

Bobby shot a 69 while everyone else was having trouble even coming close to matching par.

"You're going to have a ten-stroke lead going into the final round," Keeler said as they met for lunch.

"I hope I can keep from having another let-down."

"Can't you set your own goals or something?" Keeler said between bites. "Seems to me that when you have a big lead, you should at least enjoy what you've done.

Bobby nodded. "That's exactly the kind of thinking that gets you into trouble. You can't really allow yourself thoughts like that until it's over."

Smith and his group were finishing up their last round as Bobby started for the first tee. "Good luck, Bobby. Although, I daresay, you'll not need it with that lead."

"Thanks, Horton." Bobby shook the young pro's hand and, with Sarazen and Espinosa, started for the first tee.

"Oh, Bobby," Smith called across. "Cruickshank thinks you're going to win them all this year." Bobby didn't hear the comments; his mind was already into his game.

Even with his ten-stroke lead, Bobby bore down. He started out his last round, birdie, eagle, birdie, birdie. Keeler found himself in wonder. Many of the professionals who had finished early were now following Bobby and, from Keeler's vantage point, seemed like they were riveted to what Bobby was doing.

"He's going to win them all," Cruickshank said to Keeler as they followed Bobby to the next tee. "Is he going over there to play?"

Keeler knew that Cruickshank was talking about going overseas. "He is that I know of." Keeler said.

"My God, man," Cruickshank continued his litany. "He's going to win them all. He's playing way above the rest of us, he is."

Cruickshank got a far-away look on his face. "I'm going to send $500 to my father-in-law back home and get him to put it down for me with Lloyd's of London."

Keeler watched the man who was called "Wee Bobby" walk off. Cruickshank's statements gave him pause.

Bobby was seventeen strokes ahead of his closest pursuer in his final round. A wait was called because players ahead were bottled up, and so Bobby's expected let-down came on the last four holes. He still finished thirteen strokes ahead.

Bobby had his first meeting with the members of the Walker Cup Team on their way to England.

"They're going to have their best team yet," Bobby warned. "They do not like the fact that they have yet to win the Cup from us," Bobby looked seriously at all his players. "When we get to England, I want y'all to work at getting on your games and not be bothered by all the special events that might take our minds off of the main event." Bobby continued looking at his players. "And I don't want to be the first captain to have ever lost a Cup event, even if this is not on our ground. I will accept no excuse for poor play."

"I've got some news from back home," Keeler announced once Bobby's meeting with his team was over.

Bobby stood and waited.

"You've been elected to sit on the Board of Directors of the First National Bank of Atlanta," Keeler announced, and then he gave the news he really wanted to transmit. "And back home, they're all buying lots at $5.00 per bet with Lloyd's of London that you're going to win all four of the big ones. The last I heard, the tally of the bets placed was heading towards $3,000."

Bobby shook his head back and forth in a silent no.

"I didn't want to tell you, but I heard a few of the others onboard talking about it. I thought you should hear it from me first."

Bobby nodded. "Thanks."

At Sandwich, Bobby and the rest of the team faced a real

challenge. For the first time in a while, all the best British and Irish amateur players had come together. They had formed one very formidable team.

First-day play for the Walker Cup showed the British how strong a challenge they were facing. The Americans took a 3-to-1 lead in foursome play.

Bobby took Dr. O.F. Willing of Portland, Oregon, as his partner. They easily won their match 8 and 7 after a hard-fought morning round left them all square.

Eight singles matches, and the Americans had high hopes. Bobby faced Roger Wethered, the British amateur most considered one of the two top players in Britain. As usual, Bobby shook hands with his opponent and looked him straight in the eye. This was the way Bobby got a sense of what he was up against.

In his case, Bobby hadn't needed to do anything because his clubs did it for him. Bobby beat the former British Amateur Champion by the score of 9 and 8. After the first three holes, the match had never been close.

The American Walker Cup players won their singles matches by the score of 7 to 1. That brought the overall score to 10-2, and the Americans retained the cup.

That caused the British sports writers to forecast that the Americans would be taking the trophies that represented both the British Amateur and the British Open back home with them across the sea as well.

CHAPTER
18

The British Amateur, to be played on the old course at St. Andrews, was scheduled to begin a few days after the Walker Cup, and when it did, it gave Bobby a gift. Bobby drew a bye, a free pass, for the first round.

"Bet that makes you happy," Keeler said.

"Let's see who I get for the second round before we determine that," Bobby joked.

Bobby's opponent was the unknown Henry Roper, a miner from the Nottingham district who had never played in a national event before. When they shook hands, Bobby noticed a firmness in Roper's eyes that portrayed a solidness in the man.

Nonetheless, Bobby got off to a great start. Roper shot even four's for the first 5 holes, but Bobby started out birdie, par, eagle, birdie, and birdie. He stood 3-up. Roper hung on until the match finished at the 16th hole with Bobby 3-up.

This match contained the most talked-about shot in the tournament. On the 427-yard 3rd hole, Bobby's drive landed in a bunker down the left side. Bobby took out his mashie niblick and studied his 140-yard shot. As quickly as you please, Bobby swung and the ball was nipped ever so lightly off the sand. Seconds later, it descended onto the front of the green. It commenced to roll and, with its last breath, fell into the hole for an eagle two. Streams of people over the next two days came to the spot where the shot had been executed; some actually took sand out of the bunker as a memento.

Bobby's first round bye and his second round win left him with six more eighteen-hole matches and one thirty-six hole match to play. After fourteen years on the national tournament scene, this was still the only big tournament he had never won.

Bobby's third round match was an easy win, but in his fourth round match, he faced one of the two best British amateur golfers—Cyril Tolley, a man known to be the longest striker of the ball in the British Isles. He was a great personality in British golf and a favorite with the gallery, a fiery player who fared best in match play where his emotions drove him. He had already won the British Amateur twice, in 1920 and 1929.

Bobby's match with Tolley would require a great effort on his part. He went through his process of looking the man in the eye as they met on the first tee. As expected, Tolley didn't flinch.

It was a very tight match. Bobby always seemed to get a lead of one hole only to have Tolley come back and even the match. After four lead changes, they came to the famous Road Hole—the 17th at St Andrews.

Both of their drives were in good shape off the tee, with Tolley slightly in front.

Bobby then got a break, one of four similar ones in that round. His second shot to the 17th caught the back edge of the green and bounced into the gallery. The ball bounced off a fan and stopped in a safe place. Tolley's second wasn't too good. It wound up with the only bunker on the 17th between him and the hole.

Bobby's approach looked good but it slid and skidded on the green, winding up almost nine feet away from the hole. Tolley laid his approach shot almost dead at the hole for a certain four.

The pressure was on Bobby to do something. With only the short 18th hole left, any lead given up at this point would be most telling.

Bobby conceded Tolley's putt, and went to work on his tying stroke. Bobby looked at the stroke from all angles. Where Bobby usually was a speedy putter, believing his first look was the best choice; here, he took his time.

After choosing his route, Bobby addressed his putt and with the touch of a watchsmith, struck his putt every so gently. The ball moved slowly across the green with each undulation carrying it gently towards its target until it stopped on the very edge of the cup. As Bobby stood back up, the putt dropped.

It was all square going to the short 18th and it stayed that way after the two competitors played regulation golf on the hole.

Back to the 1st for sudden death.

Two drives ran down the middle of the fairway. Bobby's approach was on while Tolley's was slightly off to the side. Tolley's little chip was not that good, and it left him a twelve-foot-putt for his hoped-for par.

Bobby's first putt stopped directly in the line of Tolley's putt, laying him the perfect stymie which Tolley could not negotiate. The match was over.

"You're both the man I would love to beat and the man I would feel honored to lose to," Tolley said to Bobby as they shook hands.

"Thanks, Cyril," Bobby shyly smiled. "It was fun and I'm always sorry that someone has to lose in a tight match."

Bobby's next opponent was a fellow American Walker Cup teammate and the National Amateur winner from the previous year in the states, Harrison Johnston.

After thirteen holes, Bobby seemed to have this match tied down. He was 4-up. But Johnson got hot and won the 14th, the 15th, and the 17th holes. Bobby held on to win the match on the 18th hole by a halve, sinking an eight-foot side-hill putt.

Bobby got a breather on the next round. His fellow opponent got caught up in the Bobby Jones aura. Bobby won over Eric Fiddian by 4 and 3.

The next round, Bobby met another fellow American Walker Cupper who was having his own lucky streak, George Voight. This produced a very tight match with Bobby 2-down with 5 holes to play.

Both men were showing the strain of the long tournament as they got to the 14th hole. Voight shoved his drive out of bounds, and he lost 14. He lost the 16th hole too. That made them even. On the 17th hole, Voight played very well, getting his four while Bobby had a twelve-foot putt to tie. He made it.

Even-up, they played the last hole and the strain showed itself in Voight as Voight misplayed his approach. He gave the hole to Bobby for his win.

A few British reporters approached Keeler about an interview. "He's too shot," Keeler said. "But if you'll wait a minute, I'll give you some insights into his thinking."

"Is it true that he's going after all four?" one reporter asked.

Keeler nodded, although he still hadn't spoken much to Bobby about it. "If Bobby ever plays in an event, he goes all out to win it. That's why he's so worn out when the tournament is over. He puts everything he has into winning." Keeler's words made sense, and he knew it. He grinned. "So, yes, he's going after everything he's playing in this year."

Bobby's opponent in his final match, Roger Wethered, was one of, if not the, top amateur in Britain. With his sister, Joyce, the Wethered family had two of the top amateurs, male and female, in all the British Isles. Pressure matches were nothing new to them.

The fans were waiting for this match. Bobby had beaten Wethered in the Walker Cup matches—and by such a score— that everyone in the British Isles was expecting Wethered to redeem himself.

St. Andrews is a public course with no admission charges. Because of that, and because of who was playing, over 20,000 people showed up to watch. It was rumored that one or two of the small towns around St. Andrews were, for all practical purposes, emptied out by the match.

Bobby's second shot started out so badly, it didn't even clear the Swilcan Burn. From then on, however, Bobby played as only Bobby could. Despite Wethered's excellent play, Bobby had a

4- up lead at the noon-time break.

"You seem to be playing very well," Keeler offered at lunch.

"Then you didn't see the second shot that I hit on the first hole. It was horrendous."

"But you halved the hole, and now you stand 4-up." Keeler was used to having to work to win his points with Bobby.

"That shot bothered me the rest of the round. Roger's an excellent player. I'm lucky he's a little off today." Bobby's face showed tired determination.

After Bobby's light lunch, he played even better and by the 12th hole, it was all over. Bobby had triumphed by 7 and 6 and had now won all the national tournaments at least once. Up to the 30th and last green, Bobby's medal score was 2-under even four's.

Bobby's acceptance speech, in front of his fans and his wife, was very similar to the speech he had given in 1927.

"I had rather win a tournament at St. Andrews than at any other place here on this earth," Bobby started out. He praised the ruling body, the fans, and of course, the Old Course with all its intricacies. It was a course he had come to know and love.

A British reporter managed to wrangle an interview with a very-tired Bobby.

"Will this success here at St. Andrews cause you to give it your all at Hoylake in the Open?"

Bobby smiled gently. "The way I feel right now, no other tournament matters that much."

"You mean that this was the one that you were aiming for this year?"

"Precisely," Bobby offered. "I'll do my best at the Open and back home in the American competitions. But this was the one for me, the one that I had always wanted to win. In some ways, I thought I never should win this Amateur, but I'm very happy and very thankful that I did."

"So, you'll be back next year to defend your title?" the reporter continued.

Bobby looked at the man and then looked off. "I don't know when I'll be back. It may be next year or in four years, or never."

Keeler smiled at the reporter, but pulled Bobby away.

Bobby needed rest for the British Open, and he and his wife, Mary, got it by going to Paris for a few days. While they were gone, Keeler collected the cables that were coming in, congratulating Bobby on his win. By the time Bobby met him in Hoylake, Keeler had piles of cables. There was even talk about a second ticker-tape parade.

"It's going wild at home since you won the British Amateur," Keeler reported.

"Another parade?" Bobby teased. He knew how Keeler had grown to detest their Atlanta homecoming parades with his game leg.

Keeler shook his head. "They all want to meet you in New York again."

Bobby had a puzzled look on his face, and then he caught on. "I thought you said that no one gets a second ticker tape parade in New York."

Keeler mumbled, "I do believe I said that. Maybe they ran out of generals and explorers to salute." Keeler knew Bobby wouldn't be happy about a second ticker tape parade, so he changed topics. "I got a first," Keeler smiled. "They want me to do nightly broadcasts of the Open that will be carried by the National Broadcasting Company back home," Keeler continued. "So, how was Paris?"

Bobby's face took on an airy look. "Very nice. Soothing for some reason. But expensive as hell." After a moment, he added, "Thank God for Coca Cola and their business." Bobby's firm's biggest client was growing even in the tough depression era.

Bobby qualified in a tie for 20th place for the British Open, and people began to sense that Bobby might be vulnerable. As usual, it was Bobby against the field, and the field was very happy with Bobby's high qualifying score.

On the first day of Open play, however, things were made right as Bobby came in with a 70 to tie with Henry Cotton and MacDonald Smith for the lead.

Bobby found himself alone in the lead after his second round with a score of 142. But his lead was a slim one-stroke over Fred Robson. Horton Smith and Archie Compston were close. Bobby's biggest problem was his tiredness.

A third-round 74 showed his weary state. Each round's score had been higher than the one before it. Bobby was now behind Compston, who had shot a great 68, by one stroke, and he was barely in front of five others.

All of Bobby's energy was spent, but he did his best in the final round and scored a 75. MacDonald Smith cooled off in the back nine and shot a 71, which left him two strokes behind Bobby. The tournament was over. He had won his third British Open.

"Who'd have believed everyone except MacDonald Smith would have faded like that?" Keeler wondered. They headed off to Bobby's room to await the ceremony after getting Bobby out of the grips of thousands of fans.

"Winning by two little old strokes isn't much of a win." Bobby shook his head, still in shock that he had won the Open.

"It's the first time since John Ball in 1890 that anyone has won both British big ones," Keeler added. "That was twelve years before you were born."

"I have a tremendous respect for what Ball did now, believe me." Bobby nearly fell into his chair. He was glad to be off his feet. "I'm still shocked that no one came and grabbed that Claret Jug out of my hands. I wish I could finish a tournament without having to drag myself home."

"Me, too," Keeler said, and he wondered if he should say that on his broadcast that night.

Bobby was in a spot no one had ever been in before. The press started calling him "Emperor Jones."

"They passed some kind of salutation for you in Congress," Keeler told Bobby on the boat home.

"The Georgia Congress or the United States Congress?"

"The U.S. Congress." Keeler grinned. "They had to beat the second ticker-tape parade with an idea that was even more special." Keeler kept his line of thought. "There are two ships meeting us when we get close to New York. One will be carrying a guy with the National Broadcasting Company. They want to carry your whole welcoming in New York on radio."

"The whole thing?"

Keeler nodded. "Evidently they are going to have four broadcasters stationed in different spots around the city. When you arrive at those places, they will go live with your story." Keeler waited. "Oh, and we heard from Hagen. In an interview that he gave out west, he said that you were the greatest golfer in the world."

Bobby just shook his head.

"Are you going to be alright with all this?"

Bobby let the trapped air out of his lungs in a long, low breath. "I just hope they don't want much more than a few words from me when we get to New York." For Bobby, parades were harder to deal with than tournaments.

When they arrived, a National Broadcasting Company newsman begged Bobby to go on the air. After welcoming his parents, Bobby relented and said okay.

"So, is it true that if you win all four of the big tournaments, you will retire?"

Bobby shook his head. "That story was probably woven together from a few things I said back in England." Bobby smiled shyly. "I haven't even thought about the American tournaments yet. I hope to win them, of course, but retire? I just don't know as yet when or where I'll be playing next year."

Before Bobby knew it, he was in a parade of automobiles heading out of the Battery and down Broadway for City Hall. Keeler found himself walking beside Bobby and Mary's automobile. It was not something that Keeler wanted to do, but he did it nonetheless.

The arrival of the parade at City Hall was exciting, in a city that understood excitement.

Bobby was visibly tired as he awkwardly moved toward a microphone that had been set up for him. "I want to thank you all for this fine reception. I cannot think of anything finer to give a fellow and I thank you all from the bottom of my heart."

Later that night, at their hotel—the Vanderbilt—Keeler motioned to Bobby. They stood at the window of Keeler's room and watched the lights of New York pulsating with as much electricity as the crowds had generated at Bobby's receptions that day. "You're doing things that no other golfer or sportsman has ever done before."

"I have to wonder why. Who in their right mind wants to give their life away to someone else?"

"Give your life away, you say?"

"All these parades and celebrations, and all this travel to get from tournament to tournament." A weary Bobby slowly shook his head. "I couldn't be like Hagen, playing all over the world. There is so much I want to do back home. I'm happy just being at home in Atlanta."

Bobby looked at Keeler. "What do you think the reaction would be if I never won again and all these fine folks were let down? You know, I got into this big golf scene by sneaking in over time, but I don't think that's the way I'm going to be allowed to get back out."

"Allowed?" Keeler tried to understand.

"To get back out of tournament golf," Bobby tried to clarify. "By easing myself out. I love golf. I owe an awful lot to the game.

But I have another whole part of me that wants to go on and raise a family and fulfill my career as a lawyer." Bobby looked off and gave Keeler a different look than Keeler had seen before.

"Tournament golf is so different from just golf. It's the game that I really love. Not the crowds or the headlines and especially not the travel." It was quiet in the room until Bobby added, "The people I love and who love me would like me to step down from tournament golf. They worry about what's happening to me."

Keeler nodded. "Sure they do."

"Well, as much as I love golf, and owe something to the game, I owe them more, and I love them more." Bobby looked at Keeler. "You know, I can play thirty-six holes two days in a row at home and be as happy as a peach tree in full spring bloom. But out here, in competitive golf, thirty-six holes wears me damn out."

Keeler was silent; he was listening intently as always.

They continued their conversation on the train the next day to Minneapolis for the National Open.

"Every time we finish up one of these tournaments, it's a Saturday and all I can think of is how much I'd like to be playing at home the next day with Dad, and Chick, and Brad, and the boys, and having one of Camellia's grand meals. Instead, all I get is foreign food, or Northern food, and another trip."

"So," Keeler had to ask, "have you decided about your future?"

Bobby took some time to answer. "In the long run, I have to take care of my family. In the short run, I want this National Open." Bobby thought some more. "I just hope I'm rested so that my mind and body can react to the challenge of the tournament."

"What about winning all four?" Keeler finally got the big question out.

"Everyone's been telling me what the newspapers have been saying." Bobby looked out at the Hudson River Valley, which was a beautiful sight. "Since there are four tournaments to play in, it's possible for someone to win them all. But only Evans in 1916, the year that I started playing in the big events, has even won two of the four except for Ball." Bobby looked Keeler right in the eye. "I had a shot at all four in 1926. Just a little more luck in both the amateur events, and I could have come close, real close." Bobby looked out the window again. "Now, having come this far and having gotten two . . . yes, damn it, I want the other two." Bobby grinned at Keeler. "But between you and me, if we had had this talk back in December, I would have told you that the possibility to win all four was remote. The amateur tournaments are just too tough, calling for wins in so many 18-hole matches."

A very large crowd met them as they arrived in Minneapolis. As much as Bobby appreciated their interest, he wanted to get onto Interlachen, a course he had never played before, for a practice round of golf.

The heat gripping this Midwest city temporarily took the front page. Most players either cut short their practice sessions or played nine holes very early and the other nine holes much later in the day.

Bobby shot a 71 in his first round. The 1-under par effort left him one stroke behind MacDonald Smith and Tommy Armour—and one stroke in front of Hagen, who said his game was the best it had been.

"Your caddy has been hired to do a column about your rounds." Keeler grinned at Bobby.

"My caddy, a columnist?" Bobby asked, incredulous.

"Yeah, his column is headed 'By Caddy Dale.'"

Bobby laughed.

The second round contained a shot by Bobby that forever after would be known as the "Lily Pad" shot. Working his way to another very good round, on the 9th hole, which was a par-five, Bobby pushed his drive slightly off to the right. He took out his spoon, lined up his shot, and as quickly as practical, swung.

On Bobby's downswing, his left eye caught a movement at the top of the line of the gallery. He flinched. Two little girls had decided to run forward to the green.

The clubhead of Bobby's spoon caught just the top half of the ball, which took off in a straight line for the lake that bisected the fairway in front of the green. Bobby thought he lost his ball, which would cost him a penalty stroke, but the ball had other ideas.

Like a side-armed thrown stone, the ball took a skip off of the water, then another and a third. It impacted the far bank of the pond and flipped up and onto the fringe. It didn't make it onto the green, but it was really close. He finished off the hole with a chip and a putt and his wished-for birdie.

A 73 put Bobby two strokes behind the leader, Horton Smith, and three strokes in front of Hagen who had a 75.

On Open Saturday, the weather had turned for the better. It was just a normal warm summer day instead of the uncomfortable heat that had blanketed most of Minnesota.

Reacting to the better weather, Bobby shot a field-leading 68. It was the best score of the tournament by two strokes and a new course record.

Bobby's last round was played with Joe Turnesa. They teed off at one-fifteen in the afternoon, a half hour before Macdonald Smith and an hour before Horton Smith.

Keeler started worrying when Bobby bogied the 2nd hole and double bogied the 3rd. He tried to think of what he would say to Bobby to get him to buckle down, and just like that, Bobby did buckle down. He birdied the 4th hole and had no more trouble on the front nine.

On the back nine, Bobby parred through the 12th hole and was in great shape until he double bogied the par-three 13th. Keeler watched as Bobby grimaced after finishing the hole.

Keeler stood next to the 14th tee in case Bobby wanted to know how the others in the field were doing, but Bobby either ignored his presence or didn't notice him at all. Bobby birdied the 14th and 16th holes—and Keeler relaxed.

Keeler was certain Bobby was going to win the third of the four big tournaments. But Bobby pushed his tee shot off on the long par-three 17th, a hole that measured 262 yards and that had given Bobby trouble all week.

Keeler rushed to the right of the green, where there were at least 200 people stomping around trying to locate Bobby's ball.

"Hi," Bobby mumbled.

"I figure you still have either a four- or five-stroke lead," Keeler offered, looking at the ground along with everyone else.

"I must have gone through too fast with my body or too slow with my arms," Bobby explained. "But this is a ground-under-repair area." Bobby had hopes of a favorable ruling.

They couldn't find the ball. The official on the scene gave Bobby a one-stroke penalty and allowed him to drop another ball off to the side. This allowed Bobby to chip on in three and two-putt for a double bogie.

Keeler watched as Bobby stepped onto the 18th tee, which had at least three twosomes waiting to play the hole. Keeler decided to walk up by the 18th green and watch Bobby finish up there.

"How's he doing?" Big Bob asked Keeler as they met near the clubhouse.

"I think he has it. He had at least a four-stroke lead, but then he double bogied that long 17th. So, just to make sure, he has to finish this 18th well."

Big Bob nodded. "He'll do it. Then he'll have three of the four."

What Keeler didn't tell Big Bob was how tired Bobby looked when Keeler saw him on the 17th. Bobby's skin had taken on a gray pallor again and his eyes were becoming very deeply set.

Big Bob and Keeler watched Bobby's second shot hit just

short of the 18th green and bounce on. His ball lay at least 50 feet from the cup. It was another sign that Bobby's strength was gone. Usually Bobby hit his approaches flag high and sometimes even stronger when he got pumped up. But when Bobby got tired, he sometimes lost a club in distance from lack of strength.

"All he has to do is get down in two," Keeler said to Big Bob. "I just heard that Macdonald Smith is having a great final round." Keeler had walked off and spoken to another reporter who had just come in from the course, but Big Bob had stayed in place.

"There must be at least 15,000 people on this hole," Big Bob said to Keeler as they watched the throng of fans walking along in the rough.

"You should have seen St. Andrews," Keeler chuckled. "At least Bobby was hardly held up over there by the fans. Here, he's had to wait and wait."

Bobby had arrived at his ball. Since Turnesa had hit his approach into the middle of the green, Bobby was away.

Keeler watched Bobby line up his last putt. He seemed almost nonchalant, the way he casually walked toward the hole and then back to his ball. Suddenly, Bobby addressed his putt and stroked it.

Keeler watched as the ball traveled up one incline, then another, and finally on the way towards the hole, it seemed to take one small left hand turn. It dropped for a birdie. A huge roar emerged from the throng of fans.

"Well, God damn," Big Bob murmured.

"Meant to be," Keeler joined in. He watched Bobby, dead-tired, pick the ball out of the cup.

"Now it's up to Mac Smith," Keeler said to Big Bob as they walked behind Bobby up the hill.

"Do you think he can?" Big Bob asked. He knew he'd hate it if someone took this win away from his son.

"That 17th hole has been murder all week on scores. If Mac

can birdie it, which I doubt, he'll have really earned it," Keeler huffed back.

Mac Smith suffered the same fate as everyone else on the longest par-three in history. He came up two strokes short. Bobby had won his third big tournament of the year.

Keeler steered Bobby into the clubhouse to get away from all the fans.

"I have a proposition to offer you, unless you're too tired," Keeler mentioned to Bobby as they sat by the window in the clubhouse. Big Bob and Keeler sat on the window side so the fans would not notice Bobby's famous face.

Bobby nodded, signaling Keeler to speak. "The radio people want us to do a broadcast tonight from their studios on Hennipin Avenue in downtown Minneapolis. It might save us from having to do a lot of individual interviews." Keeler usually had a reason for what he wanted.

Bobby scratched behind his ear. "Just no more walking," he sighed. "When I get home this time, I'm never going to leave."

"But, what about the Amateur at Merion?"

Bobby looked at Keeler. "You know, right now, I quit. I've had it. It's not worth it to have to play like this. I'm so tired that I could lay down for a week." Bobby tilted his head. "You know, one guy walked right behind me the whole back nine picking my divots back out of their holes."

"You want me to call off the broadcast for tonight?"

Bobby's face wore a queer, tired but friendly, look. "For so long, you have kept so many reporters from having to talk to me at the tournament sites. The least I can do is this broadcast tonight."

"You're not going to tell the listeners you're quitting, are you?"

Bobby gave out a little laugh. "Not if you don't ask me that question."

The whole world seemed to know that all Bobby had to do was win the National Amateur one more time, for his fifth win in that tournament, and he would win all the big tournaments in one year. Bobby was now in a class by himself.

"What's your take on the fact that this year, of all years, three of the four national tournaments are being played on three of the courses you first started on when joining the national scene?" Keeler asked Bobby the summer before they left for Philadelphia and the National Amateur.

Bobby grazed his cheek with his hand and looked off. "Everything has meaning. I learned that a long time ago." Bobby looked up at Keeler. "Call it providence or luck if you want, but something is behind it, that's for sure."

"You might like to know what the four big wins are being called."

Bobby looked quizzically at Keeler.

"The Impregnable Quadrilateral."

Bobby shook his head. "I like the sound of 'four wins' better."

"I'm thinking of calling it the 'Grand Slam,'" Keeler added.

The world seemed to be on hold in 1930. Everyone was awaiting September, for the National Amateur at Merion to roll around. Sometimes when greatness is being achieved odd occurrences step forward to challenge it. Such was the case that long, hot Georgia summer as people waited.

Bobby had gotten a game going with a few friends over the links of East Lake. His strength was coming back and he wanted to make sure his golf game came back with it. They had only a few holes left to play when a thunderclap sounded not too far off in the distance. Since they were close to the end, they aimed on finishing.

But another bolt landed beside them in an adjoining fairway and they took off for the safety of the East Lake clubhouse. Suddenly, the rain hit and another thunderclap hit nearby. They didn't really notice; the steps into the clubhouse were just a short distance away.

Bobby paused to put up his umbrella. With the umbrella over him, he ran the last hundred yards. Just as he was ready to enter the clubhouse, another lightning strike hit. No one knew where, but it was close, real close. Bobby felt it.

His umbrella was almost taken out of his hand as broken bricks rained down on him and his friends. Two of the bricks tore through the umbrella and one seemed to graze his shoulder.

The shirt on Bobby's back was torn all the way from his shoulder to his waist. His umbrella was in shreds. The culprit could only have been one of the bricks that had been blasted off of the clubhouse chimney by that last close lightning strike. The following day some of the course workers found bits of chimney brick more than a hundred yards from the clubhouse.

"You really know how to scare a fella," Keeler said to Bobby as he dropped in on Bobby's office.

"You'll never have to remind me to get off a course when I hear thunder again," Bobby retorted.

Back at work, Bobby threw himself into the projects he needed to finish before his trip to Merion. Late one day, he had a case that required him to pick up some information at the courthouse, so off he went. He was used to having a delivery boy perform a task like this, but if he had waited for a delivery boy, the courthouse would be closed.

Bobby got to the courthouse ten minutes before closing. He quickly walked to the third floor, got the documents that were waiting for him, and started back to the office, reading while walking.

"Better watch it, mister," a voice shouted at him. Bobby glanced towards the street to see a large dump truck headed right for him. He leaped the five feet necessary to clear the spot where the truck struck the building.

Bobby looked at the truck. There had been no driver in it. Its parking brake had failed, releasing the truck to go down the small incline. It had missed Bobby by about five feet.

On the train to Merion, Bobby and Keeler sat across from each other.

"So, you're ready?" Keeler asked.

"Yep.

"The vagaries of match play aren't going to bother you?"

"Not if I shoot a better score than the other guy," Bobby laughed.

"Score? Match play?" Keeler continued.

Bobby looked at him. "Did you forget that I play against old man par?"

Keeler laughed. "Guess it's a sign that I'm getting old if I would forget something like that." They sat there quietly. "The Philadelphia Inquirer is going to do something very special about your return there."

Bobby waited.

"They're going to run at least four full pages comparing your visit in 1916 against your visit now." Keeler grinned. "I sent them some pictures."

"They're going to show me again in my dirty pants and those handmade golf shoes that I had?"

Keeler nodded. "Probably. I just wanted you to know now, so it wouldn't bother you if you saw it."

Bobby felt the impact of his arrival on the scene at Merion. It was as if the statement "Jones is here" was passed quickly from mouth to ears all over the course.

That impact even seemed to show up in his opponents.

"The one thing, big thing, I'm going to miss after this tournament is not having another chance at you, Bobby Jones," George Von Elm said when he saw Bobby.

"There's always hope for the future, George." Bobby grinned back. Von Elm was the last player to have beaten Bobby in a thirty-six-hole match. He was the player responsible for keeping Bobby from winning five amateur titles in a row.

"Not if there is no future," Von Elm shook his head. "I figure it's been costing me about $10,000 a year to travel and play this game. Due to the depression, I just don't have that kind of money around for golf anymore."

"I'm going to miss your face at these affairs, George," Bobby said.

Von Elm looked closely at Bobby. "What's this I hear about you pulling out after this tournament too?"

Bobby smiled. "That didn't come from my mouth."

The need for people to either see Bobby, touch him, or speak to him was heightened by the multi-page spread in the Philadelphia Inquirer. Wherever Bobby went, thousands followed, expecting to see history made at any moment.

For his part, Bobby had no intention of letting either his fans or himself down. He had waited all summer for this and he was looking forward to accomplishing this last goal. Nothing was going to prevent him from doing that.

Three hundred and fifty caddies joined a pool to see who was going to carry Bobby's bag. Howard Rexford, the nineteen-year-old son of a Philadelphia ink manufacturer, won the honors. He beamed his excitement all week long.

Bobby played his first practice round at Merion and easily scored a three-over par 73. The next round, he shot a workmanlike 70. He was ready.

The United States Golf Association, aware of Bobby's drawing power, charged $1.00 per practice session. Thousands of Philadelphians anted up.

For the first time, two marshals wielded a rope between them to keep fans from either walking right up to Bobby or creeping up behind him when he got ready to strike his balls. Even so, Bobby was still left with only a ten-foot alleyway through which to hit his shots—a dangerous and nerve-wracking proposition for him.

Bobby just broke 80 that afternoon by scoring a 78. He almost threw his clubs again, he felt so badly about how he was reacting to the pressure.

"I hear you're throwing your clubs again," said a phone caller to Bobby's hotel room.

"God dammit, who the hell is this?" Then he recognized the voice. "Is that you, Sweets?"

Bobby heard chuckling on the other end. "Yep." Jess Sweetser chuckled again. "Bobby, you know Merion. Probably played it thirty times. So, how about if we take tomorrow and get away from all this fuss and go over to Pine Valley. There won't be any reporters or crowds there."

Warming up slowly, Bobby failed to break 40 on the front nine. But, with a number of caddies and course personnel following the group, he found his game on the back nine where he scored an easy 2 under par 33.

The next morning Bobby was sick, throwing up in his room. Bobby decided it was too much Brunswick stew the night before. He and Sweetser had stopped at a roadside diner.

The outing had changed Bobby's game, though, despite the illness. He shot a 74, and even broke the rams-horn face plate off his Jack White driver, Jeanie Deans. George Sayers, the professional at Merion and a well-known club repairman, fixed the club.

Bobby was now loose and it showed in his game as he shot his first under-70 round. He scored four birdies after getting only one in his previous six rounds.

Bobby was accompanied on the course by Keeler, Big Bob, who had arrived the day before, and Grantland Rice. They were followed by fifty other sports writers, ten well-known golfers, and around 4,000 fans. Everyone wanted to see the lead-up to history.

"Thank you, Granny, for all the coverage that you've given my game," Bobby told America's top sports writer as they walked to his next shot.

"It's really been my pleasure, Bobby. You've been a really great story."

Like most sports writers, Rice was always after a story. "How is your game from your perspective, Bobby?"

Bobby slowed so the sports writer could hear him. "You

know, I've suffered from this game for a lot of years. Among other things, I've discovered that to play well, you must play this game by feel, which is almost impossible to describe." Bobby smiled his shy grin. "But feel is the easiest thing in the world to sense when you have it completely." Bobby looked out over the course. "Today, I have it completely. I don't have to think of anything, just hit the ball. Sometimes, during important play, I've had to rivet on one, or two, or maybe three checkpoints in my mind on each shot."

"Would you mind telling me what those three points are?" Rice continued.

"Dragging the club back, not lifting it, bringing my left hip into play at the start of the downswing, and keeping my left arm close to my body."

Qualifying for the National Amateur started, and the USGA, recognizing what might happen, decided to protect Bobby with fifty U.S. Marines.

The first day, there were only 7,000 spectators at Merion, but they were all focused on Bobby. He teed off at nine-fifteen and shot a leading 69.

The next day, he shot a 73 to miss breaking the record for qualifying score by one stroke but led for medalist honors.

Bobby's first opponent was Sandy Somerville, three-time Canadian Amateur champion, an ice hockey and football player, and very experienced match player.

Somerville played the first nine holes in even par, but Bobby had gotten off to a better start. He was 4-under for the starting nine and 4-up in his match. Bobby won again—5 and 4.

That afternoon, Bobby faced another Canadian, Fred Hoblitzel. This time, Bobby couldn't seem to get his game started. He was ten strokes over his morning round after nine holes and barely up on his opponent. Hoblitzel backed his game off, and Bobby easily won 5 and 4.

"The score was the same, but the game wasn't," Bobby told Keeler as they met for dinner with Big Bob.

"I'll bet somewhere inside you, you're glad to have those 18-hole matches over," Keeler knowingly commented.

The following day, Bobby met Fay Coleman and beat him 6 and 5 in the first of his 36-hole matches. Bobby was still not exactly on his game.

Bobby would play his second 36-hole match against Jess Sweetser, his friend and a competitor from the Walker Cup and a number of other big tournaments.

"Your game seems to be in better shape." Big Bob looked at his son.

"And I'm glad, especially with facing Sweetser."

"I saw that your group was held up a number of times out there today. Didn't that bother you?" Keeler asked.

Bobby waved away the thought. "I've learned in these big tournaments that you can't let things like that get to you or it'll take your mind off your game."

Keeler remembered something that he needed to pass on to Bobby. "There are some film people here who want to meet with you for about fifteen minutes."

"Film people?" Bobby inquired.

"That's what they called themselves. Here's a card that they gave me." Keeler gave the card to Bobby. It read: Gene Maxon, Warner Brothers Film Corporation.

"They have sound in those things now," Big Bob offered.

"Yes, but it's going to put more people out of work. Even piano players need to eat." Keeler continued. "And with the depression getting worse, good jobs are hard to find."

Bobby met his friend, Jess Sweetser, and beat him easily 9 and 8.

Now, Bobby was into the finals where he would meet Gene Homans. The excitement rose to such a fever pitch on the course, people were fainting.

"So, how are you feeling?" Keeler asked Bobby before the final round.

"Like the end of a long, long trip, and you know how I feel about trips." Bobby answered. "I was worried last night, but now that this day is finally here, I'm looking to have it over with and relish that sense of freedom."

Almost 15,000 fans were perched near the first tee when Bobby and Gene Homans arrived. They were kept in place by both the officials and the fifty Marines.

If there was another person besides Bobby who knew that day what the outcome of the match was going to be, it would have had to have been Homans when he shook hands with Bobby.

Bobby won the first hole and started his slow, steady march to a sweep of the four big national tournaments. History was begging to be made and Bobby finished the script as if he had written it.

The lunchtime break found Bobby 7-up. As many sports writers had learned to say, it was all over but the shouting.

Although Bobby wanted to win, he was very tired and this final match just seemed to drag on. Homans played better and finally played as he should, but he was running out of holes—and he knew it.

At the 11th hole, known for it's babbling brook, Homans was in a situation where if he won the hole he would have to keep on winning holes. He tried. His long approach putt had a slight chance, but he missed the hole. With that, Homans walked over and congratulated Bobby. The win was in the books as 8 and 7, in favor of Bobby Jones.

CHAPTER
19

Bobby's face showed some pain as a song came over the radio in his office. He had just bought the radio and was showing it to Keeler. He and Keeler were catching up on news just weeks after Bobby conquered the "Impregnable Quadrilateral."

"Don't you like that tune?" Keeler asked. "It's played all over."

"Do you know the chorus to that song?"

Keeler happily began to sing it. "Won't you come home, Bill Bailey? Won't you come home? We cried the whole night long."

"Don't you remember the name of my brother, who died?"

Keeler's face took on a strange look. "My God. Your bother's name was William Bailey."

"That song was written in 1902, the year I was born."

Keeler was silent for a bit, to allow Bobby to collect himself, then he changed the subject. "I have a few cables I thought you might like to have." Keeler put his pile of telegrams down beside Bobby. "A few of those cables are from very important people."

"I wonder why they sent them to your paper?" Bobby teased.

"Maybe for the same reason that every time I play golf, people expect to see me shoot around par."

"Don't you?" Bobby kidded.

Keeler laughed. "Watching you doesn't seem to help me like watching Stewart did for you," Keeler added. "Strange to me is how everyone expects it to."

"Have you heard from the movie people?" Keeler had his notepad in hand.

Bobby nodded. "We're going to meet next week. They've been kicking around a bunch of thoughts about how to make a film work."

"Well, don't keep me out of this." Keeler smiled. "I'd love to see myself on the big screen with one of those pretty actresses."

"As a matter of fact, they'll probably need a good writer to help with the scripts." Bobby laughed. "Someone who's been around the game long enough to understand it but not play very well."

"I'll see if I can conjure up some willing soul." Keeler knew when he'd been had.

It was quiet as they both sat there. "Any new thoughts about your future in golf?" Keeler finally spouted out.

"The trouble is, every time I start thinking about next year, I start getting a sick feeling in my stomach."

"Just like you had in Philly when you thought it was from the Brunswick stew?"

"Or, just like I had at Scioto in 1926," Bobby remembered.

"This has been going on for a while," Keeler offered, finally putting his pad away.

Quiet again, Bobby put his face onto his hand. "I just have to figure a way to leave the game without putting the blame on anyone or anything."

Keeler knew this was coming. He had sensed it for years, but now that it was time, he was clearly bothered by it. "It's not like you to ever blame anyone for what they did do."

"But you know how people read between the lines. I need something that is clear to explain my leaving, so no one can think of another reason for it."

"There are a lot of ways to phrase something to avoid placing blame." Keeler looked at Bobby. "Most of us who really know you understand what you've been through."

Bobby nodded. "I fell in love with the game, just not tournament golf." He paused. "I want to get back to the game that I love. I have no problem with other people wanting to spend their nights on Pullmans. I'd just rather be home in my own bed and watch my children grow. That can't be asking too much." After a few seconds passed he added, "And I owe so much to my parents. They want to see me grow up to be a fine practicing attorney and an honest breadwinner, especially after all the schooling they put me through."

Keeler nodded. "I understand your thinking. There seems to be a balance that some of us need. Others don't need a base and can do whatever they want," Keeler thought. "People like Hagen," he added.

"Isn't he on his second marriage?"

"He may be on his third, for all I know." Keeler waited. "And I doubt this one's going to last either."

Bobby laughed. "Hagen is just such a lovable character. For some reason he reminds me of a grown-up version of Peck's Bad Boy."

Keeler laughed. "Maybe Mark Twain met him somewhere. You know, Hagen's been in some very strange places."

Two weeks later, Bobby called Keeler. "Let's have lunch." Keeler appreciated the call. He was tired of looking like he was the one always pursuing Bobby.

"The film deal is going though. I should have the contracts in hand by the middle of November," Bobby glowed. "If they didn't have sound, I wouldn't do them."

"So what type of movie is it going to be?"

"All instructional. About twelve to start with, and they're allowing for more if we have a hit."

Keeler let out a very big guffaw. He knew that Bobby's life story was nothing but a hit.

"They have told a few other studios about the series, and wait until you hear this." Bobby looked at Keeler. "They have Joe E. Brown, W.C. Fields, James Cagney, Walter Huston, and even Loretta Young who want to play parts—and they'll play their parts for free." Bobby smiled. "And George E. Marshall is going to direct us."

"Where do you think I'll fit in?" Keeler had of course been worried about what would happen to him if Bobby left golf. He had been worried about that for a long time, so any news about the future was good news.

"They want you and me to work up the story lines for the shorts," Bobby grinned. "You can write a script, can't you?"

Keeler let out a nervous, relieved laugh. "Once I understand what they want, I'll be able to give them that and more." Keeler had come a long way from that man who was surprised by his own talent.

"Sorry, but this has to be kept quiet for now."

Keeler was so grateful, he was quiet for a moment, and then he said, "Can I help you put your 'exit from tournament golf' letter together?"

A youthful shy grin came over Bobby's face. "Not much you don't know, is there?"

Bobby called Keeler again the next week. "I have the letter for you to see." He paused. "I think you'll like it."

"So, you didn't need any help after all."

"You playing par golf yet?" Bobby passed back. "In case I'm out, it'll be sitting on my desk."

Keeler grabbed the letter off Bobby's desk when he got there. It was addressed to H.H. Ramsay, the President of the USGA, but it was written in such a way that it was obviously a letter meant to be published.

> Upon the close of the 1930 golfing season, I determined immediately that I would withdraw entirely from golfing competition of a serious nature. Fourteen years of intense tournament play in this country and abroad have given me about all I wanted of hard work in the game. I had reached a point where I felt that my profession required more of my time and effort, leaving golf in its proper place—a means of obtaining recreation and enjoyment.

My intention at the time was to make no announcement of retirement, but to merely drop out quietly by neglecting to send in my entry to the Open championship next spring. There was, at that time, no reason to make a definite statement of any kind, but since then, after careful consideration, I have decided upon a step that I think ought to be explained to the golfers of this country, so they may have a clear understanding of what this is and why it is being done.

On November 13, 1930, I signed a contract with Warner Brothers Pictures to make a series of twelve one-reel motion pictures devoted entirely to exhibiting and explaining the methods which I employ for various shots ordinarily required in playing a round of golf. These pictures are to be purely educational in character, and it is the ardent hope of both parties that they will be of some value. First by improving the play and thereby increasing the enjoyment of the vast number of people already interested in the game, and second, by creating an interest where none exists now among the many who find enjoyment and beneficial exercise on the golf course.

The talking picture, with its combination of visual presentation and demonstration, and the possibility of detailed explanation, appeals to me as the ideal vehicle for an undertaking of this matter.

Of course, the matter of monetary compensation enters into the discussion at this point and it is for numerous reasons that I wish to be perfectly understood on this score. The amateur status problem is one of the most serious with which the United States Golf Association has to deal for the good of the game as a whole.

I am not certain that the step I am taking is in a

strict sense a violation of the amateur rule. I think a lot might be said on either side. But I am so far convinced that it is contrary to the spirit of amateurism that I am prepared to accept, and even enforce, a ruling that it is an infringement.

I have chosen to play as an amateur, not because I have regarded an honest professionalism as discreditable, but simply because I have had other ambitions in life. So long as I played as an amateur, there could be no question of subterfuge or concealment. The rules of the game, whatever they were, I have respected, sometimes even beyond the letter. I certainly shall never become a professional golfer. But since I am no longer a competitor, I feel free to act outside the amateur rule as my judgment and conscience may decide.

When these pictures have been made, I expect to return to the practice of my profession, unhampered by the necessity of keeping my golf up to championship requirements.

Keeler put the letter down and took off his glasses. He rubbed the bridge of his nose, where his glasses were perched, and he would have wiped a tear from his eye, but Bobby walked in and interrupted him.

"What do you think?"

Keeler nodded. "It'll do the trick."

"Sorry that I wasn't here when you came in." Bobby was grinning from ear to ear. "Something important came up."

Keeler questioningly looked at him.

"An old friend just showed back up."

Keeler raised his eyebrows. There was always a Bobby Jones story to be had.

"Stewart is back. I just made an appointment with him for little Bobby, but it's not for a few years."

Breinigsville, PA USA
20 July 2010
242070BV00002B/2/P